HONOR YOUR Spirit

Listen To Your **Spirit**, Find Your **Purpose**, and Walk Your **Path**

BY CAROLYN COLERIDGE, LCSW

Honor Your Spirit

By Carolyn Coleridge, LCSW

Cover design: Erika Wilmore

The content of this book is for general instruction only. Each person's emotional and spiritual condition is unique. The instruction in this book is not intended to replace or interrupt the reader's relationship with a physician or other professional.

ISBN: 978-1533225221

Printed in the United States of America

Contents

Introduction

YOU ARE here for a reason; every single person on this planet has a reason for incarnating here on earth. It is not a random occurrence that you are here, nor is it random that you are reading this book. We are all sent here with everything we need to create our life purpose, to live our life to the fullest, and to have a fulfilling existence. Every desire we have, and the means to create it is wrapped inside of us. The trick is finding how we unwrap our mind to find our authentic selves.

How do we find our truth? How do we figure out what our gifts are? How do we create our journey consciously? This book will help you find your life's purpose, create your own journey, and support you in this undertaking. You have to listen to your *spirit*, which sends messages to your soul. Throughout this book, I will help you understand how to be aware of your *spirit's* messages, not everyone is given the same gift. We don't all have the same abilities, privileges, or desires. This doesn't mean each individual's gift is not valuable, quite the opposite, we can learn to add value to each other. One thing I can tell you, without a doubt, is that we can all live a more fulfilling life if we listen to our *spirit* and believe. It is your *spirit* that asked, before incarnating, to be challenged to grow on the earth plane; that is what we are here for. In the following chapters, I will demonstrate the remarkable ability of the soul to overcome hardships, and recreate its life. I will give examples of wonderful clients who have transformed their lives to create their purpose.

I will also describe how I had to honor my *spirit's* gifts and abilities, as my heart and soul drove me to study the mystical, the metaphysical, and the mystery of the soul. At the end of the book, I hope you will feel inspired to hear the call of your heart, honor your spirit, and fulfill your mission.

As a psychotherapist, and practicing spiritual intuitive for twenty years, I have seen first-hand the **struggles** of the *spirit*. I have witnessed and heard the pain of the soul and the tragedy of the human experience. I have always, without a doubt, been able to see the divinity in each and every individual that I have encountered. No matter how far away they appear from the light, everyone has a *spirit*. I have seen the need of the soul to feel loved, appreciated, and respected.

Many people learn and grow from their tragedies, while others take out their anger on everyone else they can, many times unintentionally. We all struggle with knowing if we are good enough parents, lovers, friends, coworkers, bosses, cooks, cleaners, bus drivers, or teachers. The question comes up over and over again in different forms. Am I lovable, desirable? What am I here for?

As you learn to honor yourself on a deep level, you realize that your soul talks to you and assists you on this journey called life. Your gut, or what I like to call your GPS (Gut Programming System), is what connects you to your soul purpose. The gut is located in the solar plexus chakra*, the part of the body right around your belly button. This is considered to be your energetic power center (chakra is an Indian Sanskrit word meaning "wheel"). There are seven prominent chakras in your body that help manage your emotional and energetic body system. It isn't a coincidence that this third chakra is named solar, as in sun, or the place where the light is within you, this is the same place where you have gut intuitions about others, and receive messages from the divine. We will talk about all of the chakras in chapter two.

Many indigenous cultures worshipped the sun as their god, that's why it is not a surprise that the solar, or sun, in us connects us to our own divine truth. Your gut transmits messages all day long: who to trust, who not to trust, call your partner, leave that job, write that book, or whatever other messages may be broadcast from your soul or the universe. Your *spirit* feels that spark, a tingling, chills, or a stomach flip, telling you to move forward on those intuitions. What is right for you? What are your passions? What inspires you? This is a natural process that happens over and over again, 24/7. The trick is to train your mind to listen to this universal broadcast. Just like a pilot listens to air traffic controllers when landing a plane, you too can check in with God, the universe, and your soul to see what steps you need to take in order to have a smooth landing in life.

With the many clients that I have seen at hospitals, in psychiatry clinics, in classes and privately, I have observed how people struggle with their reason for being, they struggle to know if they are good enough, deserving, desirable, and lovable. Our *spirits* align with the same questions, but have the impetus to change these questions into actions of creation in order to gain answers. Part of the magic of creating your own purpose is that you begin to reuse that muscle of divinity that was lost so long ago.

Too many of us grow fearful and begin to create with the muscles of manipulation, control, abuse, and competition, instead of admiring all the gifts of creation that each one of us brings to the table. Our *spirits* set up our own life experiences as challenges to our own growth, learning, and experiences on earth.We create earth suits of various cultures and circumstances, in order to experience different angles and dimensions of what our soul could be challenged with and grow from. It is a masquerade of sorts, an ongoing acting job. These experiences give us new muscles and gifts such as: compassion, patience, unconditional love, integrity and tolerance, and the soul list goes on and on.

It is my belief that if more people understood their soul, and the journey that it takes through time and dimensions throughout this universe, it would ease some of their chronic suffering and deepest pain. At the very least, it would give them an understanding of why they have gone through such difficulties.

To understand your reason for being, you need to become aware of the purpose of your earth-life in the journey of the soul. The earth plane is a school for our soul, we are here to experience, learn, and grow. There are no mistakes as to who is supposed to be here, *everyone* is supposed to be here. The universe is much too intelligent to make a mistake. The universe, which I look at as God Source, is the infinite intelligence that created everything that is in existence now. Call it Goddess, if you feel more comfortable, or a large energy light being.

Some people have tapped into their inner intuition and their hearts desires and know why they are here, while others feel that the reason for their existence should be sent to them on a scroll. That was me. I wanted my mission to come with a drum roll. We all wish that we had Archangel Gabriel coming to us and saying, "Unto you a mission is born!" while hearing bells ringing and angels singing, "Ahhhh" as the clouds ascend in the background.

The game on the earth plane is to find out what brings us joy, what we can contribute, and how we can live our best life, and create, create, create. Why are you here? What are you here to learn? Why did various painful and difficult circumstances occur in your life? What is the purpose of sorrow?

This life is a short existence of our true spiritual nature. It is just a blink in time of the eternity of our soul. I have had the unique experience of working with the mind, body, and spirit of a person. I work with the mind as a therapist, the body as an energy healer, and the spirit as an intuitive reader. This work came to me as I listened to my inner calling, which was simply--help. I didn't know how I was supposed to help, but I knew I was good at it. Our callings can, at first, be very basic and small, and then our *spirit* helps us to expand them. I acted on my calling by becoming a psychotherapist. I also wanted to help people be inspired and to respect their own journeys. The *spirit* inspired me to do that.

As a psychotherapist, helping people to grow is obvious, but what is an energy healer? An energy healer transmits healing energy, or chi, from the universe to a client, it is a similar task to the familiar: in churches, when people perform the "laying on of hands," or when nurses do something called the "therapeutic touch." I also became a Reiki master. Reiki is a Japanese healing art.

There was a series of events that led me down this path. As an intuitive soul reader, I gain insights not from the client's personality, but from their *spirit*. This was a skill that came upon me when I asked God how I could help and be of service. I later learned that my intuition had been leading me all along. As a practicing intuitive, I tune in to a different frequency in order to access information from people's *spirits*. I also learned to read the energy around a person, and the energy they are giving off, in order to help them make higher decisions in their life, with more frequency. I continue to coach them to listen to their own intuition, which is the language of the *spirit*.

Working with all three of these parts, the mind, body, and *spirit* helps me to see how each part struggles to be heard. They are all intertwined, and all assist, the whole being. The mind is stimulated and moves to heal the body. The *spirit* is revealed, and the mind becomes motivated to shift and change. The body becomes ill, and the mind and *spirit* work together for transformation.

Various ailments of the body can manifest as depression, disease, or a spiritual crisis. The body may create a disease that helps the person to develop a different relationship with their self, or with those that they care about. A mental illness may help a person learn about the process of how the mind works, or doesn't work. This illness may be used to educate others about how childhood abuse can affect a person's mental health, or it may be used to teach others about chemical imbalances.

The *spirit* may have a crisis when responding to limitations in both areas of the mind and body. It will orchestrate a wake-up call to the personality, telling it to listen up, thus getting it back on track by evolving the soul. This may happen unconsciously or consciously, but it does happen. All three parts of the personhood—the mind, body, and *spirit*--work together to bring awareness and greater growth. Healing is not always about finding a cure, it may be about accepting a disease or ailment, or it may be about what it is teaching that person in this life.

As I continued to ask the universe to help, my skills and gifts continued to expand. My gifts helped to heal myself and others. My *spirit* came alive, and I realized that it was a guiding force in my life. I was fascinated and wanted to understand all about what this *spirit* was.

So, now, I will take you through my journey, with the goal that you will start examining your experiences, and wake up to the truths that the Universe has given you, allowing you to get on the path to your passion and purpose.

1 Your Reason for Being

WORKING WITH so many clients over the years, I have seen how people try to find their reason for being. We are much more human's doing than human's being. To find your purpose and passion you have to slow down and listen to the silent rhythm of your life and the whispers of your *spirit*. There has been a path laid out for you that if you become still you will see and hear it. It is time now on the planet to be a co-creator in your life to create the desires that lie in your heart.

Before we get started with understanding your *spirit* on a deeper, more intuitive level, I would like you to take three deep cleansing breaths. With these breaths, you are opening your connection to your *spirit*. It is your breath that reminds you of your spiritual nature. Without the breath, the *spirit* does not reside in the physical body, it returns to Source. As you breathe deeply, you will become more aware of the mystical part of yourself that knows who you really are, and what your purpose really is. After this breathing exercise, you may read this book differently, with a more *spirit* focused view. You may connect the synchronicities more easily, or hear coincidental messages in the text. Listening with your *spirit* and soul helps you to find your spiritual path and live with purpose. Don't forget to breathe in deep breaths when you are feeling frustrated, confused, or stuck. I always know when someone is depressed or detached from their *spirit*. When they come into my office to see me, they are barely breathing and not connecting to truth; they are mired down in the earth plane, and have forgotten their reason for being here. If you breathe deeply and open up to *spirit*, your answers will start to come. You will feel calmer, and at the very least, you will release tension.

As you learn to honor yourself on a deeper level, you will realize that your soul talks to you and assists you constantly. Just as you are sending out thoughts to the universe that create intentions, expectations, and outcomes, your soul is always transmitting information back to you. It is transmitting signals, signs, coincidences, synchronicities, and a path of right action. Breathing helps to open up that doorway to the realm of *spirit* and connect you to that wavelength. It is important that you learn to dialogue and listen to the universe in order to begin and continue on your path.

Your heart is also a very important part of your spiritual journey. Your heart holds the passion and wisdom of your soul, as well as the essence of what you want to create. Always check with your heart for what feels right, and for what resonates with you, for what your desires and dreams are. Your soul's mind is stored in your heart.

I know it sounds simplistic, but we all came here with our mission already in us. Many of us have forgotten what our goal is because of programming from advertising, media, parental expectations, low self-esteem, or fear. We can all easily be disconnected from our soul's messages, burying our own truth. The soul is always broadcasting to us through coincidences, synchronicities, nature, and intuitive insights. Your higher self, the evolved part of your soul, receives these messages and wants to act on these insights. Often the ego suppresses these insights, or just lives in pain and denies that the answer has already been given.

There is a huge shift on the planet to become more spiritual. As our planet aligns with the galactic center, which is allegedly the spiritual center of the Milky Way galaxy, we are connecting to our spiritual heart. This was one of the prophecies of the Mayan calendar* that states that we are coming to "the end of times." Remember all of the hoopla about December 21, 2012, and then nothing dramatic happened? I believe that we are in the end of times, but it is the end of times as we know it.

If you live your life with passion, enact your *spirit*, and do what you really love--time flies by quickly. Time feels different. You become so absorbed in the task of creating that you forget about the clock, which is the rhythm of man. When you move with your *spirit*, you are following the rhythm of nature. Nature works in perfect harmony with itself, and there is a time and a season for everything under the sun and that is how it should be for us during our earth lives. We are preparing for a grand shift as more of us start moving toward the realization that we are spiritual beings in earth suits. Things are shifting at lightning speed, there are a million possibilities of creation. Go with your heart and listen to your *spirit*. Systems are breaking down so that we can learn to create on our own. We are not supposed to depend on the negative aspects of banks, government, corrupt food, bad school systems, or un-healing hospitals. These institutions can supplement our existence, but cannot sustain us.

Because of this, people are creating. They are growing organic food, home schooling their children, creating conscious businesses, and visiting alternative health practitioners. Our *spirits* are creative, and are always seeking to find answers. Our world is falling apart, in order to help us practice creating. This is why we came to earth, to create good for 'humankind', to enjoy, and to learn. We have been duped by the big demon of greed and corruption for far too long, but the great news is that all of these things can be changed.

My journey to work with my *spirit,* to shift time, to become an intuitive counselor, and a healer began by honoring the urgings inside of me. I was "set up" by my gifts of intuition and sensitivity, through my parental upbringing, as well as by my secret desires to assist in the planet's evolution. It was a spiritual destiny, yet my destiny seemed to be both created and predetermined. My journey was to find the truth about why I was here. I have had many experiences in my life that have helped my *spirit* to unfold, seek, search, and learn.

I started seeking my spiritual truths in New York City while at Columbia University's School of Social Work. At Columbia, I was studying to be a social worker and psychotherapist. It was at Columbia that I noticed that sitting in front of clients seemed all too familiar and quite easy to me. I rarely felt nervous with patients, no matter what age, race, or ethnicity. I engaged with them easily, and they seemed to open up to me quite effortlessly. I knew I was in the right field as a counselor; I was helping. I was so anxious to finish my degree and become a therapist that I finished my Master's program, in an accelerated program, with an A average in sixteen months (as opposed to the two years most people take to finish). I spent the little down time that I did have going to East West Books on 86th street in the Village, and in the Open Center in SoHo, scourging through New Age and Metaphysical books, trying to feed my obsessive curiosity about light workers,* intuitive healing modalities, sacred places, crystals, incense, and anything else connected with my *spirit.*

Let's go back a couple of years, to when I really became interested in the metaphysical, as the pain in my heart called out to me. At age twenty-four, I found out about a serious health crisis, on my birthday. I had wondered *why, out of all days, out of all the years that I had incarnated on this planet, why was my birthday the day I found out about my challenges, about life and mortality?* I had just ended a four year relationship, because the guy I was with at the time had made it clear, through his actions, that he wasn't interested in a long term relationship, and because his family was putting too much pressure on him to get rid of me. I was in a mindless job as a legal assistant in Greenwich, with snooty co-workers that were far from supportive, and the job was boring. So, all aspects of my life, my health, my work, and my relationship were in crisis.

For some reason though, I felt a connection to the divine and felt that God was trying to get my attention. The day that God gave me life on this planet, a little over two decades prior, everything in my life was going wrong. That coincidence prompted me to begin studying numerology and astrology, and trying to connect to this Source. I thought it was an uncanny coincidence that of all days, my day of birth, God was sending me a sign about paying attention to him. Irony became a bittersweet theme throughout my life, whenever irony appears, I pay attention. I felt a direct connection to Source. I felt I was being sent a message of some sort, but I wasn't sure what it was, so I began to consciously seek. I was living in Washington D.C. at the time, and a bookstore owner gave me the book, *You Can Heal Your Life* by Louise Hay, so that I could begin to learn about the universe. The woman in the store said to me, "You can't call yourself spiritual until you read this book." I had never heard of creating with the universe, or of how powerful a person's beliefs were. I was fascinated! How does this work? How do I manifest?

I practiced manifesting by calling in a love interest. I wrote down the qualities that I wanted in a partner. At the time, I stated that he should be artistic, have dreadlocks, and be intelligent, along with a couple of other qualities. I put it out to the universe with a meditation and a prayer, and about three days later, I saw a guy with dreadlocks playing his guitar in Adams Morgan, D.C. He looked like what I had imagined, and was creative, and appeared to be spiritual, as I could see that he had a big Buddha sitting on his porch.

We connected and talked and dated for about ten seconds, ok, ten days, because in my request I forgot to ask that we have something in common, and that he not be a temperamental artist. What was funny was that he felt a call to connect with me when he saw me as well. I could not believe how powerfully, and easily, my words could create, and it spooked me. This experience opened me up to the world of creative manifestation,* which is the ability to create from thoughts, words, and beliefs.

My mother and father had always talked about their spiritual journeys, and about how God had saved them from various things and had blessed their lives. My grandmother had talked to me about the other side, and about her three near-death experiences. She would have been 105 years old this year, 2016, and she grew up during a time when talking about going to the other side was not popular or in vogue, so I knew her stories were real. My family had such a passion for talking about spirituality that it was not surprising that I would find myself pursuing this field. My mother talked about her various dreams and visitations, premonitions about life events, and people, and their spirituality. She would tell me stories of astral projections, seeing relatives who had already passed, and of her visions of futures events. Spirituality was also a form of survival for my parents, as circumstances, at times, proved difficult. As immigrants, it sometimes seemed that praying to God was the only thing that could help them. So, part of my fascination with all of this was due to my family background. I never thought I could make a career out of my interest in the spiritual world.

It is important to listen to your *spirit.* Look at the things you are drawn to. What brings you joy? What fascinates you? While reading, *You Can Heal Your Life* (I ate it up like it was Spiritual food), I was inspired to create a mantra of asking God to be inspired. Around this time, I went into a New Age bookstore called 'The Yes bookstore,' in Washington, D.C. After looking around at various books, I came upon one that was entitled *Embraced by the Light*, by

Betty Eadie. I was attracted to the light on the cover. Eadie's book is about a woman's near death experience. My grandmother had often spoken about her near death experiences, so I was very intrigued and wanted to read it. I read the entire thing in about twenty-four hours. The story connected deeply to my soul, as I learned about universal laws and the words of the Christ. I knew it was truth, I knew it in my heart. The story seemed so familiar, like a remembrance. There were so many lessons in this story about how to live life by the universal laws and about how our lives have meaning and purpose. Also, with my health crisis and the other challenges I was facing, I knew that it was a time to turn to God. This book also validated my family's experiences and natural connection to *spirit*. This wasn't just my family's belief system that I had learned--it was in fact universal knowledge.

I began my quest of trying to find my reason for being, in D.C., and I continued on that quest in New York City, after moving there to attend Columbia University. It was about that time that I came across the book, *The Lightworkers Way* by Doreen Virtue, PhD. When I saw the word lightworker,* I immediately resonated with the term, even though I didn't know what it was. I found myself being drawn to the name. Dr. Virtue is a psychologist who has had psychic experiences her entire life. Her book validated my dual life, as someone training to be a therapist with an interest in spirituality. Her book and writings about indigo and crystal children helped me later in my work with children at UCLA Pediatric Pain Program, as an intuitive healer. Many of the children I worked with were very sensitive and had incredible extra sensory perception abilities that were sometimes thought of as being bizarre. Later, these children were diagnosed with physical pain. You will read about this later in my book.

I also was able to meet Dr. Judith Orloff, MD, in New York City while she was promoting her book, *The Second Sight*. Dr. Orloff is a very intuitive psychiatrist and a professor at UCLA. I later filmed with her, when I did a brief segment with her on CNN International. Dr. Orloff and I were filmed separately, discussing energy healing, along with the medium Lisa Williams and Dr. Mehmet Oz. Dr. Orloff coined the term "an Intuitive Empath," which has helped many of my anxiety clients to understand why they are so sensitive to energy. Her books have validated my intuitive experiences, as well as my sensitive empathic nature that quickly puts clients at ease. When you communicate with a person's *spirit*, you are connecting to their inner truth.

I was so obsessed with this field of study, and with learning about metaphysics, that I would often fall asleep with multiple books on my bed, and still do. I also attended Unity Church at Avery Fisher Hall in Columbus Circle, with Eric Butterworth, a popular New Thought teacher. I was inspired to attend after reading *Essence Magazine* and more specifically, *In the Spirit*, a monthly article written by *Essence Magazine*'s then Editor, Susan Taylor. Her cultural interpretations about the African American's ability to listen to the universe and create with Source really spoke to my soul. Every month, I would put her *In the Spirit* articles into a folder of inspiration. These articles helped me to understand about my own *spirit* and my ability to work with the power of positive thinking and creation. They also inspired me, and I love the feeling of being inspired. I would often wonder how I could inspire others to have that same feeling. When I met Susan Taylor in person, she didn't disappoint me. She was smart, caring, and spoke as intelligently as she wrote. Looking back, I believe her weekly column inspired me to write my inspirational newsletters every month. This was before Oprah, so to be inspired monthly by a woman who walked my path, with my color and gender challenges, spoke to my heart.

WORKBOOK EXERCISE 1

- **What** inspires you? What gives you that joy feeling?
- **What** do you find yourself drawn to? Right now,
- **WRITE IT DOWN.** Then ask *Spirit* to give you a sign.

Obviously a good book inspires me, but what about you? Is it artwork, music, a great computer program, organizing in a home, patterns and fabrics, journalism, sports games, jewelry, or essential oils? Like a magnet, see where you are drawn and what fascinates you and catches your interest. What do you feel that you can do all day long? This is what your *spirit* is drawn to, and paying attention to it can help you to start living your purpose. I was always fascinated by people and the way they think, the things they do, and how they interact with one another. I majored in sociology and psychology, for that reason. Groups and people interest me. Everyone thought that majoring in sociology was a waste. I never thought that I would be a social worker, but that study really helped me to understand groups, environments, and the patterns within people and groups. Also, learning patterns would later help me understand energy patterns as a healer, and how within a body, the cells function together. If I had listened to other people, I would have been off of my path.

As I continued to dialogue with the universe, asking questions, and trying to find my reason for being, I started having various paranormal experiences. I would often see ghosts in my NYC apartment. I had never seen a ghost before, but my mother had. I would see many different ghosts very regularly. I felt like I was haunted and was always nervous about what I would see upon waking. One day, I woke up with a weight on top of me. These beings said to me, "Don't wake up, don't wake up!" I could clearly hear their thoughts. I was pretty terrified, as I had no clue what was happening to me. I felt all of these etheric hands on me as I struggled.

When I opened my eyes, there was nothing there. Ghosts! I felt very haunted. I started praying like crazy and I sought out a spiritual healer named Celeste Meola. She said that these deceased beings were, "Seeing your light, and they are trying to soak up your energy." Light? What light? "You're seeking spiritual knowledge," my teacher said, "So when you open up spiritually, your light goes on and others on the physical plane, *and* the spiritual plane, will see you. You said you wanted to *help* right? It is in your field." That wish I had made years ago had been heard, when you make a request to the universe, it is heard. Yes, ghosts do exist.

Celeste also told me that I was a healer, and this was the first time that I had heard of this. She said that because these lost beings on the other side are searching for light and looking for healing, they hang on to me in order to heal. She said that I had to ground myself and protect my energy field, as these beings were trying to get light and *afterlife therapy*. It was all so bizarre to me, but I could feel the energy of these beings. The fact that their energy was heavy meant that they weren't higher beings. It felt surreal. She told me about the archangels and how to protect myself. Her methods greatly helped me, and the restless spirits went away once I began doing the exercises that she taught me. I discussed these experiences with my mother, who turned to my grandmother and said, "Ah, she is like us." It was just one small acknowledgement about my intense intuitive abilities, and then they went about their business.

My family has never used the words psychic, mediumship, astral projection, readings, or such. It was commonplace for my parents, with their background and history, to look at spirituality and working with your soul as part and parcel of being an earthbound human. It was not at all exotic or flashy. I don't think that they would have encouraged me to look at it as a profession, although their influence did help me, because I now look at it as a way of life. It was nerve wracking back then as I was studying to be a psychotherapist at the conservative Columbia University. I wondered if Celeste, the healer, had just been lucky. She was very accurate, but what was this healer /helper thing that she was talking about? Because of all of the profound paranormal experiences that continued to occur, I sought out a professional psychic. A traditional therapist would have thought I was nuts and psychotic, and one therapist I went to definitely did think I was strange when I described her son to her, without having ever met him.

It was about that time that I found a woman named Alana, who had a place in the Upper West Side of Manhattan. An actor turned psychic, Alana was a very kindhearted woman who would give very long readings for a minimal fee. Alana had always had psychic abilities. She was humble and astute, and her accuracy was nothing like I had experienced. She stated her spiritual guides remembered, "How bright you are and clairvoyant you are." I was surprised, me!? Clairvoyant is the ability to see with your spiritual eyes. She said that she would eventually be able to send me clients when she was out of town. What!? She later invited me to join an intuitive group that looked for lost or stolen children.

I figured she was kind, but misguided, about my abilities, forgetting, of course, that my mother was highly intuitive and a medium, and had just never utilized her gifts professionally. Not only did I think I could NOT find children who were stolen from their homes, but I was also working to become a traditionally trained therapist; I was afraid that the psychic world would not have fit into that traditional world. Psychic phenomenon, the ability to see, hear, and feel with a sixth intuitive sense, was considered psychotic in the world of psychology that I was entering. Hearing voices or seeing and experiencing people who weren't physically there was cause for a trip straight to the looney-bin.

Columbia was also very old and very conservative. Some of the books in the library even had mold on them. Psychic comes from the Greek world psychik, that means "of the soul." Psyche means "of the mind." Reading about other professional therapists, PhDs, and MDs who combined the two worlds helped me know these worlds were colliding, but there were still many excuses as to why I couldn't do that type of work for a living. My *spirit* seemed to have different plans. I would later learn how my intuitive ability and connection to *spirit* could greatly help my therapy clients in a deep way.

CHAPTER

2 Your *Spirit*, Your SOUL, and the Universe

How do you honor your *spirit*, if you don't know what it is? Your *spirit* is the part of you that inspires you to listen from within, it is the etheric spark that lies in your gut, your heart, and your mind, it is the whisper of your Soul that gets you on track. Your gut, as mentioned before, is what connects you to your soul purpose. Your gut is your GPS, or God Purpose System. Your gut sends you messages all day long, about what is right for you, what you're passionate about, and what your physical drive is.

Your *spirit* hears these messages continuously, and is motivated to move you forward. It is that tingling energy that gives you the "Ah-ha" moments and goose bumps. It is the life force energy inside of us, the gasoline that keeps our SOUL vehicle moving. Our *spirit* is what brought us down from heaven and into the earth plane. Our *spirit* resides there and here, and has the script of our life path, our purpose, and our reason for being. It feels these messages with energy sensations in our body. Our *spirit* is aware of the book of life that we wrote with God about our path. Usually déjà vu moments, chills, and good bumps are indicators that we are on our right path. Nausea, stomach pain, headaches, and other body aches are warnings that we may be off our path. So, my thinking is, *if our spirit is our guide that brought us down here to earth, shouldn't we listen to it?*

We can look at our SOUL as the hard drive or the computer and the *spirit* as the floppy disk, or USB drive. When we plug our *spirit* in, we get the information needed to help us on our path. We plug into our *spirit* by meditation, becoming quiet and asking for spiritual assistance. To be inspired is to use your *spirit* to create something. *Spirit* is the root word of inspiration. Your *spirit* is the go-to between your physical body and God's ear. Whatever you might call it, if you are reading this book, you have probably felt that there is a universal intelligence that is the glue keeping everything going together. Is it God or a directive? Is it healing intuitive energy, or, as many say, the energy of love? Its purpose seems to help keep us on track.

Many clients have told me that they are recovering from Catholicism, or detoxing from Judaism or other religions, and dogma that made them feel bad about themselves, some are just exploring their spirituality on their own terms. To be inspired is to use your *spirit* to create your dreams, hopes, and wishes. Clients often ask me how their *spirit* functions, how they connect to it, and how it leads them. This acronym is a spiritual cheat sheet that might help you understand how the *spirit* operates.

SPIRIT

S ~ Synchronicity and Signs: When you want to hear the messages of the *spirit*, look for synchronicities. Coincidences, or incidences, that coincide in your life are items to pay attention to. An example of a synchronicity is when you think of enrolling in school to become a teacher, and not knowing how to start the process, or anyone who

has done it, yet you end up sitting on a bus and striking up a conversation with a complete stranger, who happens to be the admissions officer for a teaching program, and is looking for someone exactly like you. Remember, there *are no coincidences* in life. Coincidences are the prime ingredient of synchronicities. Your *spirit* guides you through feelings in your heart, gut, and body to move you, through the law of attraction, to receive an inspiration. When your light of awareness goes on and you pay attention, the synchronicities come quicker, as the dance with the universe begins. Watch for synchronicities, they are messages from the universe.

You also have to pay attention to signs, they usually happen in threes. If you feel inspired to move to Arizona and you receive three messages about Arizona, it is something that you should pay attention to-- you may see a moving truck with an Arizona license plate on it.; you may hear a friend talking about applying to Arizona State; and finally, you might see a big billboard advertising Arizona as a vacation destination. These are all signs. Make sure you double check with your head about the logistics of how to get there, but those three signs will correlate with your thoughts about Arizona in order to get you to pay attention. Signs can be either physical or etheric, but please take note.

P ~ Purposeful and Passionate: The *spirit*'s messages and insights always seem to have purpose. The *spirit* has reasons when it gives you a nudge. Let's say that you wake up with an intuition to take a creative writing class, and you go online to search for one, you are able to find a class in your price range. You take the class and end up doing so well that you decide to write an article about the treatment of dolphins in Japan, in order to help raise awareness for this species. You end up creating a budding career and become an expert in this area. When the *spirit* urges you to do something, know that it has purpose, it may not be revealed right away, but it will move you on the path towards your destiny. The *spirit* also helps you find your passion. When you work with what your gifts are, what you like doing, and what preoccupies your mind, this is your passion. We will talk about passion in more detail later. Your *spirit's* passion helps awaken you by giving you chills, goose bumps, or "Ah-ha" moments when you get close to your passion. Your passion is something that you think about all the time. You are drawn to do it if you are sad and depressed. Sometimes, your passion can be a healing balm, if you have lost your way. Your passion is something that you may also be able to make a career of.

I ~ Intuitive and Insightful: This is the inherent fabric of listening to *spirit*, trusting your intuition. Your intuition, means "inner teacher." Intuition is the language of your *spirit,* and is another way that your *spirit* speaks to you. Intuition is when you seem to know something, without having any verifiable facts on how you may have come to that conclusion, about someone or something, and you are right. Your intuition is generally quick, insightful, and concise. When intuitions come to me, it reminds me of a leaf as it falls to the ground: the message lands in your thoughts somewhere in between the chatter, it just flits around until it has a place to sit. Have you ever had a thought that just plops into your head? If you don't catch it and act on it, it could just blow away.

All of our chatter, mind fog of negativity, fears, and inner dialogues block the space where *spirit* messages can land. Similarly, when you wake up from a dream, you have to remember it immediately, or the memory will fade. With your intuition, you have to listen to the subtle nuances of life and the quiet whispers of your heart. Make sure you write it down! Tune into the feelings that come along with various body sensations. Do you feel chills or goose bumps? The impressions or images that you see in your head that make an impact on your heart and feel significant, those are the things to act on, that is how intuition comes to you, and that is why it is important to quiet the mind. Meditation and mindfulness are key. Also, completing mundane tasks may bring about your intuitions. A lot of people gain insights while cleaning the toilet or taking a shower.

The insights that come from your intuition can generally be relied upon. Your insights are your *inner-sights* into your life. When you use your intuitions and get an inner sight, pay attention to this. This could be your SOUL mind speaking to you. Also, when you practice with your inner intuitive sight, your soul awareness becomes clearer.

R ~ Renewing and Recharging: Your *spirit* constantly revitalizes your body, mind, and soul. When you are depleted, it is your *spirit* that says rest, take a vacation, or go within. The renewing part of the *spirit* is the part that is always creating new ideas, new songs, hairstyles, designs, and business ideas. Your *spirit* will renew your faith in humanity, and also your ability to re-create in the world. After a devastating loss, your *spirit* will help you rebuild. When you are depleted, you may take a walk on the beach, or in the woods, and feel rejuvenated and recharged. Energy healing and massage both heal the *spirit*, as does walking in nature and taking salt baths. Try sitting in a sauna to recharge your *spirit* or read a spiritual text that renews you. Fulfilling the *spirit* is like putting gasoline into a car that needs to be refueled. Many empathic sensitive souls get drained easily; they need to gas up their soul vehicle, just like they need to charge their cell phone. These tasks are what will revitalize your *spirit*. Regularly recharge, rejuvenate, and renew the spirit.

I ~ Intelligent and Inspirational: Your *spirit* is highly intelligent, more intelligent than the cognitive mind may think it is. This is because your *spirit* mind uses your intuition to think, your insight to see, and your inspiration to get you motivated. The *spirit* mind is connected to the universal collective consciousness, or Source. It can help you figure out how to plan a party for 300, when you thought the guest list was only 200. You can write a great novel, when you are aligned with the creative part of your soul. It can give a message to help you heal someone's heart as a counselor, even when you don't know what to say. The intelligence of the *spirit* has to be experienced before being understood, but know that it is there. I don't care how much education you have, or don't have, there is an intelligent inspirational part that lies within each soul. This creative intelligence is what created the planet, nature, animals, etc., so surely it can guide your life as well. Listen to what inspires you, as that is your *spirit* in motion.

T ~ Truth and Trust: Your *spirit* only knows truth, it is honest and trustworthy. The *spirit* doesn't lie, but sometimes its insights are hard to understand without practice. Just know that once you tap into the *spirit's* truth, intuitive insights will abound. The universe is an all-yes environment. This means that it is positive, and prefers to say yes to all of its insights. On the physical plane, where a lot of no's and restrictions of creation exist, it is sometimes hard to trust. The duality of good and evil, light and dark, create limitations that make you grow from the contrast. If you walk with *spirit,* you will see more truth. This may spark awareness in you that you have always been listening to your *spirit*, but you just didn't know what it was. Your *spirit* will always tell you what is true. You must always trust your *spirit*. Some of its insights may be painful, or hard, in its revelations. Your *spirit* will lead you on the path to your soul's mission fulfillment.

You now understand the function of the *spirit*, but how does the *spirit* see, hear, feel, and know? The *spirit* is a live energy force that communicates to Source and to your physical body and mind. When the *spirit* feels something it is called *clairsentient,* or clear feeling of sentient beings. It can feel through urges, energy waves, pain, and sensations. Many massage therapists, healers, therapists, nurses, and even doctors are clairsentient. They feel in a deep way, and relay that to the mind. Clairsentients are also called empaths. Empaths are people who feel the pain of someone else on a deep level, like the pain is happening to them. They also use the intuition to understand these sensations.

The *spirit* is energy so it relates through feelings, this is the most powerful sensation for the *spirit.* Clairsentients, or empaths, tend to be drained by others very easily. They have to take care of their *spirit* body regularly. We will discuss this more when we talk about sensitive people. The *spirit's* intuitive knowing is called *claircognitive*. Cognizance is a term which comes from the word *to recognize*. Clear recognition is similar to your intuition, and occurs when your *spirit* just knows something, even before your mind thinks the situation through, you recognize the truth. The *spirit* sees through a term called *clairvoyance*. 'Voyance' comes from the word voyeur, *to see*.

Clear seeing is how the *spirit* sees through the third eye. The third eye is a chakra that resides in the etheric plane, between your brows. This is where the *spirit* sees visions or uses the ability to daydream, imagine, and work with creative visualization. The opening of the third eye is in the corner of your eyes, this is why some may see ghosts out of the side of their eyes. Your *spirit* is seeing the ghosts that are in other dimensions. Imagine that the *spirit* inside of you has circular vision, if the body is blocking the full view it would only get a glimpse of the apparition. This is why, when you think of the future or the past, you look to the side, you are trying to look into your memory through the third eye. You can use this third eye to create dreams, wishes, and future outcomes. Since your *spirit* is naturally creative and a connection to Source, what we think about and see, we can create. The *spirit* is a natural creative force, and it is a powerful part of us, that is often underutilized. When we get a vision of our future, have an idea, or come up with an invention, it is generally through our third eye. If these imaginings come up, *write them down*, they are coming to you for you to create. The *spirit* hears through *clairaudience* – a clear audience derived from the word, *auditory*--it is the ability to hear. Sometimes, your *spirit* can hear a message or a voice. There is a big difference between this and hearing voices like command hallucinations which tell someone to hurt themselves or someone else, this is not something that should be listened to. True clairaudience, of the high part of your *spirit*, is direct, quick, compassionate, and generally uplifting. It can also be a warning, such as if you are in danger the voice may say, "Watch out!" or "Move!" If you are of sound mind, you must discern between hearing voices and hearing an inspirational voice.

Another question you may have is, how does the *spirit* sit in your body? Where is the *spirit* located? The *spirit* is energy, so it lies inside of you and spills out. Think of how steam can permeate a substance, being both around and in something. Since it is not solid, it spills out of you, and this would describe as your aura field. The aura is the bioenergetic field that surrounds you. Bio, meaning life, and energetic, meaning the energy field or life force. It is your charisma, or your vibe. The aura field carries in it all of your thoughts and intentions, and it magnetizes what you put out into the world. This is why your aura, or your vibe, can feel different depending on what your intentions are, or your mood is.

The *spirit* resides in your body, and is almost snapped into--and held in your body by your chakras. Although the energy of the chakras are etheric.Your chakras, as mentioned before, are those energetic wheels that radiate out from different parts of your body. The chakras line up like a prism in your body, and look like the colors of the rainbow. A rainbow is a dispersion of light, and we are light energy beings. The chakras are our natural rainbows inside of us.

If you do yoga, you will know what the chakras are, and may have seen the picture of them -- (see page 35) picture the *first chakra* is red as the base color of the chakra, this is the chakra that connects us to Mother Earth, it is located in the coccyx, or lower back area. Emotionally, it helps us to be stable and strong enough to walk on the earth plane. This chakra is about survival and about creating jobs and opportunities, and it also resonates with support. When people are out of work, this chakra is usually spinning hard in order to create the energy from *spirit* to create opportunities. It is also why the lower back often hurts when a person isn't feeling supported, emotionally or financially. The energy of this chakra can also feel low if the person needs to create income. It has more of a male assertive energy, but also has the energy of creating with Mother Earth, with its red earth color.

The *second Chakra*, the sacral is sacred and is generally orange in color. It is the sexual, sensual chakra and has to do with creation. It is located where the sexual organs are. This chakra is about creating life, creating children, as well as creating articles, movies, music, artwork, or seminars. This chakra holds our emotional health, it has to be healthy in order to manifest creative opportunities and healthy intimacy in love relationships. Creation is more of a feminine receptive energy, the womb is where things are held and created. This is why I feel that women want to "create and nest an egg" it is a place where they can be intimate. It is why women become so attached to men; we take in their energy, their life force, literally, and harvest things to grow. This chakra takes in a lot of energy in the world and is a very sensitive chakra for women and men, as they create life their also.

The *third chakra* is the Solar Plexus, or our power center. This chakra is yellowish in color and it concerns the ability to stand up for oneself and to stand in power to say yes and no. It is the seat of our will, and has a more assertive male energy and drive. When people have chronic stomach issues, I know that they are having an issue with their power, either in their personal or professional life.

The *fourth chakra* is the Heart Center. The color of this area is green, and sometimes a little pink, as it is the love center. Loving ourselves and others, self-love and self-care lie in this chakra. This chakra resonates with joy and an open heart. An open heart chakra feels receptive, supportive, and loving. A closed heart chakra feels heavy, angry, and sad. It has a nurturing, loving feminine energy when it is healthy, like a good mom or dad. Often times, when a person's heart is closed it is because they have been hurt deeply, or are grieving, or feeling resentful. A closed heart chakra can disconnect you from your passion, your purpose, and your mission. Your passion lies in your chakra heart, but engaging in something that is a passion can also heal your heart, mind, and soul, even when you are depressed.

The *fifth chakra* is the Throat Chakra, it resonates with the color blue. This gives us our ability to communicate and to speak our truth. This chakra helps us to create on the earth plane. What we speak about, we bring about. This is a very powerful chakra. When God said "Let there be light," allegedly, the world was created. You will create in your world, with your own words. It has more of a male assertive energy, but it can also be loving and nurturing. We all know how negative words towards children can damage their confidence and self-esteem, it is the same regarding how we can nurture or destroy our own self-worth. Words are powerful creators.

The *sixth chakra* is called the third eye, and its color is indigo. The third "eye" chakra is how your *Spirit* sees. This chakra gives us the ability to visualize what we create in the world, through our inner vision. The ability to daydream, imagine, visualize, and manifest on the earth plane comes through your third eye. It is the seat of our intuition and of our inner guidance. It is important to envision what you want to create, and pay attention to your daydreams. Often, our daydreams are what we have the ability to create, bring into reality. This is why marketing and subliminal programming work. Advertisers know that if we see something over and over again, with certain stimulating attractions, we will eventually buy the product, see the movie, or purchase the item, because we think it will make us feel good. What truly makes us feel good is when we learn to love ourselves. This chakra has more of a feminine energy. Surround your space with positive words and inspirational pictures to keep your visions on a high vibration.

The *seventh chakra,* the crown, is usually purple or violet, and is the ability to connect to the divine source. I have seen the crown chakra portrayed as a white light, which can be associated with this chakra. The crown chakra helps you experience life from a higher and more spiritual perspective, this chakra resonates with Source. The chakras should be paid attention to so that you know what path to go on, and how to interpret your spiritual lessons. The energy of the chakras may be low or strong, depending on what you are going through. The seventh chakra has more male energy, connected to God the father, but the crown chakra also creates with all sentient beings, so it has the feminine energy of creation. If you noticed that the chakras go back and forth between male or female energy, it is because we all are made up of *both* energies. You can find a very feminine woman with a lot of male energy, and a very strong masculine man with very sensitive feminine energy. This is because we need both energies to balance in the physical plane. Yoga, a mind body exercise and spiritual philosophy, greatly focuses on balancing these chakras. If you want to learn more about the chakras, I recommend the book, *Chakra for Beginners* by David Pond.

WORKBOOK EXERCISE 2

- **Pay attention** to what colors you are drawn to or reso- nate with, and also the clothes you wear or energetic colors you want to be around. Many times, they are connected to colorful chakras and the energy you need to incorporate in your life, or challenges you need to heal.

- **Write down** what you are noticing, and look at the corresponding chakra colors.

Affirmations really help your chakras, since we create our energy into being by our words, it is important to say positive things frequently. For the *first chakra,* you should say, "I am safe; I trust more; I fear less. I am centered and grounded."

For the *second chakra* you should say, "I feel my emotions and my pain. I reawaken my passion. I surrender to this moment." For the *third and solar plexus power center,* say, "I am courageous; I am whole; I stand in my power." *Fourth, and heart chakra green,* "I am loved; I let love in, I am kind to myself; I live in peace and gratitude." For the *fifth and throat chakra that resonates with blue,* you should say, "I play in my imagination. I create my reality. I know and share my truth." For the *third eye, indigo chakra,* say, "I honor my intuition. I accept my path; I am healing body, mind, and *spirit.*"

For the *crown and seventh chakra, which resonates with violet,* the affirmation is, "I connect with *Spirit,* and invite sacred transformation. I embrace the unity of all beings."

These saying are from the chakra healing flags of www.westwindflags.com These affirmations help get the chakras spinning, and help clear negative programming. I also do energy healing, so I know how to clean the energy of chakras. I recommend wearing various crystals that correspond to the colors of the chakras. To further nurture your chakras, and clear your energy field, which holds your *spirit,* I recommend that people ground and protect their energy field.

As you become more sensitive to your *spirit,* you will want protect and care for your field, as you would care for a nice new car. It is like having a good radio signal when you want to connect to a clear frequency signal from the universe.

Photo by Maxwell Aston

There is a powerful meditation technique called *Grounding and Protecting your Energy*. This procedure should be done in a meditative and quiet state. Light a candle and some incense, relax with your feet flat on the floor, and your back straight. Put on some background music--Reiki, or healing meditative music, if you need to come back to this method when you have more time, than do so.

Imagine your heart is filled with golden energy, this is the energy of love, light, and peace. With each natural breath, the energy gets stronger and stronger, and the golden light starts filling up your whole chest cavity. The gold energy starts running through your body and aura, and it helps to put positive energy into your field. Bringing energy from your heart, where your *spirit* heart lies, down through all of your lower chakra and pelvic area into the thighs knees and calves and into your feet. Imagine that your feet are so filled with this light that at the bottom of them they create golden roots that come out of the pads of your feet. These imaginary roots can go through the floor and into the cement of the ground, and down into the earth, helping you to feel grounded on the earth plane. Make sure the energy rays go down at least ninety feet, with two roots coming from each of your feet down into the ground. You are connecting your energy in the earth so that the energies work together. Then bring energy from the earth up through the roots counting by ten feet intervals, from 70' to 60' to 50', and so on. Bring golden earth energy up through the lower chakras and your legs, past all the lower chakras and stomach, and then into the heart. Just like the earth gives energy to plants and trees, it can nurture you, let the energy sit in your heart. Imagine the earth sending you good, strong, stable energy.

Next, imagine energy coming from the heart all the way up through the throat down into your shoulders and down your apper arms eblows and lower forearms. Let the energy move into your wrists and fingers as the light moves back from your fingertips and wrist and up through your arms. The energy comes through past your chin, nose, eyes and the third eye, filling your whole head all the way through the crown and through nine dimensions of time and space, and then connecting to a big star in the sky, counting up through dimensions from the third, fourth and fifth dimensions the way to number nine where Source is. This way you are hooking to the energy of the creator. If you're having challenges around God, imagine you are connecting to a large star, or energy source. Imagine yourself sitting in this light for a while, and connecting to your purpose and the wisdom of your plan here on earth, or just let the energy give you positive insight. Sit in this healing light for a while, for five to ten minutes, and then imagine an energy ray from Source, filled with this wisdom coming down through nine dimensions of time and space, down into your crown and into your heart.

Counting up and down is a way to get in and out of altered states, similar to what hypnosis does. When you move your energy in and out of altered states, it soothes the soul and the conscious mind, this opens up for intuitive wisdom to come through. Then mix the two energies together in your heart area, the yin and yang, heaven and earth, the male and female, the passive and assertive, the father and mother. As the energy, like a circuit, comes down from above and through you, and down into the earth and up through you, and to heaven and back, the circuit of light becomes so strong that the energy flows out of all of your cells and pours out like energy rays, and you become like a light as you shine up your aura field. As the energy comes through your energy field, it can enhance your aura. Make the rays shine out of your body into an egg like bubble around your aura. Command that the bubble to let in only positive energy and deflect negative energy.

You have to cleanse your field daily to support your spirit just as you have to take a shower for your body. You can also sage your field regularly, which helps to clear the negativity in your energy field. If you want to do the meditation more deeply, you can sit in the energy of each chakra, affirm the positive qualities of each chakra, and remove the negative qualities bringing in more light. Essential oils and high vibrational sprays help to clear your field of negative energetic debris. Remember, your energy field houses your *spirit,* and clearing it is one way you can enhance it. This method in *spirit* self-care fine tunes your *spirit* instrument to function at an optimum level. Understanding and knowing your *spirit* can help you to know and live your life purpose and mission. Since the *spirit* holds the information about your goal on earth, and is the guiding force, you should pay attention to it and understand its function and care.

This care of the *spirit* is very important for sensitives and empaths, as they tend to absorb the negative energy of others regularly. Working with your energy field helps you to realize that you are part of the cosmos, and that you are more connected to the energy or the stars and the planets then you may have before realized. We will discuss this more, later in the book.

Your *spirit* has been calling you. You may have felt an insight that there is a universal intelligence that supports and guides you, it could be a higher part of yourself that knows what you want to create on earth. This meditation practice clears and energizes the chakras, and protects your energy field so you that don't get so drained in life that you miss those spiritual insights. Respect this sacred instrument of light: Your *spirit*.

What is the universe? The universe is a vast array of inter-connective consciousness that is made from love, and embodies God's heart, mind, and soul. I believe God is an energy source of consciousness, and that the universe is the emanation of his aura into the world and galaxies. I do believe God is the father of us and of all of creation. Yes, I believe in the feminine power of the Goddess, but the voice I have heard sounds masculine, with a loving, nurturing, feminine quality. I have friends who have heard the divine mother in their thoughts. Don't get wrapped up in these earthly constraints, just dialogue with the higher consciousness. This universal energy, and life force, is a directive energy, and many say it is love. When you are listening to your *spirit* and creating with your life force, you are creating with the love energy of the universe, that is how I define the universe, but you will have to come to your own understanding.

The more you tap into your own answers, the more you will learn how your *spirit* speaks to you. Ask your *spirit* now to explain to you what the universe is. The movie *The Secret,* by Rhonda Byrne, describes the law of attraction, one of many universal laws. What you vibrate, you attract. This information has made understanding the universe more mainstream, there are many universal laws, and they are listed and explained in the back of this book. I know when I ask the universe a question, I generally get an answer. I either receive the answer that I wanted, or something different.

If I look back on some of my thoughts and unconscious beliefs surrounding an event, I can sometimes see how I manifested it.

The universe feels like a copy machine--recreating thoughts, words, and deeds. The only thing that changes those patterns is when I ask God to intervene, and there seems to be a break in that cycle of my creation, not always, but sometimes. As we grow in our spiritual development, we need to be careful with our thoughts and what we create. I have also manifested many of my fears by focusing on them through chronic obsessions and worry.

The Universe will speak with you, it is the master promotion artist, and will send messengers in many forms, at the right time and the right moment, if you need the inspiration. The *spirit* is a powerful part of our being that works and dialogues with universal wisdom. The *spirit* is easy to ignore in the materialistic earth plane. We learn to squash our wishes, dreams, and desires and create material things: mortgages, unfulfilling relationships, and empty lives that are earth bound. Images and outside appearances are a big distraction from our true spiritual nature. These distractions don't mean much to the growth of the soul, unless the manifestation assists our spiritual nature and others.

Our *spirit* is not always found in church, it is within us. The *spirit* in everyone is powerful, and when you tap into it, you can find messages, peace, and wisdom. Your *spirit* talks to you through your intuition--that is its language. The language is a whisper, an "Ah-ha" moment, or a gut instinct. If you are at a crossroads in your life, if you are feeling defeated, ask the universe to send you a sign or message. It will oblige, it always has for me.

How Does the Universe Speak to You?

There are many ways the universe converses with us, and it speaks to your *spirit* on a regular basis. We all learn in different ways, and this earth is constantly asking us to get back on track in many various ways. The earth is in chaos, and it is a practice place for us to use our spiritual muscles to create more good. At first, it was an intensive summer camp, but it now feels like juvenile hall because so many of our SOULS have forgotten why we came here. The universe is our school counselor who asks what college we want to go to, and what we want to study. Here are some examples of how the universe broadcasts its messages to us.

Dreams~ Dreams are messages from your SOUL, or the Universe. The soul is part of your *spirit* that resides on the other side of the veil. In human form, your body is the vehicle and your words are how you communicate. In the *spirit* world, your soul is the vehicle, and the *spirit* is how you communicate on the earth plane. Dreams are the transmissions from your SOUL to your *spirit* and mind. Dreams can be very profound and lucid, or can be premonitions or nightmares.

Analyzing your dreams can help you understand what you are going through. Your dreams are a broadcast of your soul to your physical body and mind. I believe your dreams are your in-house psychotherapist. Unless you are using drugs or abusing alcohol, your dreams can help you figure out your dilemmas in life, they can also help with the higher meaning behind patterns. I have had many premonitions recently, especially after I started my meditation classes, which helps to give energy to the *spirit*. Premonitions are dreams that may be of the future. They are dreams in pre–motion, before it happens on the earth plane, they can be your soul's warning to you about your path. I also have been having some profound, lucid dreams and have experienced astral projections in various dimensions and times.

As I honor and respect the totality of my SOUL, more gifts seem to open up. The more you meditate, the more you become aware of your *spirit* body. Pay attention to your dreams and don't say to yourself, "I can't remember my dreams," saying this just programs your mind to close down. If you are alive, you are dreaming. The best way to remember your dreams is to ask your cognitive mind to remember them before you go to sleep. You can also bring a pen and paper by the bed to record your dreams, as soon as you wake up. Everyone dreams every night, but sometimes you close down your ability to remember them. You have to clear out the fear and be open. My father said my grandfather, Charles, used to have many premonitions, he used to discuss them with my grandmother, Ida, who herself was an intuitive and spiritual counselor. They would never charge for their gifts. My paternal grandmother was just known to give spiritual advice to neighbors and friends at the kitchen table.

Meditation helps to remove all of those cobwebs. It helps clear the way to hear your *spirit*. Your mind, your unconscious, is a store house of all of your life experiences. Your mind and your body are like a computer that takes in and records all of these experiences. It stores memories in your brain until you are ready to look at them. It stores memories in your body until you are ready to release them. These memories also reside in your *spirit* and are uploaded back to your SOUL when you pass on. Your *spirit* is a storehouse of your earthly experiences--through your dreams; sometimes, these bits and pieces of your thought process come through in a symbolic movie form, to be analyzed. Your soul also comes through in your dreams, helping you to get on course. Dreams are a powerful way of knowing what is going on around you. When you are having a difficult time in life, pay attention to your dreams!

I teach about dreams in the IOP (Intensive Outpatient Program) where I work. You would be surprised by how many people are already getting ideas about what to do next on their path, in their life. People who have never analyzed dreams and who are in crisis and deep depression are now going to sleep with intention. Listen to what your dreams are saying. What is the message they are trying to convey? Many dream symbols mean the same thing as when you see them in the waking state, and they are a good way to practice dialoguing with the universe. Get a good dream book, and begin to analyze the symbols, just like you would in the waking state when the universe is talking to you. Talk it over with a trusted friend. Bring it to a therapist or a skilled counselor that can really help you look at it from different perspectives.

A great book is *The Dream Book* by Betty Bethards, a renowned mystic who is now deceased, or I should say who has graduated to go back home to *Spirit* Land. It has a lot of great insight. I generally use this one, but there are many, many others out there. I am also a fan of Edgar Cayce's book, *Dreams and Visions*. I did training at the Association in Research and Enlightenment (ARE) center in Manhattan, Edgar Cayce's School.

I have always been a good dream analyzer, as I constantly analyze the symbols in real life, and thus understand the ones during dream states as well. One client was having nightmares, and after I analyzed the dream, the nightmares went away. No matter what book you get, your guides and disembodied *spirit* teachers, along with the universe, will work with whatever symbol they know will bring understanding to your awareness. **Program yourself before you go to bed by stating, "I want to remember my dreams."** Get a dream journal by your bed, and write all of the significant parts of your dreams down. See what the universe is trying to tell you.

Synchronicities/Signs: I explained signs earlier, when I discussed the ways in which your *spirit* speaks to you. It is worth stating again that the universe will reveal messages to you in signs, and there are a million different signs. They could come in songs, repetitive messages, through others, animal sightings, or messages on billboards, when you ask. Just ask! For example, I started seeing feathers everywhere. Literally, right in front of my path, where I was walking, boom, there was a feather. It became a game with the universe for me to ask for a feather, and then see one. I recovered up to thirty-nine feathers that I had found over several months. I would see them in the most obscure places. Generally, I would be thinking about something spiritual and a feather would appear. I thought it was funny that I would find long ones, short ones, and small ones, feathers from hawks, eagles, pigeons, and all other kinds of birds. It was always when I was asking the universe to give me a sign that I would see a feather. It was fun and I knew that I was dialoguing with the universe, and getting a physical answer. I put all of my feathers on my altar in a big container to remind myself of the presence of *Spirit*.

I was asking for proof of my *spirit* guide. I knew he was native, but wasn't sure. Alana, the reader in Manhattan, had told me about my *Spirit* guide, who was a Peruvian healer and herbalist, and allegedly my compadre in Peru when I was incarnated there. I named him Eagle Feather, as he showed me he was responding to my request to make himself known. I have heard him on occasion. Yes, *spirit* guides can answer as part of the Universal dialogue. I know that the feathers were him saying hello. Many intuitives have seen him hovering around me, he helps me with mediumship readings and protects me from danger. Yes, even I, who works as an intuitive, have doubts that all of my requests are being heard. I often wonder why I chose to incarnate at this time in this very dense earth plane that always feels so unnatural and uncomfortable to me. I am constantly waiting for the mothership to show up, and I pray this is my last incarnation.

I always felt it would be a lot more fun to be a *spirit* guide, all purple and shimmery, watching others on the earth plane, and trying to assist them on their spiritual paths from the other side. These thoughts often come up when I hear so many sad and horrific stories in my career as a social worker, an intuitive, and a healer. I too need to be inspired--helping people to begin their journey inspires me, and helps me to process my journey as well as theirs. It fits pieces into the complex puzzles of their lives. Until the mothership arrives, I will be here seeking, understanding, helping, and hopefully inspiring.

Another way I understand that there is order in all of this sadness, terror, and confusion is to test the universe for order in the chaos. I drink a lot of water and collect a lot of bottles, like a good recycler, I tend to put them in my recycle bin with plans to bring them to the recycle stand. The recycle bin is only a couple of blocks from my home, without a doubt, I always drive by a homeless person or bottle collector and give them the bottles. Now if you know anything about Los Angeles traffic, then you know it is quite busy and not easy to stop, but within the chaos, there is order, because I am always able to pull over and give the bottles safely. I never go more than a day with the bottles in my car. This shows me that the universe is listening.

Bringing together a need – There is someone who needs to receive, and I need to give.

1. There is order in a seemingly chaotic situation: LA traffic, and

2. Acknowledgement that the universe is at work, and my request to help has been heard within twenty-four hours, as all of our requests will be. I ask, and it is given.

I am also detached about whether I give away a bottle or not, so that is usually why the manifestation comes quickly; I have no real attachment to the outcome. **Detachment creates outcomes quicker.** Recently, I have been giving the bottles to the cleaner of my apartment building. Ironically, every time he is cleaning my floor, I have tons of bottles to give him. I work frequently and it seems like coincidentally, I am always home when he is on my floor. The look on the faces of these individuals is very moving, sometimes I feel like the bottle Santa Claus. People who try to be invisible, who try not to be seen, those who dig in the garbage cans of others, I try to make feel appreciated.

Hopefully, the message I convey is that there are others who are watching and seeing your struggle, and who are there to assist and support. They teach me about gratitude, synchronicity, appreciation, and courage. It is my tithing, my way of giving back to my spiritual teachers, giving is a lesson in humility. Their appreciation when I am having a bad day is invaluable. My interactions are not always pious, I can get frustrated with the barrage of people trying to catch my eye for a quarter or a dollar, just when I have gotten out of a day of working in the ER helping other people in similar circumstances. I know it isn't always the right answer, but many times I can sense if someone is running a con game. I often have to stop myself and appreciate what I have. People often ask if I am scared, or nervous. Of what? No one has ever been dangerous when I have given them bottles. I work in the ER, and I am not scared of someone without a home, I am filled with compassion for them! I often remember my father stopping his car to help strangers in an accident, or someone needing assistance, when I wasn't in the car he used to pick up hitch-hikers, never afraid, just doing a service.

The world today has gotten too dangerous for that, and he's too old, but the message of helping others was there. I guess helping random strangers reminds me of my upbringing from home. Also, in my spiritual home called heaven, I know that is how we are judged. Not by how many toys we have, or how many riches, but by how we gave to one another. By the way, a smile doesn't cost a dime. I will tithe to the universe by giving someone with little to no income my bottles, no strings attached, in order to help them on their path. And by the way, every act that we do, positive or negative, we will experience in our life review at death. We will physically feel how we have treated one another, by feeling what they felt. Empaths already have that ability to feel the pain of others, very deeply, and that is why they are so sensitive--they work with their *spirits*, and they know how others feel when something bad happens to them. The empaths are the forerunners, in the shift on this planet, to bring more light and sensitivity to one another.

At the beginning of my spiritual journey, I needed more concrete signs. I wanted the bells and whistles, and I wanted to hear and see the messages from the universe-- concretely. I needed a sign from the universe when I was struggling to understand if all of these spiritual experiences were real. I remember feeling overwhelmed with all that I had to do, when I was studying in graduate school. I was getting a two year Master's in sixteen months; I was having health problems, working an internship with poor working conditions (large rats running across my desk in my internship in Chinatown), seeing challenging patients, dealing with loud neighbors, and fighting the annoying New York roaches (they were the kind of roach that used to laugh with an "Is-that-all-you-got?" type of NY energy when I pulled out the Combat Spray. You can almost hear New York roaches saying, "Bring it on").

I could go on about all of these challenges. I would get so down on myself and just complain. Without a doubt, I would see a blind person with a cane, navigating themselves through New York City, with a smile on their face, sometimes I would see them by themselves, or with a helper or guide dog, stepping onto the subway, or hailing a cab. What?! I would quickly end my pity party, realizing with gratitude all that I had. I must have seen twenty-five blind people over the course of the sixteen months I was there. The chances of seeing so many people who had lost their sight, *at the exact same time* I was beating myself up, was a synchronistic occurrence. I knew it was orchestrated by the universe, and I knew the universe was alive, aware, watching, and hearing. I felt the universe was saying that if they can get on a subway by trusting others in a big city, and get to their destination, surely I can get over anything. Also, they were symbolic of the old Bible verse, "Walk by faith, and not by sight." Literally, the blind people had to trust their other senses, as I had to trust my sixth sense, as I navigated my new spiritual path. Also, the blind people I saw had to trust people they couldn't see to help them on the streets. I had to trust my guides and angels that I couldn't see, but could sense. Finally, my grandmother was partly blind, seeing a blind person reminded me of my dear grandmother who taught me unconditional love.

Usually when I see someone with a challenge and see their ability to navigate the world--one with a wheelchair, a cane, or maybe cerebral palsy, I know there is a powerful soul wrapped up inside. A young soul wouldn't take such a high level lesson. Look at your own symbols that way, there are always multiple meanings. What does a recurring theme mean to you? It may be a hummingbird constantly coming into your path or it may be seeing a bunch of men on motorcycles, which may represent freedom. Another example might be running into a monk three or four times, in a large city, which may bring up feelings of exploring spirituality. Maybe you have been hearing the same song, on four different radio stations, four different times, and the musician hasn't recently died, or had a major scandal around them, and the song isn't a new release. What catches your eye or your ear? *Pay attention.* Take notice of what the universe trying to teach you. If you *pay attention* to the universe, it will develop a dialogue with you and speak the language that you understand. **Play with the universal language, try to ask right now for something that you want to experience, and see how your request is heard.** Ask for someone to give you an insightful or inspiring message, and then take notice when it occurs.

When you obtain a confirmation, raise your head to the clouds and say, "Thank you," or say it in your thoughts. Once you create the vibration of gratitude to the universe, it fine tunes you to the higher vibration, and if you match it, more good is allowed to come in. There is a creative force in the universe that wants to work with you, it wants you to be abundant, fruitful, expansive, and bold. It is calling you to move forward, to find your purpose, and to keep you on course. It is the sacred call of the divine.

Animal totems: Nature is a wonderful example of the universe speaking to you. God has created nature as a gift for our eyes, senses, and *spirits*. The Native Americans often look to animals as signs from the creator, they call them totem animals. Animals seem to hold the key to the synchronicity of life. In shamanic wisdom, every animal has a meaning and a message. I have also loved animals for their unconditional love. I tend to meditate in the park, and try to concentrate over the myriad of crows. They are loud and obnoxious, and they often remind me of gangsters yelling to each other and performing a call and response type of conversation. They represent ancestors, and always remind me of my powerful lineage of seers and healers.

When I started seeing different animals, I would google 'animal totem,' and put in the name of the various animals that I saw. It was unbelievable the various animals I would see represented the exact situation that I was experiencing in life. A hummingbird means to enjoy life's simple pleasures, and that you may be accomplishing something that seems impossible. A raccoon means wearing a mask in life. I saw a hawk, and the website talked about the power of vision and intuitions and seeing life from a higher perspective. I found the hawk feather exactly when I needed to hear that exact message. Don't dismiss an animal's ability to teach us and give messages.

One day when I was running around too much an animal almost sacrificed itself to give me a message. I was careening down my street, trying to get home from a job to see a private client, when I saw this large rock in the road. I wondered what a large rock was doing there. As I approached, I saw that the rock was moving forward, but slowly. When I was right up on it, I saw something stick it's little head up, and I realized it was a turtle. I live next to a turtle pond, so I realized that this little critter had gotten out and wandered. I was concerned that it would get hit, so I pulled over and ran out into the road. Just as I was approaching it, a large semi-truck was coming from the other side of the road, there was nothing I could do to protect it, so I just prayed...and don't you know the truck went right over the turtle without hitting it. I attempted to grab the turtle again and there was another big tour bus coming toward it, so I prayed again, and the second vehicle missed the turtle. Here was my chance, I ran into the road and grabbed the turtle. The poor thing quickly retreated into his shell, scared from all of the noise and turmoil. I quickly ran to the pond and dropped it in there. The turtle just sat at the bottom of the water, I thought it was dead. After a couple of seconds, it started swimming. When I reflected on the turtle, and googled turtle totem, the translation for seeing a turtle was "slow down" and also "working with mother earth." A message I needed to hear as I was running around from job to clients.

Honestly, there is really no time constraint with *spirit*, all of the rushing around is usually, in the bigger picture, meaningless. The next day, I went to see how the turtle was doing. I found it sitting in the middle of the pond, on a rock, with tons of smaller turtles around it. It looked like a homecoming. I imagined his whole family happy that papa turtle had returned. I could hear the turtle telling its community about his big adventure: "I was sitting in the middle of the road, and thought I was going to get hit by this big mechanical thing when a big brown hand, I think it was mother earth, picked me up and saved me." The story would be the talk of turtle town for years to come, or so I believed. My friend on Facebook called me 'the turtle whisperer.' I slowed down and took time to take in the scenery, and give myself time between my work and my private clients. Nature is there as our teacher. Listen up.

One of my clients from Russia, in my *Dialoguing with the Universe* class noticed that her cat was trying to teach her something. She was dating this guy that was not good to her. She noticed that when he was around, her light cat turned completely gray! When the guy left, the cat's normal hair color returned. It was a warning that this guy would turn her hair gray! The cat was giving her a major warning sign! I remember I was seeing this really good looking marine and my little cat, who was a kitten at the time, gave me a warning--the minute the marine came into the apartment, kitty's hair stood on end like she was terrified. You know those Halloween pictures of the black cat with its back arched and hair straight up? That is exactly what she looked like! Who knows what the marine was up to, he didn't stay long in my spiritually oriented apartment, that was years ago. This was not the first time my cat has been a protector from the male species.

I was seeing this guy who was going through his own spiritual trauma, with a Saturn Return. He was kind and sweet on the surface, but had a foul mouth and seething rage on the inside. It is common for a healer, like me, to attract someone who needs healing instead of a suitable partner. The dark (lost) looks for the light (has a direction), because they are off their path, and they subconsciously understand that the light can lead them back to the path.

Even before I saw that angry side of him, my cat would ignore this suitor. One time, when I introduced him to my cat, she hissed while taking a swipe at him. I thought she was jealous, as my intuitive friend had said, but my *spirit* said something else, this guy spent a considerable amount of time at my apartment, and when he got on her side of my bed, my black panther was there to meet him, hissing! She sometimes slept in that space, and she didn't like the intrusion in her territory, or so I thought, then I noticed my kitty was losing hair, in the shape of a V down her back. At first it was a small spot, and then it accelerated to a V. The vet, over the phone, said it could be mold or something else, but in my heart I knew it was because of the relationship. My feline friend was my little protector--the relationship was tumultuous with two fire signs both wanting their way.

Even before the vet gave me the diagnosis of my cat being nervous and picking her own hair out, I knew this guy had to go. He had emotional demons he was "working through," that my cat didn't like, and neither did I. Kitty felt the undercurrent way before I did. The guy was sexy and hot, but I knew when I met him that he had an expiration date. He was one of the first guys I was with that was as intuitive as me, often reading my thoughts etc., as I did with him, so that was the pull, but it wasn't enough. Within two weeks of him being gone, my cat's fur grew back. She was over-grooming to warn me of the darkness in our midst. Trust your animals, as their instincts are superb. They are put on the planet as teachers, companions, and protectors. They are God's gift to us.

Inner knowing, and "Ah-ha" moments: You can have revelations through the words of others. I hope this book inspires you, and gives you some "Ah-ha" moments. Have you ever talked to a good friend, and got an answer to a question that has been troubling you? The person may not be consciously giving you a *spirit* message, but may say something that gives you a feeling that you must *pay attention* to what they are saying. In your heart, you know what sounds right, and in your being you know what feels right.

Sometimes, a friend will say something to you, and the hair on the back of your neck will stand on end. This is an affirmation that what you are hearing is authentic, true, and right. TRUST THIS FEELING, and move with it. Your *spirit* will use any vehicle to get you to listen to your truth. Your soul only knows truth, and the *spirit* is your vehicle to get there, but remember not all messages from friends are *spirit* driven. If they are mean spirited, or if the messages make you doubt yourself or cause you to act out in anger, most likely that is not a higher message. You may need to stay away from this person.

Your *spirit* messages are usually light, airy, and quick, and they hit you in your heart or gut. There is a lot of useless jabber going on, with text messages, Smartphones, and emails, but there are also a lot of beautiful messages coming in, you just have to be tuned in to the right frequency in order to hear the right messages. Life purpose broadcasts come on the high end vibrational radio, this is the station of light, love, inspiration, and high intentions. Remember, the purpose of this book is to get you to know, listen to, and honor your *spirit*, to get you on the right path and help you to stay on the course that you have already created eons ago, in the *spirit* world.

Songs*:* Songs can help you receive messages from the spiritual realm. Songs are the ultimate frequency of melodies to induce harmony and poetic resonance. We love music because it is energy in motion that rocks and inspires our *spirit,* and soothes our woes. I am amazed how frequently clients will hear a song that moves them to insight. It is fun to ask a question to the universe, put on your radio, and scroll through the many radio stations to see what message comes through. It is uncanny how many times a message comes through music, at just the right time.

I had a client, Lisa, who was having a hard time making a decision about whether to stay in an emotionally abusive relationship. She and Jonathan had been together for ten years, but there was a history of chronic verbal abuse. I didn't feel that it was the best relationship for her, and she admitted to always being drained when she was with him. Lisa was skeptical of intuitive readers, but her friend had convinced her to come and see me. I told her to ask the universe for a sign, and had gone through the various ways that the universe speaks to us.

As soon as she left our session and got in her car, she started to switch the radio station around, asking for a sign. On the radio was a song with lyrics that said, "Hit the road Jack, don't come back no more, no more, no more/ no matter what you say," by Percy Mayfield. She called me from the car. I laughed and said that too bad his name wasn't Jack, and she laughed even harder, saying she couldn't believe it, but his family had called him Jack growing up, which is his middle name. She went home to find him in a compromising position with another lady. That was enough and she quickly broke up with her boyfriend.

The universe is an energetic vibratory frequency, and that is why it can use music to get a message through to teach you. This is why music moves our SOUL, our SOULS are energy. Anything that pushes you to the light and your own truth, the universe will generally provide. She needed a direct and tangible message, and she got it.

I love it when the universe works with me and helps clients to see things for themselves. That is why I like having classes and gatherings. I coach people on how to tune in for themselves, to not need someone else to do it for them. The synchronicities are amazing, and everyone is a witness, proof of the presence of *spirit*. It helps clients to believe in themselves, and the power of *spirit* to provide an answer to life's difficulties.

The universe will send you messages in different ways. I always tell clients to ask the universe to send you a message, in ways that YOU will understand. The universe will honor your *spirit,* you have to learn how to dialogue with the universe; open up and have discussions with universe, like you would with a good teacher--ask questions, get evidence, explore, and gain proof. Learn the language of the universe. If you feel dense, tell the universe to be very direct. If you feel you need things shown to you in the physical plane, ask for a manifestation that way.

My way of communication has changed over the years, as I learned to trust and tune in and to be aware of the *spirit* messages, and not the egoic mind. It generally feels like a stream of consciousness in my head. Phrases come to me such as, "This client won't come back," or "They are being abused by their spouse," or "They have never ever felt loved." It moved my work more quickly, and I am able get to the core of the issue easily working around that wound, tending, clearing, and suturing that painful hurt.

When you work with the universe, you understand that in all of this chaos there is order. There is a plan in action that can be masked by our own egos and obsessions in the material world. We realize that life has built-in lessons that we may have to learn, but that there are ways to get the message so that we don't keep repeating the same experiences over and over.

Your *SOUL* and *SOUL* Contracts

What is your SOUL? I believe it is the totality of your life's existences, through time, space, and dimensions. It is the record keeper and store house of your thoughts and feelings, of spiritual and earthly experiences, from the beginning of your creation. I believe it is the store house and memory bank of it all. It is wonderful, God-filled, loving, and light. Your SOUL is **S**ynchronistic, **O**pen, **U**niversal, and **L**oving. It is the part of you that is closest to SOURCE. It is the higher perfect part of you that resides on the other side of this dimension. I believe your *spirit* is the energy that whispers from your SOUL. The SOUL, since it is all energy, sends a piece of itself to earth but regularly checks in on the aspect of itself that is in summer camp.

In life, we have many contracts for houses, apartments, cars, phones, college loans, computers, everything! We have to fulfill the contracts on the earth plane, or we will have penalties, it is the same in the spiritual world. We make a contract with love, or an agreement to come to earth to fulfill our mission, if we do not fulfill it, we may suffer the consequences. The consequences may be a bad relationship, a difficult health problem, or just a broken heart. Our heart guides us to our contracts.

These SOUL contracts are a little more flexible than the written contracts on the earth plane, because these contracts are to help us grow, and they are from the other side-- where there really is no judgement. Also, these contracts have waivers and amendments in them, they are fluid and flexible--they may change because of some of our life choices. *We do have free will.* Sometimes, we know when we don't fulfill a contract, we feel we have missed something, or situations just don't feel right. We may have *a personal contract* with relationships and challenges in our SOUL family. We may have *professional contracts,* as a teacher, doctor, lawyer or healer, intuitive or coach. It is up to you whether or not you fulfill the contract.

I think I could have stopped at being a therapist, but the *spirits* literally wouldn't let me sleep, so I explored the spiritual world. I wasn't just interested in the personality of someone, but in their SOUL, and whether or not clients were hitting their spiritual marks. We may have group contracts, as a group of scientists, or even group karma from certain races or ethnicities. The Civil Rights Movement may have been a group contract for African Americans, and for others. We also may have environmental contracts to clean up the ocean, save the animals, or find medicines that can help us cure cancer. We all have these contracts that are stored inside of us, and we feel this passion to connect to push these projects forward.

Group contracts are always there to help uplift and enlighten the planet, to help the planet evolve. It is more about the lessons we learn from the earth, and not the reverse. There are so many contracts in life, and we tune into them as we have feelings about them, that are good or bad. No one is given a gift without earning the ability to have it, and the gifts are given to fulfill various contracts. What we do with these contracts is also our karma. Remember, karma is not good or bad, it is just energy stored in our SOUL--to be learned from or released. All energy created has to be reckoned with.

Saturn Return

Now that you are on your path to find your purpose, how do you know that you are on the right one? The Saturn Return will get you there. Saturn is the task master, and the planet of maturity. Saturn will orchestrate everything to get you on your true SOUL path. When you are on the right path, everything flows fairly easily. Opportunities happen, synchronicities abound, and coincidences are predominant. Little things occur to direct you, step by step, and make you feel that things were meant to be. In the opposite way, if you are off your path, the Saturn Return can seem very heavy: fear, anger, and nervousness abound. Saturn is a wake-up call, and many people will lose jobs, have health problems, family issues, or severe emotional crisis during this time. Your soul is trying to get your attention.

We go through cycles in life, and around age twenty-nine and a half is when all of your planets are in the same place, as when you were born, and we call that the Saturn Return. Things you came here to learn as a soul will come us to look at. A lot of first time clients come to me from ages twenty-seven to thirty years old, you can feel the shadow of this window at about twenty-eight years, and sometimes at even twenty-seven. People who would never seek out an intuitive reader come to me at this time of potential turmoil in life. Both privately and in a clinic as a psychotherapist. It helps me know how to work with them clinically also.

At age twenty-seven to about twenty-eight I was haunted by ghosts, and by age twenty-nine, I was into learning about the spiritual world, thus opening up to my path of the SOUL. Saturn is the task master that orchestrates everything else in your life, and forces you to think about your soul mission. It is meant to get you in order. It is a sort of *spiritual redirection.** Also, at around fifty-eight years of age, the second Saturn comes about -- many people feel the window at fifty-six. Saturn will challenge you to ask, "Have I accomplished the goals I set at the first Saturn? Have I listened to my SOUL lessons, or do I have to try again to reestablish them?"

At age fifty-four, there are similar Saturn-like energies where life issues that you may have missed before come back around for you to look at once again. Were you a good person or partner, or did you miss a lesson years ago? Did you take the career that was safe, or did you try to pursue your passions and your purpose, which may have entailed some risks? Did you clear up issues with family and friends, or did you bury them without doing so? A pattern may come up that you need to take a look at.

The Saturn Return is one of the most challenging times on the spiritual path. This is the time to pay close attention to your SOUL, and your inner wishes. It helps you find what you are here to accomplish, and it will steer you in the right direction through certain blocks. Some people feel very restricted by Saturn and depressed.

Twenty-nine and a half is the age in which you will need to make choices in your life, about your path. Your SOUL pulls on you a little before this time. Your planets, connected to the energetic matrix of your *spirit*, are trying to understand their path. Saturn makes you grow up, and will sometimes force you to make decisions from your heart and soul, as opposed to from your personality and egoic mind. It is always very suspect to me that so many rock starts died at the age of twenty-seven, right before their twenty-eighth birthday, before Saturn really got started. Jimi Hendrix, Janis Joplin, Jim Morrison, Kurt Cobain, and Amy Winehouse all met their demise, by their own hand, before their Saturn hit.

The Saturn return can be very suffocating. It felt like an iron on my energy field. I can't imagine doing it publicly, and with everyone thinking that you are an amazing musical artist, and inside you are feeling not so good, fighting inner demons and may be using drugs to drown the pain. During this time, it is good to look at this book, or any spiritual resource, that can bring you closer to your *spirit*. Also, work with your heart energy.

At age fifty you hit your Chiron Return, which is when you master your life lessons and think about the gifts that you have been given. It is the time also of the wounded healer. When painful wounds from the past come up to heal. Are you going to be a teacher for others? This is a great time to fulfill your purpose as a master teacher, or healer. Are you going to give back to others, or invest more in the material world? Mostly, people who would never have come to a psychotherapist, nevertheless a intuitive reader or a healer, come SOUL searching during this time. These are great times to work with the universe, and find your higher calling and lessons. Finding an astrologer, healer, or seeking spiritual advice can greatly help you nurture your *spirit* and heal your soul.

3 Finding Your Life Purpose

I WAS EXCITED about this universal dialogue, the signs and synchronicities, the symbolic messages all left me in a state of awe. Every day, I would ask for signs about finding my life purpose; I wanted to combine my passion with my profession, but how? I remember walking around Manhattan, and noticing that tourists would come up to me to ask for directions. If you have ever been to that city, you know that people move at a lightning pace, and for an outsider, it can be very intimidating. In New York, tourists instinctively go to someone they feel will answer their questions, without an attitude.

I remember noticing that any given weekend, more than six, than ten, and even more than twelve people would approach me--this happened even when I was pissed off (not hard to be in New York), busy, or not wanting to be bothered. Once I noticed this pattern, more and more people would come up to me. My friend, Barbara, and I noticed that it was up to a total of eighteen people on one weekend, including entire families that would approach me for directions. Even with her Sarah-Jessica-Parker-looking-blonde-self, people would come up to me. Even she thought it was strange. I would calmly tell them how to take the various subways and buses, or how to get somewhere on foot so that they were able to get to their New York site-seeing destination. I would wonder why so many people who were lost would come to me. "I am like a tour guide," I said to Barbara, and we both had the same insight. She said out loud what I was thinking, "You are helping them find their direction," I got chills.

I realized I kept asking the universe how I was supposed to help people with my work, and that it spoke to me literally, in the physical plane, in symbols! People were coming to me when they were lost, confused, and needing help, and I was giving them directions. That is what I would be doing as a psychotherapist, and later as an intuitive counselor and coach. I was reconnecting them to their purpose and their path, helping them to find what they were looking for, even if, at that time, their purpose was to find a good pastrami sandwich (easy to do in Manhattan).

My friend Jaina, a medium, calls herself a telephone, because she connects people to their deceased love ones. The minute I got the metaphoric message, the direction seekers stopped approaching me. The tourists seemed to go elsewhere for help. It is almost like the line of seekers stopped, in order to emphasize to me that the message had been received. The message was heard, I accepted the call, and new messages were soon to come.

I also feel like I work at the bus stop. People come with questions, and a destination in mind. They may say, "How much, and how do I get to Seattle?" Translation: "Is this job right, or relationship, or health issue." I check the computer system--their Spirit and soul, and give them a print out of how to get their destination or on their path. Sometimes, when I check the computer system, it is a different destiny. Usually, something larger than they thought, but something that on some level, they knew: "I always wanted to do that, but I didn't know how I could do it." If they get nervous about their path, I assure them that this route has already been laid out, and is safe. In essence, their soul has a soul map, and they just have to connect to that destination, by taking the bus. I give them their schedule and routes, their messages from the universe, and they are on their way. Clients will know if it is the right route, because it will resonate as truth. I was a lighthouse to people who were lost.

Your Life Purpose

To understand your purpose, start formulating questions in your mind. What are your passions? What do you like doing? What are you good at? What gives you joy? All of these things are what constitute your life purpose. Everyone, every soul, was given a gift from Source, before they came to the earth plane. The gift was an ability, talent, or quality that was to be used to help raise the consciousness of the planet. I often see that when people find their passions, they feel a sense of purpose. Once they find their purpose, they become more passionate, and the universe steps up to help create intention.

I highly recommend numerology and astrology. Numerology is fun because it numerically lays out what you are here to do. I remember when I took a test in *Parade Magazine*, my numerology number was a nine. Nine is the God number, and the number of philanthropists. I see how that works in my life presently.

There are several numerology reports online, or in books that can help you to figure out, energetically, what you are to be doing. All the numbers around me come to a nine, meaning, if I add them up they would be a nine. My phone number comes to a 9, zip code 90036, $9 + 0 + 0 + 3 + 6 = 9$, my office number suites 22 and 23, 2+2+2+3=9. The suite is 22 which is 4 and 23 which is a 5, together they are a nine. My full name comes to a four, and I see fours everywhere. It is uncanny, but it makes sense as to why it all works in my life. Even my code at work has two nines in it. I was born on the nineteenth of

April, another 4! Look at sequences of numbers in your life, and you will see patterns. Do research on numerology, and it will give you a picture of your destiny. Also, look into astrology, there are thorough reports that can help you know about the hills and valleys in your life. Do you own research on a respected professional who can see your patterns and potential.

If we all did what made us happy and brought joy to ourselves and others, this world would be a better place. The truth of the matter is, if we utilized our GOD given gifts, there would be more peaceful people on the planet. When people are happy, they are less likely to fight, start wars, manipulate others, lie, or cheat. They are just focused while working on their purpose. As you understand, universal dialogue will help you realize that it isn't worth it to make poor choices, because you will have to pay it back somehow. Living your passion has the potential to create heaven on earth, and that is every soul's goal. It may not be every person's or personality's goal, but it is the *spirit's* and soul's goal. When you realize there is an energy or force working with you, you begin to understand that there is abundance, and the universe is conspiring for your own fulfillment of your destiny. Here are four other ideas on how to find your life passion.

Childhood Dreams: When you were five years old, what did you want to do? What were your desires, wishes, and dreams? Don't screen this thought or discard it! Can you think back and gain any insight: fireman, teacher, writer? Even if it is silly, write it down. It may be a clue to another mission or related activity. If you can't remember your wishes, or even your childhood, try to ask somebody who knew you well and that you trust. What did you like doing, or what were you good at? When you were five, you were less self-consciousness about your wishes. Many times during my classes people would say, "Oh I wanted to be a counselor, but I decided to do something else." You may be in your forties, but don't want to go back to school. You may be able to be a life coach, or a spiritual counselor, or Reiki healer. Don't restrict the universe. Write down your passions, there is a way to create it. Take some time to contemplate your childhood dreams. When I was about seven-years-old, I found a baby bird in our yard that had fallen out of its nest. My whole family was rushing to church, but I refused to get into the car until my dad put the baby chick back into the nest. My father later spoke up on the pulpit about my caring and nurturing nature. It is not surprising that I later took a profession that helps the downtrodden. I usually don't let up, until those that are lost or wounded get help. Whenever my family went on trips, my father said I blessed the walls and the rooms of the hotels that we stayed in. I would thank the walls for keeping us safe during the time we stayed in the hotel. Somehow, I understood energy and how it was stored in walls and rooms, and about leaving positive energy. Look at your interests or your childhood habits. Your life path may lie there.

Financial Freedom: If you had five million dollars, what would you do? Money is a big factor in why people don't pursue their dreams. Everyone is looking for security. I understand the desire to have fringe benefits, but guess what? Those days are becoming a distant memory. Hospitals are closing ERs, companies are getting rid of pensions and are letting go of employees. Many banks are collapsing, and executives are laundering money. The universe though, has a built in security plan. If you align yourself with your heart's desire, the universe can, and will, make you prosperous. Prosperity is not only financial, it is of *spirit* too. **It is the universal law of abundance.** We are limitless and abundant beings, it is our divine right.

I recommend that you read up on the law of prosperity and abundance. If you understand that if you tap into the unlimited supply of the universe, you can have more abundance, you may be willing to pursue your purpose. I recommend books like *Think and Grow Rich,* by Napoleon Hill and Catherine Ponder's books *Open your*

Mind to Prosperity and *The Dynamic Laws of Prosperity* to expand your knowledge and understanding of how you can work with the universe to create abundance. I have worked freelance for ten years, with no full-time job, just believing in and working with the laws of the universe of abundance. I have been an on-call social worker, an energy healer, a speaker, and intuitive counselor—all at the same time. I have worked in clinics and hospitals, and have worked at events and parties as a reader. I have done speeches at churches and expos, and energy healings at various events around LA. The money came in when I was open to living my purpose and passion. I have even done television appearances on cable and have been on radio shows.

There were multiple ways to earn a living, when I listened to the call. I have two rents that I pay each month, over $2400 dollars, and somehow I have never missed a rent payment on my freelancer's salary. I did that to prove to myself that working with the universe can work. If I could trust myself and secure gigs, it gives proof to others that may prompt them to create their own purpose. I wanted to practice seeing if the universe would continually provide me work. The universe will provide synchronicities and coincidences to lead you along the right path. You must trust and believe.

Soul Messages: What soul messages have you received? If we are off of our path, we will receive universal nudges, prompts, and wake-up calls to get us back on path, back on the journey of our *spirit*. Sometimes, those messages will come from another person. You may lose your job and have time to do some soul searching. You may complain to a friend about your job, and she says, "I know an opportunity that is open at my company." You may be feeling lost in your life, and then have a powerful dream telling you how to move your life forward. You may also hear a song that gives you a message that you needed to hear. You may be prompted to draw, paint, dance, or engage in some other dream that you have put on the back burner. Your soul transmits messages all the time. Your

SOUL sends out universal light, and light is knowledge, so listen. It is important that you listen to your soul messages each and every day, and begin to work with their energy by taking small steps forward. The goal of a permanent job with great benefits is becoming fantasy, many people feel like their creativity is squashed in corporations. We are being called to become co-creators with the universe. The breakdown of these systems is spiritual because we, as souls, are being called to being co-creators with life understanding the laws of the universe and learning how to create with them helps you to find your passion and fulfill your mission.

Connect to Source: The creator has put us all on this planet to express our creativity to the fullest on the earth plane. If you don't have a connection to God/Goddess and all that is, you can call it the universe, the force or Yoda, for God's sake, just connect to something larger then you. Imagine that you are connecting to a big energy source, plugging into a universal inspirational socket. Recovering Catholics, or those detoxing from judgmental religious backgrounds, sometimes don't like the concept of GOD. I have worked with many who have suffered abuse within traditional religious communities, churches, and temples. I understand!

I was raised an Episcopalian, and actually don't dislike the church, but I felt there was something more for me. My path felt different. I had to somehow link the commonality of most traditional religions and connect to *Spirit*. I was to listen, grow, and learn from my *spirit*--I had to tap into the knowledge that was in me, and the energy that was coming towards me. The bottom line is that you should ask in prayer to be connected with or be shown proof of something out there that can guide you. Go within your heart, connect to your own insights, and ask for your *spirit* to speak to you. Spend time in nature and see the beauty all around that Source has created; there are many ways that you can connect to Source, and have a sense of *spirit* in your life.

Meditation is another way to hear the messages from the realm of creation. It is better to meditate in a group, where there is more energy of *Spirit* present. "When two or three are gathered in my name, I am present," said Jesus the Christ.

Honoring your *spirit* feels like a tall order, but it doesn't have to be. The task can be very easy, if you are doing what you love. Remember, the creator stuffed our gifts inside of our heart, so that is the first place that you should look. After you find out what is in your heart, balance it in your head, and then move forward. Many clients I have worked with have found their path after listening to their heart.

WORKBOOK EXERCISE #3

- **What messages** is your *spirit* giving you that you are dismissing? Write them down!

Excuse number one for not honoring your *spirit*: not believing in the messages you receive, and then rationalizing in some way that you can't live your dreams or goals. Some common limiting thought forms are: it has not been done before, I don't have any money, no one will believe that I can do it, I don't believe that I can do it, or I can't make an income at it. I have said all of these things before, and have avoided doing things that were my passion out of fear of what other people, my family and friends, would think. You have to trust that these ideas were put into your heart for a reason; your heart is filled with passion. Passion is energy of movement, so it doesn't serve you to be passionate from the sidelines. You must put your passion into action to see it blossom into creation.

Reading testimonials in books, of intuitive therapists and inspirational writers, helped validate my experience as a psychotherapist with deep intuitive gifts and a love of inspiration. Could I make a career out of this? Could I do both? I decided to put my intuition into practice. The counseling part seemed very easy, as I mentioned previously, and I began to notice that I would gain insights about people on a deeper level than other counselors had. I often heard clients saying, "I've never told anyone this before," or "I never thought about that before," even though they had gone to counseling for years. I often found clients tearing up very strongly, with soul sobs, deep crying that came from their authentic core. These insights seemed to help them to release severe wounds that they had been carrying for a long time.

Some days, about 90 percent of my clients were crying, I would have to ask for more tissues, and had boxes piled up in my office. It took me a while to figure out that I was connecting with their souls, and giving them *spirit* messages. It wasn't something that I conjured up how to do, it just happened. The gift was already in me, I just had to be an open vessel in order to let it flow. Many times, *Spirit* speaks to you by offering you a purpose or a gift in something that can be lucrative and satisfying to your personality, as well as a help to others. It could be great art work, a funny script, amazing dancing, singing, or inventing. Don't dismiss it. Your *spirit* often guides you on your path with signs, synchronicities, and messages.

I continued to ask the universe to show me what I was to do with my gifts and my therapy work. My first profound experience in connecting with the *spirits* of clients was when I was interning at a vocational program for young adults in Manhattan. These clients were labeled as being learning disabled, but they taught me that they all had fantastic gifts, no matter what their disability was labeled. These young adults inspired me not to focus on their personalities, but to connect to their *spirits*. They taught me how to listen to my heart, to throw the theories aside, and to trust my intuition. It proved to be a profoundly educational experience, for me.

Healing Art

There was Jose, a nineteen-year-old who had been diagnosed with AIDS. He would often ignore me in the mail room support group that I led. The purpose of this group was to help these young men become mail sorters and assistants in big city law firms, many of them would leave the program to secure jobs in Fortune 500 companies. Jose though, had a passion for art and would often grab scraps of papers or matchboxes that he would design elaborate fantasy art and other magical creations with. At this time, in the early 1990's, the treatment for HIV was not as effective as it is now. Many people died from AIDS and as a young guy, with poor healthcare, and limited treatment options, his life was doomed, so I would let him draw in class. This practice gave his *spirit* life. He would never look up at me, even if I asked a question. He was always just drawing and creating. It seemed to soothe him of all the health (and other) problems he had.

I realized then, as I continued to support someone's passions and God given gifts, that I could heal help to their *spirit*. The *spirit* truly heals the person, but I could assist by connecting them to their own *spirit*. Artistic ability is a powerful gift. When I let a client get in the zone, they are in the realm of *Spirit*, with no time and space, which is why artists often become lost in their craft, losing awareness of time and structure. His gift of art made his illness seem minimal. I heard a year later that he had passed, never to have his art recognized. I made sure I recognized it, by letting him explain his creations. He would often crack a slight smile while describing his work, partly, I believe, due to an adolescent rebellion, that getting away with something the others guys couldn't do in group gave him joy.

Children or young adults who die young are often sacred beings and teachers. I often honor their wisdom and gifts, and really listen to them. I also make sure that they realize their time on earth was important and meaningful. These interactions with clients I call *soul nutrients**. The soul nutrients are the ingredients that need to be observed by my *spirit* to teach me about my own soul's growth. Soul nutrients are the qualities or situations that feed the soul so it can grow.

The Green Man

At the same program, I worked with another young guy named Carlos. Carlos was sent to me to help him adjust to becoming a food service worker. Carlos was often bored in our counseling sessions, and he had a distant look. He was labeled mildly mentally retarded. On the surface, I could have made the assumption that he could not engage in treatment, and that he had no interest in working with food services. The referral to social services was made because he was non-productive in the food service training, but my intuition told me that it was because he wasn't passionate about his work and he wasn't living his joy.

Everyone has a mission here. Sometimes, it is just being a good friend, being a good worker, or being available, supportive, and loving. Carlos would often stare behind me at a voluminous green plant that was in an aquarium in the session room. When I would sit with him, I would often see flashing lights around him. They looked like flashbulbs to me; there were many lights, probably about six or seven. I didn't know what the lights were, but I felt stillness and a presence around him. He was the kind of person that resided in a quiet meditative state. He was a young man with a good heart.

I remember reading, *Embraced by the Light*, by Betty Eaddie, in which she explained that we should not judge the disabled or mentally retarded. Many old souls choose to use challenging bodies to teach others to learn about tolerance or compassion. I had also read in Doreen Virtue's books that *spirit* guides and angels often express themselves in flashing lights. See how the connection to me following my passion by reading the books I loved gave me knowledge that helped others?

While seeing the lights, I became quiet and listened, and felt the wisdom. The impression I received was that I needed to look toward where he was staring, and listen to his heart. When I looked over my shoulder to his view, I noticed the aquarium. I asked him why he was so interested in the aquarium. He smiled and said, "I love plants. They are so green, but something more needs to be done with this one. It is going to die." I said, "Tell me about it."

He proceeded to get up, and started to prune the plant and talk to it. He said that he could take care of it, and knew what it needed. His whole demeanor changed, and his smile lit up the room. We spent most of the session with him pruning the plants and explaining to me that they needed love. I love the joy of assisting someone in finding their passion. It is almost like finding a lost treasure. I proceeded to ask the supervisor if he could work on this project of fixing the plants in the aquarium. With a lot of hemming and hawing, he eventually let Carlos do this as an extra project. Carlos was so happy. Carlos was now cooperative, enthusiastic, and engaged in sessions. He would work very quickly in his food service training so that he could get to work on the aquarium.

When I later followed up during a family session, his mother said to me, "My son, what did you do to him?" I asked what she meant, and she stated, "He is going around and fixing up everyone's plants in our apartment building in the Bronx, and all over. He is like a changed young man." She continued, "We are Puerto Rican Americans, no one has done gardening since my great-grandfather, who he never met!" I thought "Ah-ha! We found his gift, his passion, his reason for being."

God gives everyone a gift, what a wonderful gift to be an attendant in God's gardens. Carlos' garden creations were beautiful, especially for someone who had no formal training. He indeed appeared to know what the plants needed. Later, he told me that he didn't feel as sad as he used to. Often he would drive home with his parents to the Bronx, and he would look at the tall plants in the windows, and would fantasize about how, if given the chance, he would change them. He said to me, "I smile inside Ms. Carolyn, every time I see plants! They are so green."

I thanked his guidance for coming through as flashing lights in order to help me to find his purpose. Judging from the amount of lights around him, I believe he was a very old soul, since he had so much spiritual assistance. He helped usher in the way for me to read clients' souls and go deeper and deeper into assisting them to live their purpose and find their truth. These interactions were more soul nutrients. You can often feel the presence of a profound soul in a physically challenged body. Naysayers might rationalize and say that what I am doing is unconventional, seeing the lights and listening to guidance that doesn't come from me, but I would see over and over the result of helping people with my intuitive gifts. I realized that God brought me these people for a reason, and that reason is to reach people who may have been brushed aside previously. *Honoring somebody else's passion activates your own divinity.*

Working with disabled youth, I learned about compassion, tolerance, non-judgment, and unconditional love. They may not have been perfect in the shallow, earthly, egotistical way, but silently and unknowingly they were powerful and perfect teachers for the soul. We come here to enlighten and enhance our soul, so what a gift it was for me to be their counselor. In essence, they were my teachers. On your spiritual path, it is very important that you learn to curb your own perception of what is valuable and important in the world. **If you learn the soul's language, you realize that it is the downtrodden, the unlikely, the abused, and the invisible that often hold the seeds to your** *spirit's* **nourishment and growth.** Look to the unseen for clarity, speak to those silenced for insight, and seek in the darkness for the truth.

The universe loves dichotomy, and irony. It teaches in symbols and metaphors. It seems that through these symbols and metaphors we are to figure out the puzzle that is our existence. The money, the grandeur, and flamboyance appear to be fun and may be important here, but they do not translate to spiritual evolution in the *spirit* world, unless they are pursued for the sake of others. We will be judged only by our own *spirits* based on how we have treated one another. It is better if we treat others well, because we may recreate the things that we judge. "It is done unto you, as you believe," said Jesus the Christ. This quote has two meanings to me: first, if you believe that you will be treated badly, you will. If you believe that you are no good, you aren't. If you think you can't accomplish something, then you won't.

Another way to look at this quote is that it is done unto you, as you believe. If you believe someone who has a learning disability is dumb, or someone who is disabled is a cripple, then who knows, maybe in your next life time you will be treated the same way you perceived them. It is done unto YOU (you experience the same thing as you believe about them), as you judge about them. What you judge, you nudge. As you look at certain passages, you may hear and see multiple meanings. The soul is multi-dimensional so analyze things multi-dimensionally.

A Mending Amanda

Messages from the universe can often come from others who are mislabeled by schools and institutions that do not respect spiritual gifts, individuality, and diversity. I remember this African American girl, named Amanda, that I would have sessions with in the same vocational program. She was labeled as slow, but read about five romance novels a week with a great retention of characters, plots, and storylines. I asked Amanda, "How can you have mental challenges, when you were reading so many books?" She said, "I am not slow, I was just in foster care, and didn't have anyone to advocate for me. I got tired of fighting, so I let them put me in any class."

Amanda also had flashing lights around her and had a breath of knowledge. Her lights were a purple color, and so I knew she was a high spiritual being because of the number and color of the lights around her. Purple is a high vibrational color, connected to the crown chakra. Somehow we happened to talk about spirituality, and she stated, "Earth is not our home, it is only a temporary existence." I wondered how someone, who was considered learning disabled, could have such a wide breadth of knowledge in spirituality and metaphysics. Again, I was being told that the soul and *spirit* are more wise and profound than the cognitive limitations of the mind. Amanda and I had many great discussions and counseling sessions. I can't recall them all, as this was eighteen years ago, but I remember she grew more and more into her own as a smart young lady who had been mislabeled. As much as I could, I encouraged her to pursue her dreams. She said she wanted to be a social worker, like me. I encouraged her to do whatever made her feel good. "I don't want kids in foster care to be mislabeled, it's wrong." She wasn't bitter or angry when she said this--it was just a factual revelation.

Amanda eventually graduated from the program, and moved on with her life. Her wisdom, presence, and insight stayed with me long after she left. That is how you spot an old, wise teaching soul, their resonance lingers on. After "training with the soul nutrients" from her soul, I was interested in investigating what the various colors around a person meant. This gift of seeing auras comes and goes, and it seems to be present when a client's soul really wants to show me something that they want interpreted. I feel auras and words very strongly attached to these clients.

A good two years later, I moved to a clinic in the West Village in NYC, helping people in the work place. I worked with several gay male clients dealing with AIDS, trauma, addiction, and abuse, it was the 90's. I seemed to be doing really well with the one-on-one counseling, having many of my clients referring their friends to "the nice young black lady, who was compassionate and insightful." This was during the AIDS crisis, so many of the sessions were very intense, and sad. Many of my clients were struggling with being harassed and targeted during this time, being blamed for the introduction of AIDS into society. My *spirit* related to their *spirit* being blamed and disliked for just being.

The *spirit* is colorless and genderless, with no religious dogma, and no age requirement. When you listen to others' *spirits*, they feel heard. I loved the clientele where I practiced being a great therapist, but not the environment. My boss didn't like the fact that I was outshining her; it appeared that she especially didn't like clients asking for me over her, since she was the founder of this program. Funny, I was warned by others not to take this job, because of her, but I didn't listen to my gut, and later my *spirit*. Always listen to your gut!

She made my life difficult there. Her being an African American woman was disappointing, but black on black crime in the workplace is something of cultural dissonance that, unfortunately, happens quite often. Self-hatred, projected onto an easy target, someone who looks like you. (take note here, when you work with peoples' *spirit*, you move faster and quicker to truth, and others may be intimidated with your gifts).

Stressful work environments are commonplace in social services, but the ones that are often overworked (and underpaid) can be most difficult. This woman also tried to control me, a method that never works for an Aries. She tried to control my counseling too. Her aura was misty and gray, so I knew that she was not that evolved, or ethical. I also didn't want to be trained out of using my newfound gifts.

I was feeling burnt out and exhausted, was completely underpaid in an expensive city, and the little part of my *spirit* that felt solace in helping others was being stepped on. I remember my white coworkers telling me that our boss spoke badly about me, and other black employees, behind our backs. We heard from others that she was in the process of getting rid of us, for no reason.

I began to feel defeated and asked the universe for clarity. Ironically, while walking down Flatbush Avenue in Brooklyn, wondering why I went into social work in the first place, I heard someone call out my name, "Ms. Carolyn, Ms. Carolyn!" a small voice echoed down Flatbush Avenue. It was Amanda, the young client that I had worked with several years before. She ran over to me to say hello. She appeared happier and more confident. "I wanted to tell you, you helped me so much. I have gone back to school, and am getting my BSW. Thank you so much for changing my life." I laughed, and said, "Just when I was thinking of changing my field." She looked both horrified and confused, and stated, "What? You can't do that! You have helped me so much. You saved my soul!" Then I looked confused. Saved her soul? That word--Soul. We both heard the D train approaching, she gave me a quick hug, and whispered, "Thank you," and was gone.

Once again, Amanda's kindhearted old soul message opened my heart to my path, my gifts, and my journey--more soul nutrients. It was an emotionally mending interaction. It is a rare occurrence when a client comes back to you to tell you how you have helped, an angel's message, and a spiritual intervention sent by the universe, telling me to go on. What a powerful soul she was, and I will never forget her being a messenger in *my* life. Right when I was thinking of throwing in the towel, and gathering my applications to business school, an angel came and gave me the message to keep going. Who would think someone who was labeled mildly mentally retarded would do that? She is a profound soul and a powerful messenger. Good for her, she had to overcome authority figures who thought that she could not go for a traditional education, but she did it. She believed in herself, and listened to her inner messages. Don't ever be fooled by the outside appearances of people, or dismiss the ways in which their *spirits* can help you. I ended up forcibly leaving that job, and began working in a clinic with high-risk kids, as well as seeing people privately, as I quietly continued to explore my spirituality and intuitive gifts at a spiritualist church, and the Edgar Cayce Institute in Manhattan.

This observation, to look into the *spirit* of someone, proved to be a recurring theme in my life. I found messages that seemed to speak to me, right when I needed them, because I paid attention. I also did the same for others, giving them messages right when they needed to hear them. I realized I was doing *spirit*-to-*spirit* communication, speaking to the highest, most evolved part of a person's heart. Dialoguing with the universe, you too will hear these messages.

As I look back on that challenging working environment, I remember that the boss had asked me a question about a conversation that I had not been a part of, yet I knew the exact words that were exchanged in that meeting. She looked at me all freaked out, and asked, "How did you know that?" Unfortunately, I had used my intuitive mind, instead of my cognitive mind; I wasn't yet good at toggling back and forth. Intuitive insight doesn't always resonate in the corporate workplace, or with others who are hiding truth and living a lie. **There will always be challenges and obstacles, even when you are completely on your life path.** This spiritual school, on earth, can be difficult, but if you are listening to the universe and following your path, he will send you a message, a person, or a book telling you to go on.

These were times where I wanted to get my MBA, and make some "real" money. Recently out of college, I also endured a lot of judgment from my peers for picking such a "mindless" field. Many of my classmates from college went on to medical school, law school, or business school, or decided to pursue PhDs. Smart kids take that path, not the path of a social worker, is what I was told.

After a while, my classmates and I had little in common. It is not easy to stray away from the herd, but I had to. Those other fields didn't speak to my intuitive, sensitive soul. I worked as a legal assistant for a cable company. Can you hear me snoring? No law school for Carolyn. I also worked for an economic research firm, doing marketing, and that is when I knew that getting an MBA would be a waste of time. I spent most of my time there counseling my coworkers. I remember sitting next to a coworker, Kirsten, a Swedish secretary, who spoke seven languages. We would gossip together all day about the spiritual world. Those conversations were light, fun, and inspiring.

I had the opportunity of transferring to France, working in the same company, for a year. It was such an earth plane opportunity, meaning that it would be party time, since the marketing job that was available wasn't very challenging. I would move to France, single, in my twenties, and everything would be paid for, I would even get a bonus when I moved. A great international experience, but my heart was not in to the work. I am sure I would have had fun experiences, but from what my boss said, everyone smoked in the company, meaning in the office. During this time, I was getting into my healthy conscious body, and eating up the book *You Could Heal Your Life* (by Louise Hay). I was working out twice a day, hanging out with the body builders at a gym, right next to my apartment building.

After my health scare, I had gotten my body into tip-top shape. I was meditating in the park every day, and was a vegetarian. I decided at twenty-seven-years-old, right before my Saturn Return, to walk away from that corporate strangulation company. I was wondering what I should do. Since it was a French company, I had six weeks of vacation time. Looking back now, I can see how the universe steers you on your right path with messages from others, blocks some, or other different forms of spiritual interventions.

A Gift from Spirit

I went to a bookstore to attend a workshop on how to meet your angels. As I was sitting in class, I felt this strong presence behind me. I kept turning around, and saw a guy that shined. He seemed slightly familiar, and yet, I hadn't met him before. I was listening to the instructor, but felt this presence behind me very strongly. Later, after the workshop, I was looking at the books in the angels section of the store, and this book about how to connect with your angels fell off the shelf. I commented to the shiny guy, who was wandering around in the same section, that the book must have wanted to talk to me. The minute I spoke to him, he began to engage me in this profound conversation about angels, the universe, and manifesting. He said his name was Paul. We talked for so long, I lost track of time. Before we knew it, the owner of the store told us that it was closing time. It was my first experience with time warping. Time warping is when you feel like you have been talking to someone for ten minutes, and suddenly three hours has passed.

After we left the store, we went to get something to eat at an outdoor café. I was starving as I didn't eat before the class, but as we continued talking, I suspiciously lost my appetite. He talked about auras and other things, and about how you work with universal laws. He said that when you give, you receive. At that time, he pulled out a wad of dollar bills. We were in the middle of Washington, D.C. and I felt uncomfortable with his display of all that money. Some homeless people had asked him for money and he generously gave them a dollar bill. Many more people came as the word spread. He easily and effortlessly handed out one dollar bills, almost as if to exemplify what he was saying about giving. Several people, ten or twelve at least, came up to him to ask for money, which he gave to them. He had no wallet, just a handful of money. I told him that in the middle of a city, he really needed a wallet, and that he shouldn't expose his money the way he was. He was rambling on about hanging out in Guatemala with shamans and learning Spanish. "Wait," I said, "I have a wallet that I just bought from a Guatemalan vendor. What a coincidence." I handed it to him, and said, "Here, cover your money."

He thanked me for the gift, and opened up the wallet to put his money in, and inside the wallet he found another wallet. He repeated, "When you give, you receive," and he handed back to me the second wallet that had been stored inside. I had never noticed that there were two wallets in the one that I had given him. When he was giving away the money, I noticed that his wad of dollar bills didn't seem to be getting any smaller. The Bible story of Jesus being able to feed thousands of people with one little fish ran through the back of my mind--the symbolism of the infinite supply. What I did notice, when talking to him, was that looking into his eyes was like looking into the universe. They were deep and soulful, or maybe it was just that I had never met someone I felt so spiritually connected to. My path was still new to me. About that time the owner of the restaurant said to us, "We are closing the restaurant do, you want the food to go?" I was shocked again, as it seemed like we had just sat down.

As Paul dealt with our check, he said, "Whatever you want in the universe, you can have, just ask." As he said that, he was fiddling with his hangnail. As he got his money, this woman came up to him on the street and said, "Hang nail? I have a nail clipper." She opened her jacket and it had all these nail clippers attached! It reminded me of the hustlers in New York, who sold watches out of their coats. I had never seen that kind of vendor before, and have not seen one since. The vendor said it was only a dollar, so he purchased the nail clipper. He showed, by example, that what you ask for, you receive. His energy seemed accelerated, as if things were thought and manifested quickly. He was a profound SOUL who encouraged me to listen to the universe, by his example.

As we left the restaurant, I wanted to continue these mesmerizing conversations, and I was going to take a taxi back to Maryland. He lived in Virginia and was thinking about that long ride. It was only four hours until dawn, so I told him he could stay with me. His energy was innocuous and healing; he seemed safe. We took a ride back to my apartment, and the Indian cab driver kept looking at him through the rear-view mirror. Finally, as Paul was leaving the car, the driver said to him, "You carry a lot of light." I didn't know what the cabbie meant, but I paid attention to that comment, because it struck a chord in me. Paul spoke about how the universe worked, like he knew it personally. He was reading the book A *Course in Miracles*, by Helen Schucman, as was I. It was a gift from my father, and we were on the same page! What a coincidence.

He wanted me to continually read from the *Course* out loud. "Your voice," he said, "is healing--the tone, the vibration, its essence shifts peoples' souls." I continued reading the book. By six in the morning, we hadn't eaten, and had not slept. I wasn't even tired. He wanted to go to Yoga in Takoma Park, so we hopped on the red line and took it there. It was the first time that I sat through a formal meditation. It was a new experience, and felt so healing. While walking back from Takoma Park, he showed me how to move clouds with thoughts. We would puncture holes in the clouds with our fingers; it was focused intention with thoughts and energy. We would focus on a cloud, and push our intention to make a hole in it. A circle would actually dissipate in the cloud, and it looked just like a smoke ring!

He was a friend, and a traveler, a guide, who stayed with me for three days. Together we read *A Course in Miracles*, and he showed me how thoughts and right intentions could create in unison, with the universe. I remember that during the three days that we hung out, I didn't really eat. I lost my appetite. His knowledge was so profound that food didn't interest me. I was fed by *Spirit*. I was twenty-seven-years-old, and it was right before my Saturn Return, which I described before; I was forced to think about what I REALLY wanted to do, and NOT do. What does my family, those in society, and others think is right for me? This is the time to go deep within your heart.

I had read that, many times a master teacher comes in before your Saturn Return. I remember that Paul encouraged me to go to Columbia to pursue my social work degree and become a psychotherapist. He kept saying, "You are beautiful and have helped me so much. You gave me food and shelter." He didn't tell me to go to grad school, but his compliments about my pseudo untrained counseling and intuition made me feel like I could really help people. The choice was to go to France (to party) or go to New York (to study). I remember debating this decision with him back and forth, arguing that I was well established in D.C., and didn't know anyone in New York. I told him that I didn't want to feel alone. Paul turned around so I wasn't able to see his face, and said, "No matter what you do, and where you are, you are never alone!" The message was so loud and profound that it shook my apartment. It was like every cell in the room reverberated with this voice. The voice was stern, loving, concerned, and nurturing, and it was NOT his; the voice spoke to me like a parent would to a child. It stunned me, and scared me. I said, "Who was that? It sounded like God!" He replied that we can all channel God. I thought to myself, not like that, and inquired, "Are you a channel?" He told me that people had said that. When Paul said that, he didn't look me in the eye, and it was probably the first time in our visit that he didn't. I believe this visitor was able to channel God's message to me, and I could hear it because my energy field was high. I was eating clean, exercising twice a day, meditating in the park, and reading *A Course in Miracles*. He also carried the Christ presence. It surely made an impression.

After the meditation class, we took the red line metro to Takoma Park, and ended up at a Buddhist store, where he told me about reading his book on Milarepa, an Indian man who became enlightened.That night we went back, and continued to read from *A Course in Miracles* while chatting about spirituality. He said that he had to go home to take care of things, and he planned to come back the next day to cook me a vegetarian meal, to thank me for all of my hospitality. We parted ways after about thirty-six hours of being awake together. I went into a deep, much needed sleep.

The next morning I woke up to find him (his *spirit*) staring at me from over my bed. He had on a long white robe, and was smiling at me in pure joy. His hair looked different, curly and shorter, and he was etheric. He was in my room, as clear as day. When I finally fully woke up, his presence was gone. I had never seen someone astral project before, but what was stunning about this is that he looked different, so peaceful and almost angelic, and he was wearing a fancy white robe. When he finally got to my house later that day, I commented that he had been in my house that morning. He didn't look surprised, and just smiled. It was like he knew he was there in the morning, but didn't acknowledge it. He continued talking to me about the universe, but my analytical intuitive nature was rising. He constantly told me that I was a gifted intuitive, that I was beautiful, and about how much I had helped him, over and over again. Every word, thought, and gesture was encouraging toward me. Were we channeling *Spirit* for each other? When I asked him who he was again, he stated, "I am real, just like you." After my insistence, he explained that he had to go. "Our time together had ended," he said. *Spirit* was definitely present.

I never really heard from Paul again. I received just one letter, with no postmark, telling me how beautiful I was, and how my intuition and kindness was needed on the planet. I remember taking a piece of his hair from the comb he had borrowed, and putting it in a container. I still wasn't sure who this guy was. When he left days later, I checked the container, and his hair had disappeared too. I had taken a picture of my visitor, but it never came out, there was just a light in the image. I rationalized that my film was warped and damaged. Who was this wise stranger that came to me and channeled profound truths? Was it a person on their path who, for the moment, ascended into their Christ self in order to give me profound messages or maybe an intervention from *Spirit*? I believe that mortals can serve as channelers, and that you can be visited by an intermediary between the realms. What was true was that messengers kept steering me back to my path, to find my higher purpose, because I asked. **Right now, just ask about your purpose.**

His Spiritual intervention did assist me in taking "the road less traveled." The path I was taking was a combination my spirituality and my psychotherapy training. It was both my passion and my interest, and it spoke to my heart. If you have to make a decision about your future path, use your mind, but always go with your heart. Your mind creates your life, work, worry and fear, and your heart creates passion, trust, and creation; your heart is where your spiritual path is created from.

Many times our parents (or society) try to dictate what we should be doing, even though our heart is saying something else. Society can try to steer people into the wrong path through methods of fear. The opinions of others may not resonate with your heart's desires. I had many experiences like this throughout my life, of people telling me I couldn't do something, even though I was an A student in math and science, in an accelerated prep school, and my mother's dream was for me to go to medical school, all those years of education seemed suffocating. To top it off, I am squeamish. Medicine was my mother's dream for me though, not mine. When she was pregnant with me, she said she would hold her stomach, and say, "This is my healer," meaning doctor. I tell her "Well I am a healer, next time be more specific." We laugh...now. Make sure when you are honoring your *spirit*, it is your dreams you are listening to, not the dreams of your parents, teachers, or other influential people.

There were other experiences that deterred me. My mother was a high school chemistry and biology teacher, and had a passion for teaching sciences to minority students, who society had said couldn't do it. She later became the first black teacher to head a science department in Connecticut. She was so good at teaching that she won the prestigious Olmstead Award for Teacher of the Year, from Williams College in Massachusetts. She even shared the dais with the director, Martin Scorsese, who also received an honorary doctorate that same year. She was also eventually awarded an honorary PhD from Yale Divinity School, for her scholarship work with students. In the 1950's she had gotten into three medical schools, but as a foreign student, was not eligible for a scholarship. My mother would teach me chemistry formulas, and I was really good at them. With her help, I would receive all A's on all of my chemistry tests.

I was devastated though, when my high school teacher asked some guys in my class to see if I had cheated on the test when the teacher left the room. A couple of them, over privileged and petty, they made fun of me mercilessly. The fact that this teacher asked this of my classmates, and they told me, really hurt and enraged my *spirit*, especially since I was the only black person in the class. All those hours I spent studying, and he automatically assumed I had cheated. Out of a school of about 2,000 students, there were only about six black students in three grades. Every rampant stereotype was present, continuously and chronically.

My mother went to this teacher and let him know that she was a chemistry teacher, and his eyes about popped off of his face. He later changed his attitude toward me, but the damage was done. It was no different in trigonometry, where the teacher announced to the class that I had gotten the highest test grade in my class, a 97 percent, beating out the two Asian girls. His announcement included the questioning of how I could beat them, he thought he had given me a compliment, but of course, I was insulted. I was taught unconsciously, and subliminally, that to be intelligent was shameful and embarrassing.

My English teacher though, always praised me and supported my writing. He was very kind, and almost every time we had a spelling bee in our small thirty person class, I won. My parents had spent a lot of money and scholarships for me and my sister to attend prep grammar school in Fairfield, Connecticut. By the time I got to the suburban high school, I was very prepared, but the English teacher was only one of the few that complimented me. He wrote me a wonderful recommendation for college. He saw my gifts and supported me, and he praised my *spirit*. I say all of this to tell you that, you will have some teachers, mentors, parents, and coaches who don't believe in you or your passion, and you will have some who do. You have to believe in you.

Right now, think about what *your* dreams and passions are, not those of your parents or the limitations imposed by guidance counselors or teachers. My mother and father were incredible advocates for my intelligence. They also had to combat chronic and constant racism. If you come across these obstacles, try to reach inside of you to find strength with *Spirit* or with the universe. Find a good mentor. Create one from observation, if there is no one around.

For example, I left my prep school to go to a public school in eighth grade. The school had a "level" system, and even with my receiving all A's in a prestigious private school they wanted to put me in level two. My mother looked at them like they were crazy, and yelled and pushed until she got me into level one, but because of racial stereotyping, all of the black and Latino kids who were bussed in were automatically put into level two or three. I happened to live in the area of the school, but had not gone to a public school before this time. At the end of the year, all of the students had to write a speech. I wrote one about the experience of transitioning to the school, comparing it to a literary journey.

One morning the principle asked me to come to her office; I thought, "Uh-oh." When I got there, she was so excited to meet me and told me that my essay was stellar, and that I had won. Out of 300 students, and with a high average score, they picked my speech. She said that I would be doing the graduation speech. I was like what!? Remember, this was my first year in that school. Prep school had paid off. I was happy, because it had been hard for me to fit in.

When I got back to my classroom, my teacher had a different view. In my level one class, there were only two black students. I thought I would be praised, but instead, in front of the whole class, she said that I didn't deserve to do the graduation speech, and that my parents must have written the story for me. She didn't know why they had picked me and didn't know what the principal was thinking. Once again, my intelligence and my hard work were shamed and ridiculed. The mostly white students all turned around and looked at me. Even they were shocked. Some were compassionate, but most snickered. I was mortified once again. When I went home and told my parents, they were saddened. My mother went to the principal and didn't mince words. The principal was on our side, and reprimanded the teacher.

In the end, I did the graduation speech. It was nerve wracking, but rewarding. I got up, at thirteen-years-old, with my little hairband and afro, and gave my speech. I was very taken aback that many older black ladies came up to me afterwards, took my picture and said, "I never thought I would see a black girl doing the graduation speech here. We are so proud of you." Old ladies cared about me doing my graduation speech, wow! I noticed a pattern where when I had done something well, people tried to dismiss me. I was often smart shamed.

If you see yourself in this situation, it is important to still persevere. It could be because you are from the wrong neighborhood, or have an accent, or are part of a culture that has been stereotyped, or because your parents don't speak English, it could be because you are a very attractive female and people think you are a bimbo, or because you have a parent who has put you down, so you are sensitive to authority or criticism. Maybe, you have a learning disability or a movement challenge. Whatever it is, check your heart and *spirit* and keep moving. These insults and indignities are recorded in *their* book of life, or karmic energy. They will have to pay for their meanness, sooner or later.

People are always fearful of what they don't understand. People will always project their own limitations and slant onto the world and onto you. Don't let it sway you. If you listen to your own inner voice, you will be led on the path that you were intended to create. Stand up and honor yourself. Find some authority figure, someone who is kind and safe and will support you. Look for someone to model yourself after. Your *spirit* may have set up these events to help develop the various spiritual muscles of dignity, respect, tolerance, and listening to your *spirit*, over all others. Nowadays, speeches and writing are areas in which I continue to do well. I think my writing and speaking abilities at that time were more than those authority figures expected. Many of my black friends have had the same experiences, so I wasn't alone in this intelligence profiling trend. You may have too may have gifts, strange hairstyles, enjoy alternative music, building ideas, using green products--and if you are on the leading edge, there may be a lot of naysayers. That doesn't mean you should not pursue your gifts. I had put writing and speaking on the back burner, because I had so many negative experiences with it. It wasn't until my mother showed me my seventh grade yearbook, and I had three short stories published in there, and had won the third grade reading award, that I realized it was an early gift that I had let go because of embarrassing criticism.

Think back now. Were you really sensitive, in a crazy alcoholic family, were you a peacemaker? Maybe, you are a healer and intuitive. Were you the nursemaid to a mother who was beat up by your father? Maybe, you have an incredible empathy. Perhaps, you will become a nurse or psychotherapist. Did you draw little pictures all over, collect quotes, or hallmark cards? Perhaps, you are a motivational speaker and an artist. **Look at your hobbies, they may be a career.**

Think about your interests, they may be a gift. Delve into your experienced traumas, there may be a seed of inspiration, and a clue to your purpose. I went with my interests and obsessions, listened to my *spirit*, and my soul had a plan. These things happen for a reason. Your life is a divine story, and your experiences are the tapestry of your soul.

The Living Earth

Georgette was a client who came to me for a reading. She was a petite and friendly Japanese American female, who was already following her life's passion as a landscape photographer. She decided to work in this field because she loved nature and always enjoyed being outside. She was not a trained photographer, but easily picked up the ability to take real life pictures of nature. Before becoming a photographer in her late twenties, she was a high powered executive for a brokerage firm. She hated the stress, pettiness, and draining work. She decided to take a leap a faith, and start living her passion. Georgette had never been trained in photography and learned everything on her own. She loved nature and natural settings, and was able to really capture real-life, natural pictures. She used her skills as a business executive to help promote her business and create. Within a year's time, she had become the number one landscape photographer in a major city, with a cover on one of the finest photography magazines. When she came to me she was already doing well, but was concerned about whether or not she would make enough money. She called herself an "over-achieving Asian girl."

Image was also important to her and her family, as was making a "respectable income." Her culture had strong opinions about what was considered successful. She was unsure of how she was able to create this beautiful photography; the pictures she took looked alive, like nature was speaking directly to you. I would often see symbolic messages in the pictures, there were glimpses of little gnomes and twinkling of fairies. The pictures, in my opinion, brought you back to the magical kingdom, and your soul. Georgette also had a special ability, where every time she wrote something down, it would happen. What a powerful gift she had manifesting!

Through working with me, she realized that she had many intuitive gifts, and that she would readily get messages from *Spirit* and nature. Georgette came to my manifestation and meditation classes regularly, and began to meditate every day. This has helped her to become connected back to Source. I shifted many of her limiting beliefs through Thetahealing*. She became more and more confident. She was living her life purpose, knowing that there was more to come as she expanded her life. Georgette receives more insights and now trusts that they are messages from *Spirit,* and she moves on them. She hired a PR firm and marketer for her business, and through doing so, she ended up landing a major landscape contract for a major magazine. I am sure she will continue to do great things, as she continues to listen to her heart and her *spirit.* I recently saw that she has a following on Facebook; she took some great funny pictures of her dog. One time, at the end of class, she emphasized that I had really helped her find her way back to her true purpose. "You have to write your book. Everyone is trying to find their purpose." Georgette is married now, with a beautiful baby, and doing very well.

Working with clients, I find that whenever they feel depressed, sad, or unhappy, somewhere along the line their *spirit* has been shattered, abused, depleted, or ignored. This is a vitally important part of ourselves that we often overlook, because our personhood or personality is generally our driving force in how we make decisions. Remember we are mind, body, and *spirit.* Now, on the planet, we have to listen to all three. To get back to hearing and feeling our *spirit,* we sometimes go to Yoga, Tai Chi, or engage in meditation or prayer. We go to a spa, we meditate, and we shift our focus inward and upward. We let go of the concerns of the material world, and listen to our inner wisdom.

Have you noticed that in this day and age of iPods, iPads, Smart phones, and email messages it is hard to hear our *spirit*? We usually don't pay attention to it, unless the universe knocks us on our back. This assault by the universe can be a in the form of a bankruptcy, divorce, trauma, accident, illness, or death. That is when the universe is sending a signal from our soul, transmitting a sign to our *spirit*, telling us that we may be off our path. "Wake up," it says, life is deeper than this superficial existence. Our soul is crying out for our attention.

When these things happen, people generally either breakdown, or get stronger. Remember, you have a choice in how to react to difficulty and dire circumstances. That is why I believe understanding the SOUL is so vitally important to human existence. If you understand that there is a reason for everything, you may not feel that you are a victim of life's fastballs. You may step back and ask, what was I supposed to learn with that? Once you master the lesson, it generally disappears.

Earth is a school. This world feels very real, because we have to learn lessons. The cinematography, lighting, sound effects, and actors on earth, and in your life, are like those from any blockbuster. It is like when you go to a movie, and the movie is so good you feel like you are living in it--this is how earth is set up by the *spirit* world. Our script and our fulfilling adventures lay in our heart. Our *spirits* signed up for these experiences, but our personality often comes in with blinders on, and our *spirit* memory becomes blocked. Some of my work is to give a spiritual lens to life, and unblock that person's limited view.

Punked

One of my clients came in after this sort of trauma wake-up call. She was referred by a friend. She was a punk rocker, and had kept herself clean after years of touring, drugging, and partying. When she sat down, I saw a man in *spirit* come up behind her. He looked warm, but

I thought he had an alcohol problem. I described this man, who was very supportive of her, a kind and sensitive soul, who drank to avoid life. I told her that this man said the two of them had played together, but he toured. I heard Spanish. I said, "Is your dad deceased?" She started to cry uncontrollably. Her dad had just died. She had a stone face, so at first, I didn't know if I was right. She then began to take off her jacket, and showed me a tattoo of her and her dad playing together in a garden. She tried to punk me and as she was skeptical of readers. He had died young, and was never honored for his gift of his music. He was a fairly successful Mexican session musician. To me, Marilyn looked white, and had no trace of an accent. Due to this, she passed into the punk rock scene with no one connecting her to her father. Looking at and hearing her, there was no way I could have known that her dad spoke Spanish. Her last name was Anglo, though both of her parents were Mexican, so she was impressed I got those details. The death of her dad had devastated her, as she was very close to him and they were just developing a healing relationship.

When she came to see me, she also had growths in her breasts. I was concerned, as energetically, the growths seemed large. I referred her back to her doctors. She didn't resonate with doctors very well, but she stated that she would go after I did a healing on her. I was very nervous about her health. She then said that she felt suicidal, because she felt purposeless and full of grief. She mentioned that the rock club where she worked was closing its doors, and she would soon be out of a job. She had endured a triple trauma, and all aspects of her soul were on high alert. Her body was experiencing health issues, as was her mind, through depression and suicidal issues. Her purpose and passion had been activated, because she also had to figure out how to gain employment. Then there was the spiritual aspect with the loss of a loved one, her dad whom she would never see again. This is where the holistic work of what I do really helps people.

Marilyn felt that she was worthless, because she was just doing mindless bartending work. She would get frustrated that when she spoke Spanish, some of the drunken patrons would talk down to her. "They think I am their servant!" I felt the presence of God, who is always hurt when we don't remember who we really are, it is almost like we believe that we are the roles we are playing, instead of the person underneath the costume. God's sadness welled up inside of me, and I had to tell her not to ever put herself down like that again. I had to get her *spirit* on course again because it is the guiding force for her mind and body.

I tuned into her father (when intuitives say tuned in, we mean that we are tuning into someone like a radio, on a different frequency air wave). Her father seemed to cry in *spirit* also. I gave her messages about her music that her father had heard on the other side. I also heard apologies from her father, as he toured a lot, and then tried to make it up to her with elaborate gifts. He wasn't home a lot. She was a great musician herself, but was afraid to go back to that field, because of her dedication to stay clean. She felt it was too risky.

We did an energetic clearing on healing, self-nurturing, and love because of the issues with her breasts. I also worked on removing limiting beliefs with Theta healing that were stored in her SOUL, about living life and her purpose. She had challenges centering on self-esteem and her self-worth, because of the bartending work she was doing in a music venue. We discussed what her purpose could be outside of touring; what it was that could give her a sense of meaning. I helped her to learn to dialogue with the universe, in order to find out her next step. She would religiously come to my 'Dialoguing with the Universe' class, and worked on gaining her own universal messages. She kept getting good hits and messages. She would meditate, and slowly, she became less suicidal through the healings and the messages from her dad. I instructed her to connect to the universe and ask what her next step was. We worked on affirming the positive and her *spirit* journey. She decided to put these teachings into practice.

One time, she was shopping at Macy's, and saw a woman who she felt drawn to. Part of my coaching was that before she went out, she was to ask the universe for a sign of synchronicity or a message. Her *spirit* was leading her. The woman said she was a music supervisor, and oversaw music that was to be published. Marilyn was shocked. She thought this was a good way to submit her music, and still be in the industry, but not have to play or be a part of the madness of the druggie rock world. She kept chanting and visualizing, and luckily, was at the right place, at the right time, and ended up becoming a manager of a well-known rock venue. She was making more money than she had before, and was able to secure full health benefits! She was doing very well, and could even throw out the drunken patrons who were rude! She loved it.

Later, since she had good health benefits, she was able to have herself checked out, and reported that her breasts had no signs of lumps! I was elated, as she had worked really hard on healing herself. She later invited me to an event at the place she worked. It was beautiful and elaborate, and I was so proud of her. Her mother and her husband were there as well. Her husband came up to me to tell me thank you. I was startled and asked him, "What for?" He said, "You brought back my wife. You saved her!" I told him that she saved herself, by remembering her value and worth. She connected to the universe, and was able to find her path. These are the true testimonials that come from the family of clients.

WORKBOOK EXERCISE #4

- **What** were your **childhood dreams**?
- **If** you had financial freedom **what would you do?**
- **What soul messages** have you gotten from your heart?
- **What messages from** *spirit* have you gotten that you are dismissing?

CHAPTER

4 Understanding and Knowing Your Gifts

PART OF my gift seems to be helping people find their purpose and removing the roadblocks that keep them from getting there. I often get clear visions of people engaging in their purpose. Clients will often say, "Oh, that is my dream, but I could never do that!" Many people seek me out, because they feel purposeless or stuck, and they have gotten off of their path of right action. Somehow, the messages from the outside, messages from advertising, friends, family, and media, make them feel as though they are not good enough. They stay in relationships, jobs, and lifestyles that are not helping them move forward, or allowing them to live the life they have dreamed of.

The universe is always teaching us that if we open up, and begin dialoguing with the universe, it will start clearing a path so that we are able find our right destiny. The wisdom of the soul often speaks in metaphors, symbols, synchronicities, and even sometimes, in premonitions and dreams.

I have written this book because I was trying to understand why I was here, and I am trying to do the best with my gifts. The hardest part of writing was trusting the very sensitive part of myself, the part that was able to read people in a profound way. To me, being sensitive seemed like more of a curse than a gift. I didn't know what to do with it. I had always wondered why I picked up vibes from people. How was I able to know their inner traumas, see their profound sadness, and know their desires? Why did people, even those I didn't know well, tend to tell me their deepest, darkest secrets?

Many times, these individuals would dump their deepest fears, insecurities, and experiences on innocent bystanders. Dating was a nightmare for me, as I was in the height of intuition training and could hear the deepest wounds of suitors, who were then too embarrassed to continue the relationship. There were constant messages coming from others about what I was supposed to be doing. I remember working in a psychiatric inpatient unit, and my having my coworker always staring at me. I thought I had my shirt open, or something, because of the way he used to stare. He was a nice guy, and great with the kids, so I had to pull him aside and ask him what was he staring at.

He finally divulged that after years of doing drugs, he saw auras, and my aura was massive and had various colors with a lot of white light. He said to me, "Everywhere you go, you bring a lot of light, and that could be challenging, if people are into darkness." No one had ever read my aura like that before. I thanked him for this message and felt more comfortable working with him after that. Remember, messages can come from anywhere, and from anyone.

I remember family and friends saying to me that I was sensitive, not to be too sensitive, and not to read into things. Later, I found out that I was right about a lot of what I had told them. I have learned the hard way though, to be quiet with my insights, because they are sometimes really personal and take people aback. When I became a therapist, I realized that this ability really helped people on a deep level. I was receiving messages from their own *spirits* that wanted to show me what they wanted to heal. I look at this work as very sacred, and as a privilege.

As a sensitive being, I absorbed the energy that others were discarding, and would often become drained if I was around a lot of people. As I was opening up intuitively, being in loud clubs felt to me like the volume was turned up way too high, and it was a distracting energy to my crown. When I felt uncomfortable around particular people, their truth was later revealed. I figured out that I was reading their auric fields. When I felt drawn to someone, it was usually because of their good natured quality. Everyone can be that in tune, but many tune out and talk themselves out of their insights.

Later, when I became an energy healer I would learn how to block other's negative energy, and keep my own. I understood I was an Intuitive Empath, it finally made sense as to why I was so intuitive about people, and why I became so drained by others and needed to do energy healing. I also learned how this healing could possibly become a career. I realized that there was a recent trend with more people admitting to their sensitivities, and not allowing them to be something to be ashamed of. There are highly sensitive persons, or HSPs (Highly Sensitive Persons), and empaths, or those who are overstimulated. I believe that the universe has a plan to send more of these people to earth, in order to shift the denseness down here. Sensitives usually have many great spiritual gifts.

Later, when I worked in clinics, I realized that many sensitives had anxiety disorders. When I talked to them about being sensitive to noises and crowds, smells and different energies they said, "Yes! That is me!" There are a lot of natural ways, that anxious people work with their aura field, to reduce anxiety. I also have them sage, breathe, and if they feel drawn, work with essential oils. I have seen these people actually get better, and anxiety symptoms greatly reduce as they come to understand their true nature. I sometimes even have them hold a hematite stone, which is a good grounding stone that helps them get back into their body, as empaths can get very distracted and scatter-brained, because they are usually thinking about the future, instead of the present moment.

What is a sensitive? Sensitive people are the ones with the big hearts, who feel very deeply. Sensitive people are here to help transform the planet, by making others more sensitive to the abuse, cruel actions, mean words, and general insensitivities of the world. Eventually, harsher *spirits* will grow up and realize that when you do something mean to others, you are really doing it to yourself. We all have a contract to help other people, and we all our connected. Most importantly, the energy that you put out comes back to you. It is just a matter of time before it cycles back. Some people don't know the universal laws. Sensitive people can become very irritable and agitated, as they tune in and pick up things around others, things that they can't comprehend on the cognitive level. They can also become mean and aggressive, in order to push people (that may be hurting them) away, or to mask their own sensitivity.

If you are a sensitive person, most likely you are here for the earth changes, the shift to a higher vibration. You are probably a lightworker*, bringing light to the planet. A lightworker is someone who is aware that they have a mission on this planet, and who knows that they can make a difference in some way. To bring light is to bring knowledge to others. Remember, light is what created the universe and the planet. As energy beings, we are made of light. Lightworkers are aware that they work with the light of the universe, in order to bring knowledge, love, and understanding to the masses. As a lightworker, your sensitivity is a gift. This planet has fallen into massive darkness, and your light and your gifts are supposed to be shining.

You are most likely an artist, a dancer, a writer, a designer, an actor, a fireman, or a surgeon, and you are good at it. Your sensitivity is not a curse, but you have to understand it. If you listen to your heart and to those urgings, the wanting to know and understand your life purpose, you become more sensitive. You also can have a piece of helping the planet evolve. A true life purpose always helps others, either as assistance in another's growth or their transformation. Doing your thing always seems to inspire other people.

How do you know that you are sensitive? You may have heard someone say to you, "You are too sensitive. Don't be so sensitive!" Many people on the spiritual path have heard this criticism, over and over again. It is usually meant as a put-down to someone who has a high sense of intuition and a sixth sense of knowing. This comment is usually stated with disdain and contempt, seen as a major flaw in an individual's personality. You may have empathy for the homeless, or for abused kids, or issues with the welfare system. In fact, many lightworkers have heard these exact words, especially as children, and it has caused them to close down this gift. "Toughen up! You need thicker skin!" is usually quickly followed by another comment meant to shame and dismiss the individual's perceptions.

Sensitives are usually quite gifted intuitive *spirits* who pick up the less perceived sensations of life. Lightworkers on the planet have heard these comments a lot, because they are generally trying to raise their vibrations, as they evolve towards spiritual mastery. If you are on a conscious spiritual path, you become more intuitive, thus more sensitive. To be intuitive, you must be sensitive. Intuition, I believe, is God's voice. It is subtle. *Spirit* speaks to us daily, in quiet synchronistic whispers. Sensitives have the ability to perceive the subtle nuances of truth in the physical plane. Hopefully, they pick these signals up, follow them, and begin to connect to their soul's conscious growth, living more fulfilling and abundant lives.

One of these sensitives is a client that I have worked with, her story of self care shows how sensitives can make it and still help others.

Chronic Ping

Regina was a happily married white women in her mid forties, who has been struggling with chronic fatigue for over 10 years. She was a sensitive soul and an Occupational therapist who was working part time in a government job. She found the job very draining along with the population she served. Immediately I could see holes in her aura field like indents or pockets. I asked if she had an abusive parent. She said, yes,' My mother was extremely abusive verbally and very negative." Her energy field looked like she had been used to taking in negative words and absorbing it. Every pocket looked like a negative ping of someone pecking into their aura field, with cruel intentions.

As an empath, she was so sensitive that she easily absorbed other peoples' negatively as she would her mother's as a child and she held onto it. I picked up age, 28, and at that age, she had a bad job and relationship experience that put in the bed from chronic fatigue for 4 months! At the time a negative energy had entered her field through her neck, which I later removed through theta healing. She exclaimed. "I had severe neck pain when I was 28 right before I couldn't get out of bed."

I later discussed saging her energy field. She never even heard of that. I sampled a few scents of essential oils with her which she loved. Empaths generally crave essential oils, nature energy. I then saged her field and she felt so positive. She stated" it was like a weight was lifted off me. "
I always did healing on her and she always felt tired but renewed the next day. I told her how to ground and protect her energy since she was way to open to 'taking ' in peoples negative energy at her job where she worked with vets. She was so sensitive that after she went to the zoo, she felt completely drained as it was hard for to see the animals, incarcerated. It was her compassion empathy that was wounded.

After about a month of saging she was shocked that she literally was up all night with the sage and would feel a lot better. She had a lot more energy. When she protected her field she felt ten times better. She reported her chronic fatigue was 70% better just after the treatments. She was really suffering I felt from chronic pain, the negativity that empaths take in from others without clearing her field. Just like you get those pings on your cell phone when you get a hit, empaths get pings in their field. She also began to set boundaries with friends who drained her and spoke up to people who hurt her. She had a healing energy field without understanding and doing the work to protect herself.

After 10 years she then left the job and is working with children with her kindhearted and good natured self resonated with the energy of the young. Her chronic fatigue is almost completely gone. Health care professionals really need to learn how to manage their fields so they don't burn out. Many of them are empaths and lightworkers. Lightworkers, those seeking truth, have a conscious plan to raise the vibration of the planet, and bring in more positive qualities of kindness, goodness, love, and compassion. They also have to balance the warring yin and yang energies that are on the planet. Yin, the more feminine principle is receptive, intuitive, nurturing, and creative. Yang, the more active principle, is assertive, pioneering, instinctual, and building. When harmonious, these energies dance together--manifesting birth and death, darkness and light. In conflict they create evil, abuse, terror, and chaos. You must have both energies co-creating to move toward wholeness in the physical realm.

Working with people's emotions, I have noticed that sensitive people are often the ones who can be emotionally abused by others. Their sensitivity is viewed as a weakness. Intuitive sensitives are sometimes the kinder *spirits,* who fight for animals' rights, want to spread peace, or speak out against toxic GMOs. They understand, on a deep level, the law of karma, and that what you sow is what you reap. They understand how one bad action, decision, or deception can create a long energy strain of bad outcomes for the creators and others.

Since sensitives have been criticized for just being who they are, they are often closed down and leading sad, isolated lives, denying emotions in their soul. The bullies and the abusers, entities that are heralding the dark energies, don't want to lose their ego oriented existence, so they harass the sensitives in order to keep the veil of darkness alive. The ego thrives on chaos. The sensitives are here to pull the curtain back on the wizard, to reveal the tricksters, and to shine a light on the darkness. It is the mission of many—maybe, you have heard the call, and maybe, now it is time to honor your gift of sensitivity. Sensitive people will bring this planet towards a higher vibration. We need the armies of sensitives to trust their guts, create their dreams, fulfill their missions, and listen to the intuitive voice of the universe, rather than the abusive voice of the darkness. You were made sensitive for a reason.

The universe is supporting you, but to truly hear your path, you must protect yourself from the harsh energies on the planet. Here are some easy ways to do this:

1. **Trust your gut,** and start believing in the still small voice that is inside of you. Praise yourself when you intuit something and you were right. Always honor your *spirit*.

2. **Speak your truth.** Sensitives must not hold in their emotions. It becomes toxic to their bodies, as negative feelings lay dormant in the body temple. Let out the negativity in constructive and healing ways. I had a client, Luisa, who said that she was always having dizzy spells. I couldn't feel much about her head, but a feeling of a head being banged. She wasn't a timid female, and as a former gang banger, she often didn't mince words. She just had a hard time saying her true feelings, as it wasn't something that was allowed in her culture. Women's feelings were not honored. When she discussed all of the fights that she

had been in, the dizzy spells made sense. But she insisted, "All of the workups from the doctor were negative!" Later, she realized that she didn't want to do the dishes and be a house wife, and that her husband had restricted her to this traditional family role. Whenever she yelled at her husband about her housework she became dizzy. Finally, she had enough courage to identify that her body was telling her what she was afraid to say. She eventually began to feel compassion for her husband, as he was going through a tough time, and wasn't able to express that he felt that he was losing his manhood by losing his company. Underneath her tough exterior, she was really sensitive, and the pain went to her head. She had also suffered many head injuries as a gang banger. As the couple healed together, she said she was doing more of her own business doing makeup and hair styling, and less of the dishes.

3. **Protect yourself from negative energies**--you can do this by removing toxic people from your life, or by removing yourself from abusive relationships or situations. It can also be done by trying to be more positive and inspiring to others, instead of being critical and pessimistic. Birds of a feather flock together.

4. **Meditate regularly**, with grounding and protecting exercises (See picture page 33) . Meditation raises your vibrations and heightens your intuition. You begin to grow stronger with your gut instincts, and you receive more messages on how to create your life purpose. As you live your life purpose, you feel less tired and depressed, and more uplifted. Your sensitivity becomes a gift, as you now have a focus and reason for being here. You can also do walking meditation or guided meditations.

5. **Connect with God/Universe**. Say prayers and ask God questions. What do you want me to learn today? What is the higher purpose of this? How can I serve? God likes to hear us speak to him/her. I believe that God created us in order to see his/her own expression and become more inspired...so don't leave him hanging!

6. **Receive energy work** such as Reiki, Pranic healing, acupuncture, or massage. Sensitives must work with their energies, and remove toxins that build up in their energy fields. It is like a shower for your auric field. Your auric field is part of your spiritual sensory. Sage and incense clears energy in your home. Since sensitives have a tendency to be psychic sponges, you need to remove the maladaptive energies. Take baths with Epsom Salt, or rosemary, and lavender oils. To clear your home space, burn frankincense. Don't forget about getting into nature, a great energy clearer of toxic energy in your aura.

7. **You are sensitive** for one reason, to work with the universe. "The meek will inherit the earth," Jesus the Christ, which means anointed or crowned, said, as he had a direct opening of his crown chakra. The more sensitive you are, the more likely you are to have a heightened antennae to Source. Don't cloud that transmission. Tune in to K-GOD- Keep Good (God) Open Dialogue. It's a great radio station that can help you feel fulfilled and if you remain open you will receive your daily inspirational messages.

8. **Keep the Yin and Yang Balanced**, especially the qualities of gratitude and forgiveness. Gratitude puts you in a positive space to attract better outcomes, and like the Yin energy, pulls in better life outcomes. Forgiveness is about actively releasing negative energy. To *give* energy *forth,* and not hold onto it so it corrupts you. The yang is about actively releasing stagnant emotions. Energy must be in balance for creative lightworkers and sensitives. There has to be a flow. Leave the swamps for the egoic alligators of the world, stuck in their own muck. You want your life to be like a river. With the light acceleration on the planet, sensitivity is absolutely necessary to listen to and pull down the higher vibrations. These vibrations are full of light and love, and of beautiful qualities. To be an open channel to divine expression, whether it is through art, music, writing, or inspiration, you must be sensitive. So, next time someone criticizes you by saying, "You are

so sensitive!" say to them, "Yes, I need to be, in order to hear God's voice, it is the quiet whisper on the planet, and I don't want to miss my loving instructions. I am on borrowed time. Unlike you, I don't want to mute the sound!" The spiritual side of you is sensitive, caring, genuine, and loving. The sensitivity of your *spirit* receives the signals from your soul to evolve. If more people opened up to their empathic kindhearted nature, that earth could slowly shift to be more peaceful.

As an intuitive healer and reader, I learned to listen with three layers of my ears. I listen with my heart, my mind, and my *spirit*. The heart tells me how to work with a person, and how to assist them on the path with the earthly things. The mind tells me cognitively and analytically how to address various issues and problems. The *spirit* tells me who this *spirit* is, and what their soul wants. The *spirit* helps me cut through all the layers of projections and intellectualization of the mind, and communicate *spirit* to *spirit*. Thus, I know the truth of the matter regarding where the client is as a soul, and their soul's destiny.

I generally don't get the whole soul picture. I don't think we are privy to everything on the earth plane, but I hear, see, and feel the piece of the soul that the soul has manifested this lifetime. I have always heard the unconscious of people, even before I was trained as a psychoanalytic psychotherapist. When I was little, I used to call it the undercurrent. When people were saying one thing, their body, facial expression, and my inner knowing told me something different. My mother was like this too, highly intuitive. My father was a pastoral counselor, minister, and social worker, and trained as a psychoanalyst at the Blanton Peale Institute in the 1960's, so he was always listening to the unconscious, and talking about it.

Maybe, I was trained to listen with my heart, *spirit,* and mind, rather than with my ears. It helps a lot in healing and counseling individuals, because it is cutting to the chase and getting to the truth of the matter with where they want to go, and what they want to accomplish. Working in numerous, fast paced HMOs and EAPs (Employee Assistance Programs), this ability really served and helped me see many patients. I remember interviewing at this prestigious and high profile EAP, on Wall Street. It was my first job out of graduate school. I was sitting with the managing founder during the interview, trying to impress her with short term and solution focused theories. She scrunched up her face, rolled her eyes and in "New Yawk" direct discourse, stated, "Enough of that jabber, just use your intuition! It is really high!"

In my mind, I was like "Amen!" and I was off! Since our planet is speeding up, with our thoughts and manifestations creating at lightning speed, my intuitive abilities seemed to be growing and increasing to assist other's souls in growing more quickly. You only have three to eight sessions in an EAP, so when I worked there, I listened *spirit*-to-*spirit,* to find out how gently to examine their issue, and give them insight. The *spirit* is what heals. There is always a place for a really good therapist for earth focused folks, but the planet is having a soul crisis on such a profound level that people are yearning for more. Many people need assistance on a spiritual, soul level. Thus, my gifts of hearing *Spirit*, and many others, gifts have opened up. As many, many others have had their gifts open up as well.

It did take me a while to combine the two, but I see how the universe was constantly steering me towards my LIFE path and purpose, and combining my interests with my vocation. While I was at Columbia, studying for my Master's degree and interning, I was trying to combine psychotherapy with the profound spiritual experiences I have had.

I have mentioned before that I regularly saw ghosts in my apartment on 112th Street in Manhattan. Ghosts would often wake me up in the middle of the night. I remember that one time this young black male ghost woke me up. He bumped into my bed. My bed jolted, and

I saw him standing over the bed looking at me. Now since he was a ghost and I felt this jolt, I must have been slightly out of my body to be able to feel his shove, and for us to be on the same energetic plane. I was shocked that he was in my room. He was wearing a Yale sweatshirt, and I had never seen him before. He just looked at me and said, "Sorry." It scared me, because he was solid not ethereal, but I was finally able to fall back into a deep sleep.

The next day, I was trying to figure out what was going on. Who was that guy in my apartment, and why did I see him so clearly? *I asked this question, out loud to the universe.* I brought my clothes to the laundry room in my building and was pulling out my college sweat shirt that said Wesleyan on it, an older black lady, also doing her laundry, started to speak to me about her grandson, "Ah, my grandson was to go to Wesleyan, but instead he went to Yale, down the street." I felt chills run through my body. She went on to say that he used to live with her in this building, but he died of a drug overdose. My eyes became really wide. I asked her to describe him, and when she did, I knew that it was her grandson that had come to see me. As a counselor, I find that ghosts often want to talk to me while I am sleeping. Until I protected myself energetically, they used to want to get some free afterlife therapy! The woman said, "My dear, you look like you've seen a ghost." I thought *if she only knew*! I asked the universe, and there was my answer.

This visit was my opening to the realm of nightly visits from disembodied beings. They often would try to engage in a conversation with me, or would just sit there and stare. It was quite unnerving to say the least, and I still haven't gotten used to it. I don't really engage with them, unless they come through in a reading. These experiences also made me know, without a doubt, that there is life after death. It made me look at therapy differently. I realized that the soul transmits time and space, and there were souls still searching for help or closure after they died. I realized these experiences happened to me for a reason. I was an intern for the universe. Through working in different environments, I had a lucrative stipend and the expansion of my SOUL was a bonus. The universe was teaching me and helping me to assist in the planet's evolution. Grief counseling is different, if you feel the presence of the recently deceased in the room, and can transmit messages from them. The tricky part was closing it down in a clinical setting. *Spirit* always leads me, tells me what to say, if to say it, how to say it.

My internship continued as I kept asking the universe for an understanding about my work. One night, I woke up out of a deep sleep, and saw this Asian man with a little hat and beard, who had floated into my room. I was 28-years-old, right before my Saturn Return, and he looked like a negative film on my wall. He smiled, and when he saw I was frightened, he disappeared. I thought he was Japanese, but then later, from his hat and beard, I realized he was Chinese. It was unnerving to see a man in my room, even though he didn't have a body, only a head. I asked the universe to give me a sign, and to tell me if he was real, and if this man was a part of my path. I forgot that I had made this request.

The next morning, I walked into Manhattan, down Fifth Avenue. I saw a man on the street selling little Buddhas, and was immediately drawn to him. I walked up to him and he said, "You need a gift," and gave me a little alabaster Buddha! People in Manhattan don't give away anything for free. I was shocked, but it was a gift from the universe. Not exactly the Asian man I saw, but close. Next, I asked the universe to show me more. I kept walking and somehow, all of the sudden, all of these people were congregating around me. After a brief while, I realized that I was in the middle of Korean Buddhist festival, and was part of the parade. The parade participants laughed, and I quickly got off of the parade route, and onto the sidewalk.

Then my friend, who was running a Goddess circle, called me and said that we would be studying Amatersu, the Japanese Goddess. I thought, *ok, I have received three tangible signs—a gift from the universe, a Buddha, movement forward on my path (me in the parade), and then an invitation from the universe to attend a class.* Well, that is how I interpreted it. I began to explore Japanese and East Indian spirituality, and became a Reiki master. I again realized that the universe will dialogue with you in tangible signs. It usually happens when you ask, go about your life as usual, and are open.

Finally, an intuitive named Marie, who kept telling me to do readings, said that a friend of hers, who was a profound medium, was trying to build up her practice. This woman, Diana, was giving free readings, and would go to your home to do them. She would read the space where I lived, and she thought we should talk. Diana came the next day, and said she immediately had to give me a message. She said that I would be doing healings and readings, helping people on a deep level. She said the information would just click in my head, like a ticker tape. As she was sitting in my grad school dorm room, I thought she was nuts, and I stated that I wanted to be a therapist. She acknowledged the out of body beings that seemed to gather in my place. I still appeared skeptical, and she then stated, "Well the Asian man you saw last night floating in your room is telling me it is your destiny." Chills! Ok, now I was listening. While sitting with her, I began to see her aura and receive information about her. It was the first time that I had seen an aura so clearly. Four signs in twenty-four hours! That was the spiritual jackpot. I asked for and received a response, and I was listening.

Til' death do us part

Helping clients spiritually in a clinical setting was tricky, but it often was very healing to the client. For example, I had a client whose spouse had died. He was in so much grief, for several years, that it was unbearable. I met him in an Intensive Outpatient Program. He was a born again Christian, so mediumship was not something that he would have been open to, or that would have been appropriate in this setting. During our session though, I felt a feminine presence swoosh into the room. I got an impression of a petite woman with a meek personality. This man felt that he had neglected his wife, he was immersed in his work when she was alive, and that he didn't give her enough attention. She had had a difficult childhood, and needed a lot of love. He felt his neglect was what led his wife to become an alcoholic, and what, ultimately, had led her to drink and drive one night, causing the fatal collision that killed her.

He had held his grief for three years, with no change, because he felt that he was not a good Christian husband and that he had neglected his husbandly duties. The deceased wife's presence pressed against my *spirit* and gave me a different story. She showed me pictures in my head, and I saw that she was having an affair with his business partner, and that they had felt so guilty about it that they had gotten drunk, so she drove home, and was killed in a car accident. She was the one who felt guilty in death.

I told him that it sounded like his wife was a saint. He felt she was, but this martyrdom was preventing him from seeing the truth about who she was, and it was making his grieving energy stagnant. I asked if his wife felt distant before the accident. He agreed that she did, and I asked how distant. He revealed that they hadn't been intimate in several years. "She didn't even want me to touch her!" he said. I asked him, "Didn't you say your wife was very affectionate, and needed a lot of love? Don't you find that weird?" Through tears, he agreed that yes, it was. I asked him how an affectionate woman might stay celibate for so long. "Do you think she was having an affair?" I prodded.

I was concerned that he would get very angry at me, but the *spirit* of his wife urged me on, so I said these words with the direction of *spirit*. He said, "I have never told anyone this, but I did think so. I can't tell my Christian friends this, but something seemed off with her." I asked him if he knew who the affair may have been with, and he responded that he had always suspected his business partner, but had never gotten proof. "Funny thing is," he said, "he didn't even go to the funeral, and hasn't really been able to look me in the eye since she died."

I reflected that this sounded like strange behavior, after his spouse's death. He looked up and above me, and said, "I bet you it was him!" Everything just clicked in his head. "Wait," he said, "when we do deals that he knows that I don't agree with, he doesn't look me in the eye. I called my partner after the accident, and he asked if she was killed on Mulholland Drive. I said yes, and the funny thing is, if she was at work, she would never have taken Mulholland Drive because it is in a different direction, but his house is on Mullholland! When I asked my business partner how he knew about where she was, he said his wife had called him looking for me, but that didn't add up, because I had already texted her saying that I had gotten home early. I was too shocked about the accident to put everything together, but now it makes sense!" He received an "Ah-ha" moment, and stated, "I feel chills all up and down my arms! He was hiding something from me!"

Instead of being angry, the client said to himself: "It wasn't my fault. *She* must have felt guilty. She did this to herself. It wasn't *my* fault. It was her own doing." He said it felt like a weight was lifted from his heart. A peace settled around his energy field. As he started putting various scenarios together, I saw his head playing through all the times his wife and partner were unavailable. His whole countenance shifted. The patient left and went home, and then left me a message the next day. He had confronted his former partner, stating, "You and Stacy..." and before he could finish his sentence his business partner sobbed, and said, "I am sorry, so sorry." The truth was revealed. The client stammered, "I never expected such healing, but thank you. My soul is at rest." I heard a soft whisper in my ear, saying, "Thank you. I am free too." This shot chills down his spine. His wife was no longer a martyr, but a deceased human being who had made errors. He was still sad, but within a year's time, he had met a wonderful woman that he went on to marry. He had put the guilt to rest. He sent me a new marriage picture, and I swear I could see his ex-wife's *spirit* in the background!

During this intervention, I didn't tell this client, who was in an Intensive Outpatient Program setting, that I had seen his dead wife, and that she was planting this information in my head. That would have been inappropriate. I didn't know what to say, but knew I had to be a transmitter of truth. The psychiatrist I was working with at the time was so excited to see the patients' change in emotional health, he nearly busted in my room during a session to compliment me on my good work. He himself was an energy healer. My guides urged me on, knowing it was the right time to have him release this grief, and move on with his life.

Spirit leads the way. I was a therapist with a message from beyond. The client just thought I was very analytical and objective. I knew something different. I didn't break rules in various settings, just recreated them to assist in soul healing. This was one of the first interventions I did. I was working for a company, but interning with the universe.

Right now, ask the universe for a sign of whatever question resides in your heart. Ask to be given proof that you have guides or angels. Ask if there is proof of life after death. Just ask! Ask for your gifts to be revealed! As I continued to play with the universe and ask for signs, more would come. I was still struggling with how I could incorporate counseling and my intuitive experiences, regularly. I asked the universe, "Now what will I be doing exactly? What was I to call myself--a soul therapist, intuitive, a path pusher or all three?" I began to believe that I was meant to be doing this work, and often had people seeking me out to help them to heal from painful trauma, or to find a way to their path.

Wine and Spirits

Ryan was a young guy who sought me out at the age of twenty-eight, when he was struggling with his relationship and life purpose. We spent a long time talking about his relationship, which I felt was holding him back. With a quick scan of his energy field, I observed that his sacral creative chakra was stuck. The second chakra is the sexual creative energy, and sometimes, when people are in unhealthy relationships, it will block creativity. His girlfriend was beautiful, on a physical level, but that was where the connection ended. He was paying her rent, and she was buying hand bags.

Ryan was a budding spiritual guy, so this shallow relationship was not serving him well. He came from an Irish-American family that had done well in the wine industry. He was encouraged by his family to continue in the lucrative family business, but he wasn't feeling it. Once when I was meeting with Ryan, I saw a man show up in *spirit*. I described him as a bald guy, with glasses, who had died in his mid-fifties. "Gerry," he said, "he was a neighbor." I heard music, and he said that he, Gerry and Gerry's son used to jam together. I said, "He loved your talent! Are you doing your music?" He said, "Not as much as I should, the wine business takes up much of my time."

Ryan also had a little studio in his home. Gerry said a series of things that Ryan recognized as true. He commented on his singing voice, and also his ability to play the guitar. This *spirit*, Gerry, was unrelenting. Ryan was very concerned about his family name, and with disappointing his family. We discussed his passion versus his family obligation: wine versus the *spirit*. He was coming up on his Saturn Return,* so he had to make a SOUL decision from his heart. When you go with your heart, and that is what Saturn will force you to do, opportunities will move along synchronistically. Usually when you don't follow your passion, you will run into blocks. Saturn is there to steer you to your soul's right path.

Ryan went home stunned that his neighbor had come through, but also inspired by that *spirit* spark. He came in one more time, months later, and he said he finished the album and it was doing well! We did a visualization to help him learn how to manifest. I created this scenario of him having a great gig, and then walking off a stage, sweating, with a towel in hand, and stepping into a big tour bus. As he was getting on the bus, a music company executive would come up to him from behind to ask him to talk about a record deal. Ryan liked the visualization, and would practice visualizing at home.

Months later I got an email from Ryan thanking me for the insights and for the session. He said that his music was doing really well, and that he had even booked a major commercial that used his music, through the visualization process. I was shocked, because I really didn't know his work, because I am very busy, and also for ethical reasons, I never Google a client before they come see me. I don't want what I see to bias my read on them. I wouldn't have found anything back then anyways, as he wasn't doing his music.

I finally Googled him, and was floored. His music was really, really good, and he already had 80,000 likes on Youtube. I emailed him back saying, "Is that you singing? You are really good!" I was later watching TV, and heard his music on a couple of shows. He mentioned, "Oh yeah, and after one gig this guy came up to me from Warner Brothers, with his card, and said he wanted to talk to me, just like our visualization!" It was uncanny. He continues to do well. I often play his music during my workouts. He is very talented, and was inspired by a *spirit*, an old friend from the other side. He took a payout, and left the wine behind.

I saw how just opening up to *spirit* can greatly help someone. I would always pray to God saying, "If this work is for me, let it come. If it is not right, take it away." Always, more people would come, and more opportunities would be presented. When you work with the universe, you have to be integrity-driven, and you have to invoke Source. If you want to make a lot of money, without integrity, some of these principles will not work. You can't screw someone else over, because you are working with the law of attraction and a magnetic universe, guess what will happen to you? These principles are for people who want to evolve their soul in a positive way.

WORKBOOK EXERCISE #4-A

- **What** do you think your gifts are?

- **What** are you **HIP** to — meaning, Hobbies, Interest and **Passion**??

- **Where** is your attention drawn?

CHAPTER

5 *SOUL* Attributes

TOXIC SOUL qualities–Through listening to the souls of many people, that are lost, wounded, and depressed, I have learned what soul qualities are toxic to the soul's growth. Usually when I sit down with a client, their *spirit* will guide me, or the client's higher self will give me information, to help the client start releasing heavy doses of crazy negative energy that they have encapsulated themselves in.

Selfishness/Greed: This is very unnatural for the soul's growth. Only thinking about yourself doesn't resonate with the truth that we are all universal, connected, and one spiritual energy, separated into many. When you do something for others, you are literally doing something for yourself. I like to look at it this way, if you had a petri dish of cells, and you picked one cell from the dish, the other cells would all move and respond to the action in the dish. This means that if you steal something from someone else, it will affect the whole. Eventually, you will experience someone stealing from you. You may not know when it happens, or how it takes form, but energy is intelligent, and it always returns back to its source. Just like in a petri dish, a ripple goes out from your hand, and the source of the energy goes back to the where you originally put your hand in the dish. The energy comes back to source.

Selfishness is thinking about yourself and not how your actions, words, and deeds affect other people. It is not giving unconditionally to others. Especially those in need. If you have a sandwich and a friend is hungry and forgot their lunch money and they ask you for a bite of sandwich, give them half.

Greed is obvious and it is the ultimate act of selfishness. It is accumulating things, over the care or concern of others. It is a "by any means necessary" mentality. When you have these qualities, you don't realize that you cannot take your money and belongings with you to the other side. Making a lot of money does not make you greedy, it is what you do with what you have, and how you accumulated it.

For example, if you make hundreds of thousands of dollars per year, and a friend who is ill asks you for a hand, and you turn your back on that friend, and you had caused them ill will years before, clear the karma and give them a loan. If you are greedy and selfish, you may find yourself stuck with a bad investment, an unfair lawsuit, or a nasty divorce. You may lose more money than you originally were stingy about, as the accumulation of bad energy spirals backward to the original creator. If you know the laws of the universe, you can avoid this. We are not judged by what we had on earth, but by how we treated others.

Manipulation: This is a very difficult verbal pattern of emotional abuse, by telling lies, persuading others, and by hiding your true intentions. Usually the motivation of the manipulator is selfish, and at the same time, it involves inducing guilt or fear or lowering the self-esteem of others. I don't think people understand how damaging this is, not only another person, but also to themselves. I often hear this pattern in love relationships, and in relationships between employers and employees--the classic car salesman. As an Aries, I prefer more direct communication, say what you mean, and mean what you say.

Manipulations sound, to me, like fingernails on a chalkboard. You will find younger people (the indigos)* will also be turned off by this pattern of speech. The *spirit* doesn't like manipulation, so if you want to enhance your connection to your *spirit,* you better move away from this pattern. Direct, honest communication with a balm of kindness, or good natured humor, works wonders. I know that in business manipulation is a common pattern, especially in sales. Can you say telemarketers? You can be ethical, honest, and true in business, and have a win-win philosophy. It also depends on how serious you are about spiritual evolution, and how clearly you look at this quality. The laws of the universe work with us to help us learn from how we treat other people. What we do onto others, will come back to us quickly and succinctly. It is not a theory, but universal law.

Anger: Anger is an emotion that can be necessary on the earth plane. I know a lot of spiritual people don't like anger, but if you see an abuser getting away with abusing kids, or other unfair injustices, you should get angry, and then change that emotion into constructive action, in order to move forward to make changes. Too many of us get caught in the anger, and lose the lesson that it is there to be an impetus to higher spiritual action, to change a bad circumstance. Drugs and alcohol are a prescription to anger, both street drugs and prescription drug addictions. There are more and more prescribed addictions, which can result in anger if people don't get their fix.

Some people are raised in angry environments. I have seen kids raised in gang families where anger is the prescription to communication. Anger can be a catalyst to losing jobs, relationships, and continual conflicts in life. We can overcome anger in various ways-- express the pain, discuss it. Move through it, and try to come up with an answer to move forward. A simple book on anger management, or a class, can do wonders to change this maladaptive pattern, if it overcomes us. It may help you become aware of speech patterns and interactions that you thought were normal behavior. Meditation, especially mindfulness, helps a lot with calming the mind and pausing before anger ensues.

For the last year and half, I have been teaching mindfulness meditation to work-stressed people, and in anger management classes. There were about twenty to thirty people who were activated because of work place harassment, job changes, and lay-offs. Most of the people come in pretty depressed and anxious; some are full of rage. Through mindfulness techniques, I help them to stay in the moment and to work with their breath. I also help them to learn how to deactivate anger, while it is happening. I instruct them in how to become quiet enough to locate where their own *spirit* resides so that answers to their next steps will come through. Instead of Plan B, if they are in an unhappy job, I tell them to create a Plan P for purpose. Your *spirit* generally surfaces in between your thoughts. I have seen extremely angry people become more peaceful, as they work on going within.

Addictions: We all have various addictions in life, and they are very hard things to let go of. An addiction is putting your trust into another substance, such as money, sex, power, material items, or food. If you are in the midst of a serious addiction, honoring your *spirit* is a hard prescription, but listening to your *spirit* is probably the string of hope that will help you out of it. You may want to try Al-Anon, NA, Gamblers Anonymous, or get into an alcohol treatment program. If you have a serious addiction, you may not be able to even find what your real life purpose is, but ironically, your *spirit* is trying to get to you through your legal problems, relationship difficulties, financial problems, and other crises. There are many good programs out there, whether you have insurance or not, created by people who have been there, and who will not have judgment.

Whenever I have worked with someone who is addicted, I have seen a lot of pain. These are often very sensitive people, who don't want to feel the memory of some heinous experience. Most likely, if you had heard the stories that I have heard, you would understand why they may have taken this path. If you were having the exact experience, and had the exact DNA, upbringing, and history, you would probably make the same choice. Addiction can greatly ruin your life. There is a choice, and you can heal an addiction. You have the ability to tune into your deeper *spirit,* and work on letting it go. Support is essential. Don't try to do it alone when there is help out there.

Abuse: Verbal, physical, emotional, or sexual—This is where my classic training in social work shows up. Verbal abuse, including yelling, screaming, puts-downs, and degrading comments don't help the receiver, or the person who is doing the abusing. Physical abuse, including slapping, punching, hitting, stabbing, etc., is obvious abuse, because it against the natural flow of creation, which is the function of the universe. Emotional abuse can include putting someone down and lowering their self-esteem, or having one person try to control the other. Manipulation is usually a part of this pattern. Twisting people's vulnerable feelings can be called emotional abuse.

All different types of abuse have to do with one person trying to control another. Having control is usually a way for an insecure person to have a warped perception that they are somehow in power. It is not natural for one person to have control over another, because it is against the flow of the universe, and the law of free will. If you find yourself in this situation, as an abuser or victim, it is important to realize this and to stop the pattern as soon as possible. The karma connection of people who are in abusive situations is pretty strong. That is why domestic violence relationships are so hard to break; there is a deep soul lesson in this bond. One person has to learn to stand up for him or herself, and the other has to release control, or stop the abuse.

I understand that it is not always easy to get out of it, but for your own soul's salvation, you must. It is not right to be abused. The effects on children who witness abuse are life-long. Getting counseling for this can be helpful. Sometimes, alcohol and drugs are involved, including prescriptions drugs, as part of this pattern.

Sexual abuse is one of the most prevalent, and severe forms of abuse out there. I have counseled and worked with many women and men suffering from sexual abuse. It leaves a deep hole in the soul. It is almost like a soul murder. The insecurity, shame, and pain that occurs after this act can linger on for years. Also, the maladaptive acting out by women by becoming promiscuous, strippers, domina-trixes, or porn stars, and getting paid for re-abusing themselves, is pervasive. Many eventually realize that they feel deeply empty inside.

After abuse, this justification erodes the soul, and in the process, it puts a fake Band-Aid on deep trauma. It is easy to become drug addicted, in order to numb out the pain. I have seen how victims of abuse believe they are gaining false power. When a child's or young person's boundaries are violated in that way, they either try to recre-ate boundary violations on others, in order to identify with the aggressor, or they create more boundary violations on themselves, but gain only a momentary false power. Some women justify that the money they make, by stripping or other maladaptive sex practices, will heal their wounds. The wounds usually become reopened, as they recreate further pain by degrading others or themselves. They then fall into a pattern of manipulation and turn to drugs to numb out their *spirit's* messages.

The creator's gift of sex, when it is misused, generally comes back to hurt the person in some other form. Sadly, the first *abuse is never their fault*. Unfortunately, with not enough mental health treatment services for these women or men, they try to self-heal, and continue in the cycle of abuse. Having my office in West Hollywood near the Sunset strip, I have worked with some women like this, many of them need money, and don't want to dig deep into the pain. Energy healing has proven to be helpful. This work is complicated and is too much to get into here, but anything that goes against the SOUL, and your own *spirit*, can be very damaging to the person. Sexual abuse is one of those issues. I have done some SOUL retrievals, bringing back parts of the *spirit* that were fractured during the abuse, and it works wonders on this terror. Some women fight against this abuse, and turn against maladaptive behaviors to become success stories.

A Shattered SOUL

Cristela was a bright woman, and a licensed therapist, who found me through *Psychology Today*. She was originally from El Salvador, and was in a job where she felt disrespected and dismissed. Ironically, she reminded me of me when I was in that type of job. I worked with her and clearly felt her father. She confirmed that her father had crossed over years ago. I didn't get good energy from this man, but I knew he had something to say to her. Then she told me her story in her own words. "My mother was fifteen-years-old. My dad was in his thirties. I don't know exactly how old. She was going to school, and looking for a job. He told her he had a job available. He sold textiles. I don›t know the details but I know that she was drugged, or intoxicated, tied up and raped. Cruel! Being raped was a shame to her family, so she was instructed to stay and marry her abuser. My grandfather, her father, was an alcoholic and would beat my mom. My grandfather had broken my mother's ribs and jaw before, so he was no joke. It was like trading in one hell for another. My grandfather was sexually abusing my mom's sister too, and I suspect my mom as well. It was a mess!"

I have heard this story about women who were forced to marry their abusers, a generation or so ago, again, very tragic and demoralizing. I have heard this story in all cultures and it occurs much more than we think. Cristela's mother was taught not to value and protect herself, so she didn't know how to protect her daughter. Cristela was sexually abused by her uncle, in her own home. As a skilled therapist, she understood that he had groomed her, and later ritualistically sexually abused her, from ages six to nine years old. Even after the abuse was exposed, her uncle was allowed to stay in the home. Her mother, of course, who was kidnapped and raped, couldn't protect her. Her mother hadn't healed from her own tragic abuse and marriage, and didn't know how to protect her daughter.

Later in life, Cristela's rage surfaced when she went to a psycho-therapy environment that was abusive. The environment proved to remind her of her home environment, as they were dismissive and rude. She began to get sick, and began to lose her hair. I was sympathetic to her, because I had been in a similar environment, where there were unfair practices and an undercurrent of racism and disrespect. She was very spiritual, and I immediately saw that she was a healer. She said that she had dreams about her hands being hot. I also saw pieces of her missing in her aura field, and I gave her the ages that were missing, the ages expanded from when she was a child and sexually abused to during her adolescence. Not only was a part of her missing, but the attributes that she really needed were not available. These attributes of strength and courage, adolescent risk-taking, as well as other parts of her personality were suppressed, in order to be able to survive living in a house with an abuser. Her soul appeared shattered.

She was shocked that I hit the times right on the head, and explained the parts of her personality that were missing. She felt like parts of those times in her life were incomplete. I connected to a six-year-old aspect of her, who was wearing a white dress, and was creative and curious. "That was me!" She said. "I was sooo creative and nosey, but the abuse closed me down." I explained to her that an aspect of her at age six was living happily in another plane. I wanted to bring that part back. This is a way of reintegrating a part of ourselves, symbolically and energetically, to help to make ourselves whole. I complimented her on not acting out against him in rage or joining a gang, which she was encouraged by peers to do. She also didn't get into drugs. She put her energy into school, getting a BA, and a Master's degree, and becoming licensed as a therapist.

Cristela had done a training with me, in one of my intuitive development classes, for therapists. She was open to the spiritual insight. I was lucky to work with a therapist, as they are clear on what works and what doesn't work. The SOUL retrieval I created is a meditative technique given to me by *spirit*, where I literally go to another realm and call in the parts of them that have left. Picture a glass that drops and shatters; that is how a fragmented soul looks like to me. It is like holes are missing in their personality and aura. People who have missing time, or can't remember their childhood, or have been in accidents, or various traumas, are a good candidates for SOUL retrievals. There are various methods by many practitioners that perform this procedure. Through a meditative state and energy healing, I call back various aspects of them to reintegrate into their body and *spirit*. Those parts actually dialogue with me, and then decide whether they will meld back together. This is a healing meditative procedure that has proven very successful, when the person is ready. Usually the person feels stronger, more centered and whole.

Cristela said that after the soul retrieval everyone began to look at her differently. They all thought they knew her. I feel that this is because there was more light, from the other side in her field, where we all know each other. She started to date more, as she began to gain trust and strength, and she found that she was able to set boundaries, and be vulnerable with men. Aspects of her adolescent rebellious nature served her well when she told a guy to back off, because he was too aggressive. When her creative side was reintegrated, she quickly became bored at her job, and felt that had to do more. She sent me an email that the work we had done together really helped heal some old issues, to have more confidence, and to be more open to a loving relationship. She definitely gained the attributes of **strength and courage**.

Betrayal: Who hasn't been through this painful experience of the heart and soul, that has set you up for you to learn forgiveness? The action of betrayal hurts the soul on a deep level, because its occurrence generally happens between individuals or groups who share a bond or trust. That is why it hits so deep. Who hasn't been betrayed?

Children who suffer abuse from parents, couples where there is infidelity, teachers, or guardians where they are supposed to help you, but betray you instead. There is always someone who is being taken advantage of.

Cristela's difficult experience at a clinic reminded me of working in a crazy psychotherapy environment where I was betrayed. Lisa and I were bonded as friends, and she said I reminded her of someone who was recycled. She was smart and supportive, and we learned from each other's cultures and differences. She often identified herself as a triple minority, and would discuss with me the various struggles that she went through. Always the compassionate listener, I had heard her story and let her discuss her conflict with our boss, who had made some very culturally insensitive statements to her (and later to me), and then the both of together. As with any emotional abuser, our boss' pattern of action didn't stop there. Lisa and I had discussed the situation several times, and supported each other, having "each other's backs." Lisa also told me about the abuse she had suffered by her brother, and her brother-in-law, that had left her leery of men.

During our time of working together, she confided in me that one of our coworkers told her that he would get so mad at her that he thought about assaulting her. Yes, another therapist. He said he was just kidding, like that excused the behavior! Since I worked in EAP, I helped her negotiate how to deal with this harassment. She later minimized it, but I knew with her history, it was very difficult for her. Our boss, who often made racial comments, wasn't helpful either. In group supervision, he made another racial comment about me which was based on a stereotype. It was bad enough that he did it individually, but to do it in a group, in a therapeutic setting, where we were supposed to be sensitive, was not cool with me.

I had to deal with these racial injustices for most of my life, in groups where I was, often, the only one. The most difficult thing was that no one supported me. A clinical supervisor, who was supposed to be unbiased, was throwing out stereotypes, and encouraging that energy in the group. Ironically, he was a minority also. So, generally, because others were different in the group, he had no understanding on how isolated the racial comments make people feel, and the hurt he caused felt more intense. I noticed this pattern with him, seeing that he even minimized the emotional fragilities of the patients that we discussed. He was especially demeaning toward women who were sexually assaulted, almost ridiculing them. As a therapist, already licensed in another state, I was horrified. This was a red flag regarding his emotional insensitivity.

I then had a strange experience, in which I saw visions of his abuse by an older, mean sister who was also abused. His scars weren't healed, and he was taunting young, vulnerable patients, as he wished he could have done to his sister. I rarely have visions about coworkers but I knew my guides were warning me. Later, he wanted me to collude with his lack of compassion, which was something I wouldn't allow. I refused to be abusive to my patients because of his unhealed projections. There was another energetic issue which bothered me: he had a lot of dark energy around him. In my mind, I thought of him as a vampire, sucking the life out of people who were vulnerable, and intimidating and scaring people and patients so that he could feel powerful. I avoided his energy, because my guides told me to stay away from him, because he wasn't of the light.

I wasn't exactly sure what this meant, since this person was supposed to be a healer of sorts, as a therapist. On a good day, he reminded me of a predator with low self-esteem. His energy felt dirty to me. Finally, I had to confront him about his insensitive comments regarding women and minorities. I advised him that I didn't want to work with him individually. He made it clear that he didn't like black people. Some of his derogatory statements included: questioning why I had the last name Coleridge, alluding to the bell curve, talking about when I fell while I was break dancing, saying that I lied about having a license in another state, and saying that Lisa and I wouldn't have to study for the verbal part of our licensing exam, because they always pass minorities because the state needs more minority social workers.

He also implied that I got some kind of free ride at Columbia (scholarship), because I was black, completely negating my hard work and studying; this was when I was paying $600 dollars a month back, of my $40,000 dollars in student loans. He wouldn't believe me. The only scholarship I received was from Euna Coleridge, my mother, with a default loan by my father. When I confronted this bigot, he set up a supervision meeting, and had the managing partner waiting for me. He made up some ridiculous allegation using the company's policy, and stated that I was not coming to supervision to see him. This was completely untrue, just a bunch of lies. I was shocked that a clinical supervisor would LIE, just to taunt and harass me.

He also said that none of the other therapists at the clinic liked me. He was trying to play into all of the racism I had disclosed as a supervisee, and he used all that I had previously disclosed against me. He then got the head clinician involved, a true sociopath, who wrote a scathing evaluation about me, stating that I had issues with being at the clinic and that I was somehow problematic as a therapist. Somehow I think they thought I was going to sue them, which wasn't even in my awareness. As I mentioned before the 'light' can be very threatening. Now, you know we were evaluated by our patients, and I had scored a 94 on this patient report scoring system, which meant that people who were depressed, anxious, bipolar, or borderline, etc., had to take the time to evaluate me as a therapist when they received a survey at home. I stated that it wasn't just me, and that Lisa also felt uncomfortable with the culturally insensitive comments as well. **It was the truth!**

And do you know what Lisa said? She cowardly lied when he asked her if he had said anything culturally insensitive to her. She said "no!" Lisa then became mad at me for speaking my truth, and honoring my *spirit*. Judas was born—the one friend that I had been there for basically, sold me out. She said that because I was dark, all of this was happening to me, but with all of her issues of abuse, she became friends with the guy who said he wanted to assault her, which brought to the forefront her cultural background where women had little power. Her passive aggressive energy didn't resonate with me. After moaning in my office about this guy, day after day, my frien-enemie turned around and supported the very abuser that she despised, a typical identification with the aggressor scenario, in which the aggressor had more power. She couldn't stand up to authority. It felt like a lynching, and Lisa may have not have done the hanging, but she surely supplied the rope. *Do Not bear False Witness against they Neighbor.* So now the supervisor had permission to go after me because there were no witnesses to the comments.

So, this supervisor then wanted me *to continue to work with him* after he had written me up and gotten the union on me. Most people would think that was a conflict of interest. I didn't really want to sit with him and talk about his hatred of women. He literally pulled me from working with my quirky Middle Eastern supervisor, because he thought that we, as minorities, would conspire against him. The middle eastern supervisor, sensitive because of 911 stereotypes supported me and said he had said a lot of racist things to her too. At least she spoke her truth because it was right. I didn't want to do supervision with bigoted Dracula, and he forced me to. To me, it felt like an emotional rape. I was in a position where I had to get my hours for licensing, because I had moved from another state. I was already licensed in two other states, therapists can relate to this.

This work began to feel like it wasn't worth it. I was beginning to think that I should let go of being a therapist, and focus on my other spiritual work.

Of course, when you resist something, your body feels it, and acts out the resistance. I was struggling with fibroid tumors at the time. My OB/GYN, who worked for the same company, told me to have surgery to remove it. She literally tracked me down, and kept calling and calling me. The harassment at the company lasted about six months, and during that time my tumor when from four centimeters to almost twelve centimeters, growing at an alarming rate. Basically, my whole stomach was a tumor, covering my second chakra, and my solar plexus, my power center. My OB/GYN was shocked, and I KNEW it was from being in a stressful work environment.

My periods were horrendous. On heavy days, I would have to change a tampon and a pad every hour for twenty-four hours, because I was bleeding out so much. Every hour, and I mean all through the night, I had to remember to put on a timer. So here I was at thirty-six-years of age, seeing patients and running groups of about ten patients a day. I liked my clients, but not my work environment. My mind was being attacked with harassment, and my body with the tumors, and my *spirit* by someone making up lies about me that were completely untrue. See how they were all intertwined?

The universe, though, will always support what is right. As a sensitive soul, I don't like working with someone who is a liar. As an overgrown *Indigo*,* it is hard for me to deal with lies, and a lack of ethics in the workplace. As a healer, I am sensitive to dark energy, and to sit with someone like this for an hour is like being in spiritual hell. I have never had such a visceral reaction to someone, which was especially difficult after he had told his bunch of lies. I was definitely wondering what the universe wanted to teach me. I stood up for myself, and got punished. If I left, I would lose my health insurance. If I didn't get the surgery, I could lose the ability to have children. I loved kids, and kids loved me. I had taken enough, but if I lost my health insurance, it wouldn't serve me to have a twelve centimeter tumor in my uterus. My OB/GYN was relentless. She kept calling me, and promising me that at thirty-six-years of age, she wouldn't take out my uterus. She mentioned my fibroid had grown incredibly in three months.

That night, I had a dream about this doctor and the experience felt like a real meeting. In this dream, I immediately saw a picture of the OB/GYN's children on her desk. We were meeting post-surgery, and she said, "Oh, I took out your uterus, because I really don't care about you, and I had my kids, and it is just your bad luck." I remembered feeling shocked in the dream. When I woke up, I saw a large purple light in my room that telepathically told me to remember this dream. When I went into the OB/GYN's office, I was really nervous, and then I saw the exact picture of her children that I had seen in the dream. Before she even came back into the office, I made up an excuse, and left. How could I know what her kids looked like?

I cancelled the follow-up appointment, and started a more holistic program of healing. I went to Optimum health Institute in San Diego a raw detox program. I never really got rid of the tumor, but I was able to reduce it slightly, and a lot of the symptoms dissipated for a while. I tell you this story to let you know how the mind, body, and *spirit* are intertwined, and how your emotional mood and job stress can affect your body, your health, and your *spirit*. My *spirit* was attacked and demoralized from that job, a job where I dedicated my heart and soul, and where I help patients with their growth and their souls' journey.

This was a job where, in a staff of about forty, I was the only therapist that would stay late, three nights a week, for the patients. Where, in this psychotherapy group, we all meditated, and I would ask them to think about what the heart and soul told them. I listened to their soul messages in our group sessions, wrote down all of their message, and then went home exhausted to type them up to present them at the next class. I was tired, since my hemoglobin was at about a five, out of a healthy twelve. I was doing intuitive consultations, and spiritual readings at night, during this time. The clients loved me when I was in my glory, but I couldn't stay there if I was no good, and if my *spirit* was under attack.

This man made it clear that I was not welcome there. I even had a meeting with a union representative that proved futile, as this woman turned on me. I later found out that this older black woman was insane. More black on black discrimination in the workplace. I felt the pressure of my life sinking in. After a meeting with the union rep, who stated that I needed to be on probation for another six months, for something that I didn't do. They even made a rule, that I was not allowed to call in sick!! I refused to sign it. I asked God to please give me help.

I left this meeting feeling disillusioned and off my purpose and went down to my office to work with my client. My client had this electric purple aura around her. It was so clear, it was like *spirit* wanted to show me who this person was, but more importantly, what my path was. It was so bizarre to see this, but God intervened and showed me the future. It was a miracle, as I didn't have to meditate or tune in to the person since the purple light was so vivid. She was enveloped in it. Many times I have seen how God had intervened. I said to my client, "Do you work with God?" This client who I had worked with for several sessions, started to cry. She said that her husband had forbidden her to think about God, or to teach their kids about God, and after she divorced him, she never went back to the church she loved, and wasn't able to educate her kids about religion. She needed permission to re-attend. She kept asking how I knew that. I couldn't answer her, and just told her that it was my instincts. I encouraged her to go church, and she cancelled the next session, saying that this was exactly what she had needed to hear.

I also knew I was to work with the energy field of my clients, performing energy healing. I realized that working with the spiritual world was a gift from the creator. The message was clear from the universe: it was time to move on. Ironically, during that time, three clients booked sessions with me, and told me how much I had changed their life. They had just randomly booked their appointments and made a list of the positive changes that I had helped them make. These were messages from the universe supporting me. All of that time, during the harassment, few of my coworkers really supported me. They turned their backs on me, because they didn't want to feel our supervisor's wrath. Everyone avoided me. I couldn't understand why the administration attacked me, but I was aware of the shady abuse of clients. My supervisor actually saw my client behind my back, and two weeks later that client attempted suicide. I truly believed he had kicked her over the edge. I found this out later, as her partner had unknowingly booked an intake with me, and told me what had happened. I thought I was in Looney-land, pun intended. As I asked the universe, I heard this poem from my guides:

When you shine your light, they can't see you.
When you speak your truth, they won't hear you.
When you plea your heart, they won't feel you.
Still, shine your light,
speak your truth,
and plea your heart.
As they are watching you,
the universe is watching them.

Basically, their karma will come back to them. What you do to others will come back to you. I also had a vision, that not only did this emotional terrorist have karma with me, but also with every client that I had a contract to help, and had to stop the sessions to leave. Ironically, seven years later, at the end of a cycle, I met a senior therapist who had stories about this same person harassing her. She literally flew across the room at a CEU event to ask me about my experience with him, after I had announced the company that I worked for. Three years after that, five more people told me that they avoided working in that clinic because of him. I was really concerned about the patient care. If a situation like this happens to you don't feel like you are alone. When people are abusive, there are usually multiple people that have been abused. If you come forward, others generally will too, but not always. Many of my coworkers later felt his wrath and after being at the company for twenty years, they were harassed out also. I saw how karma had come back to others when they knew something was wrong and they didn't stand up for the truth. His lies, manipulation, selfishness and emotional abuse aligned him with the dark side. When you align unknowingly with the dark forces, you lose all sight of what is right and wrong. You actually call in dark energy, which always will betray you (Watch any movie and you see this theme that plays itself out).

Like I stated before, divine retribution is real and the fact that I saw proof of this really spoke to my soul, and now I can give you proof of that. What comes around goes around. It is not just a well-known term, it is universal law. I realized then that as a lightworker, you may have some trials and tribulations that seem to be incredibly unfair and difficult. Source may need to get you out of one secure situation to get you back on your path.

I remember hearing a passage in the bible where Jesus stated that if you go into a town and are unwelcome, just dust the dirt of that town off of your feet and move on. I never felt welcomed there. I remember I went to an astrologer and she was very clear, saying to me, "Your guides needed to get you out of there. You have a bigger mission." Sure enough, I had my first article published, got a random call from a producer in Beverly Hills who wanted to put me on a show, and I made $1500 dollars doing readings from my couch with a bloody tumor. I remember though, putting that energy in my heart. My heart is how I move through life. Betrayal hurts deeply. My heart was hurt. The lack of ethics and lack of integrity was disgusting. It was the health issues that honestly were the most devastating. A job is a job.

There is another important concept of something pulling you off of your purpose: maybe the universe is trying to redirect you. Sometimes, when you hit roadblocks, it is because you had made agreements before on the other side, and you are not fulfilling them. A car accident, divorce, job loss, or illness may give you time to reorganize your life to get on track with your purpose. These situations make you stop, think, and become clear. When I went into meditation, I realized that at twenty-six years old I had vowed that within the next ten years I would work for myself. Well, I was thirty-six years old, so someone, maybe somewhere, had heard that request. I call these experiences **Spiritual redirections.*** Your *Spirit* may be redirecting you to your higher calling. Some people like to call these situations "initiations." They may feel like tragedies, but these incidents can initiate you onto your true path. Remember the universe is a "yes" environment.

When you are doing something off your path it may be rough, uncomfortable, and toxic. God may have known my triggers. He knew I didn't want to be analyzed psychologically by a bigot. He knew I wouldn't go there. I already had a license in two other states and this supervision was to have me relicensed. Who wants to go over personal and psychological issues again after sealing that coffin? Especially with someone you don't like. Columbia was challenging enough, with its conservative old school analysts, and most therapists in Manhattan are psychoanalysts. Also, being African American, a lot of supervisors projected their racial unconscious conflicts onto black supervisees. Instead of understanding, they stereotyped and pathologized. I didn't want to go through that again. I embraced spirituality because it is universally loving, and it is where I feel understood and accepted. I also knew that I didn't belong there, so spiritually I knew I had to cut the karma with this person.

Clearing Karma

I remember studying HOPONOPONO, a Hawaiian art form of self-healing. In this healing modality, you realize we all are one. You take on the responsibility of wrong doing globally by a uttering a couple of statements. The statements are: "I am sorry," "please, forgive me," "thank you," and "I love you." I told this abuser I was sorry, not because I did anything wrong, but because I was practicing the Hoponopono. It was also honestly a reaction formation.* Being overly nice to a person you really can't stand. I wanted him off my back, and I wanted to be able to have children and I wanted to get my license. You have to pray for the dark side. Mr. Banana Brain thought it was an apology for doing wrong. You know what I really meant: "I am sorry you didn't see my light. I am sorry you're contracted with the dark, and used manipulation and selfishness to get what you wanted. I am sorry you were abused as a child and take it out on every other woman. I am sorry you are a bigot because you will be me in your next life time. I am sorry you will reap what you sow." No, okay, I wasn't sorry about that! Ha! But, you can't teach all about higher spiritual truth.

Of course, he didn't realize what I meant. I just didn't want a karmic connection with an unevolved soul. When I said demon, I am doing it for the dramatic effects, but I do believe that some people contract with the dark side out of laziness, deviousness, selfishness, mal-intent, and self-hatred. That is why you don't really want to engage with these negative people on their level. *I realized it wasn't really about black and white it was a fight between the dark and the light.* It sounds pious to turn the other cheek, but it is also for your soul survival, as it frees you of living this creation again and again and again. This does not mean that you cannot stand up for yourself. By all means, fight the good fight and stand up for what is right. Make the choice from the highest good, and you will always be free. That is why it is important that if you have been severely abused, you have to make a choice to release that person, that event, and that trauma--or else you will hold onto that energy and become what you hated and feared the most. He didn't. A shamanic therapist I saw urged me to go to the board of behavioral sciences. I was most concerend about my health.

Forgiveness is the key, and hopefully the universal understanding *that no one gets away with anything.* I struggle with the concept of forgiveness a lot and that is why you see it so much in the book. I remember when I contemplated this situation, I heard one of my guides say to me, "Why take part in another's demise, their situation is already set. Detach." The dialogue went on: "If you wish them wrong, in the *spirit* world it is almost as bad as doing it, thoughts are deeds." To this I retorted, "Get out of my head." Just like a bad B movie, when you contract with the dark side, there is NEVER an alliance. The dark side doesn't understand loyalty or support because the dark side's motivation is selfish, destructive, and low energy. I am not going to collude with the dark side for some work place politics when sometimes it is just best to walk away. I was also concerned about my spirit's emotional health. When my *spirit* is challenged, my ego first comes up to protect me, and then the analysis from my soul will come clearing the way for understanding.

It is very important that you check in with your intentions. Your intentions are your energy vectors that you put out to the universe. If your intentions are pure, you will have pure outcomes. If they are selfish or unethical, eventually you will reap the karma for sending out dark energy to the universe. People who carry the light on the planet, lightworkers as they are known, are often very threatening to the chaotic and dark energies on the planet. If you are doing something in the dark, you don't want the light exposing you, revealing what you are doing. There may be some trials with the dark side. They are not aware of the misery and chaos they are causing (forgive them God, as they don't know what they do). Meaning, they don't know the universal laws and they are creating their own spiritual demise.

An important soul attribute is patience. Patience is not easy if you have been wronged, but you must believe in the spiritual fabric of creation, and that energy will only correct what was not done for the highest good. Sometimes, the outcomes take a long time because the universe needs time to show the negative evidence, so to speak. Situations are not always fair, but they are just, meaning that the universe will justify the wrong into a right, because it is law.

I knew that in this situation I had done nothing wrong. My soul was clear and I was good with God. I bring this up because I see a lot of people who are being challenged by old institutions, environmental conditions, abuse, fraud, and injustices. Company policies that are out of date, and government regulations that are unfair are every-where. Food that is manufactured for profit, with no nutritional value ails us. Educational systems that are archaic and out of date clash with the new energies of these evolving young souls, stealing their innocence and hope for the future. Healthcare systems that don't heal perpetuate drug abuse and only mask the symptoms, leaving people to suffer; I could go on.

Always take the higher road. Go with what is in your heart, and do what is right. These could be spiritual redirections. There are always answers to life's dilemmas. Two wrongs don't make a right, just bad karma that you will have to eventually undo. But when things are very wrong, I know the feeling of wanting revenge or feeling vindi-cated can be overwhelming. I have fantasies of being part of the spiritual audience in the next life, when that person that has done me wrong has to reap the benefits of what they may have done to me and others. I imagine watching from the sidelines, more evolved (of course), with a bag of popcorn, observing as it comes back to them. This is my ego talking. I know in my heart that it wouldn't feel good. My soul would be saddened by the recurring karma that has put this situation into place. Hopefully I would be out of the picture; detached, disconnected, and neutral. So, I try to practice that now.

What someone does to you with mean spiritedness and dishonor is not your karma, it is theirs. The spiritual attribute acquired is FORGIVENESS. Forgiveness doesn't mean that what happened was ok, just that I won't let it mess up my and God's plan. It is not to absorb other's toxic projections. The ironic thing is that it wasn't an enemy, it wasn't a random act of violence, and it wasn't something that I did with malicious intent. I just spoke my truth. As a fellow therapist, I was concerned about all of the other patients that this person would emotionally damage, because they were so unhealed.

WHAT INTENTIONS DO YOU HOLD IN YOUR HEART: To help or to harm, to lift up or break down?

Jealousy is defined as an unhappy, or angry feeling of wanting to have what someone else has. "Haters!" Jealousy is a wasted emotion on the spiritual path, both energetically and emotionally. When you put your energy into someone's else's life, focusing on it, and envying it in a negative way, you dissipate your energy, and miss the messages, insights, and signs that *spirit* is sending to you, repetitively, to help inspire your *spirit*. Jealousy can create a dark force around your field, and can attract negative *spirit* energies, which make you act out bad behavior towards the person or thing you are obsessing about. Television and social media can encourage jealousy as an entertaining attribute of the human condition, but it can sabotage your spiritual growth. Be inspired by what someone has achieved, and keep stepping towards your own success. You don't know how they may be suffering inside.

Humiliation: Another toxic energy to the soul is humiliation. This is the degrading of one person to another. This energy is very damaging, not just for the person who is receiving it, but for the person who is enacting it. I love the famous Martin Luther King Jr. quote:

"You cannot degrade another without degrading yourself." It is the antithesis of honor. It not only lowers the person's vibration, but that of the others on the planet. Guilt and Shame are also a lower vibration with goes along with humiliation.

Please check out the book *Power versus Force* by David Hawkins, MD, a psychiatrist, revolutionary thinker, and futurist. He describes how there are certain levels of awareness called the scale of consciousness, which shows how feelings and attributes can affect the resonance of a person and also the planet. He tests this theory through applied kinesiology. Each level of consciousness coincides with human behaviors and emotions and God. For example love is at 500 and guilt is at 30. Courage resonates at 200. Two hundred, the level of courage, represents a profound shift from destructive and harmful behavior to life-promoting and integrity driven qualities; everything below 200 is very weak using kinesiology, meaning it is not good for you or humanity. 78% of the world's population resonates below 200!! But one person calibrating at 600 *counterbalances the negativity of 10 million people below 200.* Six hundred is the vibration of peace. Hawkins believes resonating with higher spiritual qualities will help yourself and mankind. Some of the lower qualities are anger, guilt,desire, fear and grief and higher qualites are courage neutrality, acceptantance and love. Hawkins has many great books.

Positive energy is a hundred times greater than negative energy. This is powerful, so if you are projecting more positive energy, then you are really doing something good. People that like to partake in humiliating, embarrassing and denigrating others not only affect their own karma, but the energetic field of the whole earth. Older souls know that they are here to help themselves, and the planet, and generally stay away from this type of debasement. You lightworkers are aware of this too. Why not leave a little light on the planet? If you have the ability to sing and help people heal, then sing. If your ability is to speak and write poetry, then write. If your gift is to help animals, this is a sacred gift.

You can see though, that society is not tolerating this kind of nonsense anymore. With camera phones, and reality TV, we are beginning to see what was before on live TV, "caught on tape" type shows only revealed when someone was on the scene to be able to capture bad behavior. Individuals that have been getting away with heinous atrocities and unjustified crimes now have to atone for their wrong doings much faster as the videos go viral. Also, with DNA being processed, society is being given the record to prove false imprisonment and accusations: the truth is coming out. From Enron, to executives on Wall Street, to greedy insurance companies receiving lucrative bonuses, to crimes of violence, the truth is finally being revealed. We are beginning to see reality for what it is. This sets us up for our life review where at the end of life, we experience and feel everything that we have created and ways we have treated others. We feel their pains hurts and triumphs. Many who have had near death experiments talk about the life review.

That is what I believe 2012 was about: our ability to see the light and the truth, when the mask of illusion comes falling down. So, there is no longer a time lag between when something happens and when the truth is revealed, in the technology society. We won't have to wait years for the truth to come out. It is the beginning of (a newer) reality, happening right in front of our eyes, as it is caught on tape. If the indigo kids*, who are in their twenties rise up busting the old systems and speaking the truth, things will begin shifting. When the energy vibration or resonance of the planet raises, time will move more quickly, and it will feel like there is no time. The others with the ability to see auras will start seeing the truth and the other legions of people who start healing with *Spirit* as we approach the galactic center, closer to the center of the universe.

Our earth goes through cycles also and its' orbit finished a 26,000 year cycle which touched the allegedly galactic heart of the galaxy. Our heart knows truth and it wants to do what it loves. This is part of what 2012 prophecies were predicting. When you do what you love it feels like there is no time. That is my interpretation of the end of times. Gregg Braden a Hay House author has a lot of great information on the galactic center. There will be less projections, and manipulations, and deceptions which all waste time. Lies happen in layers, as you have to make more lies to cover up the original lies that were created, cascading into an avalanche of lies. This pendulum swing towards the truth (and nothing but the truth), is just beginning, and it is not going to reach perfection right away.

There is a reason for everything, even the greed of bureaucratic agencies. The negativity and greed pushes others towards the light. For example, managed care has been a savior for some and a nightmare for others, many others. For many people it has made them open up to alternative healing methods, like acupuncture, tai chi, yoga, and energy healing. Also, it has forced educated consumers to become their own health advocates, learning to trust their own guts, eat differently, and slowly transform their lives.

As we take more responsibility for our own health, along with listening to the *spirit*, we begin to become less victimized by systems. We begin taking responsibility for our own lives, seeking out reiki masters, pranic healers, naturopaths, and raw food experts; we begin to eat organic foods, drink wheatgrass, and perform body detoxes. We learn about our health, pray, meditate, and seek alternative methods in becoming our own health advocates and soul healers, and connect back to Source, the power of our own divinity. The strict and greedy healthcare systems have taken us back to our own understanding of our health, intuition, and our own bodies. You may also see food co-ops opening up, allowing consumers to have more control over their foods, forcing people to be more of a community, and giving people the ability to eat healthy.

I have gone to Optimum Health, in San Diego, a raw detox, almost every year for several years straight. It is a place for body, mind, and *Spirit* healing. When I clear out all of the junk food, I feel so much cleaner. I admire people who can discipline themselves to eat raw, organic foods all the time. Our higher spiritual journey is for us to listen to our *spirit*, and take responsibility for our own lives on different levels. This is, of course, if you are aware of your own path. Sometimes, people have learned to eat differently and more nutritiously, while others have learned to start listening to their emotions more, or doing creative visualization when they were diagnosed with cancer. *Love Medicine and Miracles,* by Bernie Siegal, is a favorite book of mine about visualization and the healing methods of a traditionally trained doctor. Healing modalities serve the heart, mind, and soul--not just the body. Learning about different ways to heal, from various cultures, helps you to search into the realms of the *spirit* from different angles. It also opens you up to different belief systems, and helps the planet to connect through inter-globalization. This helps earth beings come closer, as we learn that we are all one, and that we have a lot to teach to one other. In the madness, there is a plan.

Your *spirit* is trying to learn something in all of these difficult and painful experiences. What is it trying to learn? Could it be one of the following: compassion, understanding, joy, strength, discipline, patience, fortitude, or tolerance? Learn the lesson, and move on. If it is too painful, like the death of an innocent child, there is no need to understand the situation fully, but understand what soul quality was awarded. No young soul would ever go through really painful situations. That is the story of the older soul. When I was pushed out of my job, I walked away. I didn't need that energy of hatred, and it affected my patients. After leaving that job, I worked freelance for ten years. No full time job, just various "gigs," never really struggling with money, and having a fair amount of time off to lecture, have classes, and do what I wanted. I am not a person who likes to work 9-5 all the time. It feels to constraining to me. My creativity gets squashed in such a sterile environment, and my freedom feels threatened. Others like the structure, God bless them. They love it, need it, and thrive in it. It is important that you know your *spirit's* essence, your likes and dislikes. What makes you sing, what gives you peace, what helps you thrive and create? Write out a plan, listen to the universe, and move forward.

Toxic *Soul* qualities can be healed. Forgiveness, both of self and of others, is the key. This is the planet of forgiveness, because there is so much injustice that goes on, so much is wrong here. The earth plane is very different from the *Spiritual* World of love and light. Forgiveness of others and self is so important. Mostly, I hear that forgiveness of self is the most difficult. Why did I go out with that person? Why did I let that abuse happen to me? Why did I steal that money? Why did I hit my kid? It doesn't matter what you did or didn't do, it doesn't matter that you know it was wrong or learned later, or maybe you have been blindsided by an occurrence outside of your control—realize whatever it was, it was a situation that occurred and you need to acknowledge it, grieve it, and then move forward to forgive.

The traditional understanding of forgiveness seems to be interpreted as saying that "it was ok for something to happen." That is not the correct understanding of forgiveness. What forgiveness really means is "to let something go, to understand the situation, and to remove the toxic energy that may end up ruining your life." You cannot hold on to the energy of what someone did to you. That energy will eat away at your *spirit*, your body, and soul. Perhaps, understanding the totality of the soul, and how the situation is a lesson learned to help you gain certain attributes, might better help you to understand forgiveness and learn of your soul evolution. The belief is that your soul may have attracted these experiences for you and for others to learn from. It becomes a bitter pill to swallow when some stories are so tragic. I feel sadness when I see children being snatched by strangers from their home or from the streets. I have seen the passion of these individuals' families who were left behind, and desperately want their child back in their own bed.

Some families, who have lost loved ones, have used the passion from their pain to create The Amber Alert and *America's Most Wanted* by John Walsh. Ameena Matthes, a woman in Chicago, now works with victims of gang violence after getting out of the gang world herself. Children who have been killed in the line of gang violence inspire many programs that are created to keep other children alive and whole. I recently bought a lunch from *The Homebody Industries*. Their philosophy, founded by Greg Boyle, S. J., a former pastor and Jesuit priest, is "jobs not jail." He helps former gang members in Los Angeles find employment by transitioning them out of gang life. Children who have grown up in foster care, age out at eighteen years old, and find that they don't have a place once they reach this age. Because of this, *Peace 4 Kids* was started. Spiritual understanding and philosophy can help us make sense of this madness. No, the earth is not our home, and we are here only to grow our souls. Sometimes these older souls sacrifice their time here to teach others through their example. The more tragic the occurrence, it seems, the more profound the teaching. Our *spirits* obviously have a lot to learn if the souls of children still come down to teach. Or possibly, the more tragic the trauma, the more it will get our attention. We have to take responsibility for the madness that we created collectively. Putting more light and awareness to others and teaching by example, learning the universal laws helps with this. Teaching and learning through education, in any little way we can.

Remember, your mission does not have to be big, or public, just heartfelt. Just being happy is a mission, because you inspire other people to find happiness. I work with this guy Romero that is always happy. I ask him, why are you so happy? He says "It is because I am a Christian; I love Jesus, my family, my job, my health, and my home." Just the basics. I don't know him well, but I bet Romero's mission is to be that sunshine. Every time I see him, I smile. Mission accomplished. He recently just asked me about my book after not seeing him for two years just when I was to publish it. I told him he is in it and he smiled and offered to send my book around his church.

Our soul and our *spirit* have the answers to many of our problems. It is looking for the outlet, the healer, the minister, yoga, words of truth, or any other avenue that can demonstrate to you what is out of alignment; once you know what is wrong, you have the ability to start fixing it. Sometimes the message comes through an actual disease in the body that is manifesting. Many illnesses can be looked at as maladaptive belief systems that are stored in a certain part of the body, and then turned into a pain an ache, and sometimes a disease. We all have vulnerable body areas, whether it be the back, neck, stomach, or head, and it can create an energy block and hold the energy of disease.

I recommend looking at Louise Hay's book, *You Can Heal Your Life*. In the back of this book, there is a chart of diseases, and the corresponding belief systems in the body. See if the book resonates with you. I understand that disease can also come from toxins in our environment, air, mold, hormones in food, dirty water, and many other forms of pollutants. I don't disbelieve that we can bring in ailments from past lives and past traumas, to work through healing in this lifetime too. If you have reoccurring sore throats in your throat area, check out the wisdom within your own heart. Is there somewhere in your life that you are not speaking up for your own truth? Is it with your partner, at your job, or with friends or family? Look back on your childhood. This is where patterns are started. Maybe it was a past life memory of being killed for speaking of intuitive truth. It also could be an ancestor's memories stored in your DNA, that you are now responsible for healing. No matter what the source of the pain or ailment, if you are on a path of spiritual growth, ask for an understanding or clarity from the universe. If you are ready, the answer will be given.

Positive SOUL Qualities

When we move through trauma in our life, it is because our soul wanted to expand, not generally our personality, but our SOUL. We acquire certain spiritual attributes that help us grow. Here is just a small list of some positive soul qualities that your soul is working on when it comes to the earth plane and experiences with trauma or tragedy. Within every pain, there is an opportunity for growth.

Compassion: With passion. Compassion means to give of your heart with love, light, and well-being. It means to look at someone with love and reverence, understanding that this person is a divine emanation of God's light and heart. To work with compassion is to know that we are all the sum part of the whole, and that as we help one another, we are in essence helping ourselves. Many painful experiences will teach you to view other people with compassion. The planet is working on becoming more compassionate, always. There are lessons of learning compassion. Neglected children, runaways, homeless people, the mentally ill, abused women, the disabled, child trafficking, the unemployed, or the starving can inspire within us a compassionate response.

There are a lot of things happening on earth to help you gear up your compassion for yourself and for others. Learning and activating compassion makes your soul grow. Our souls create these opportunities to help others, to observe and find ways to fix the problems. Sometimes, other souls will teach us through their vulnerability. Please note that if you Judge, you nudge. When you judge others who appear less than you, you nudge that energy into existence, giving the negative energy the license to appear and grow in your life. Simply, someone else may judge you when you are feeling vulnerable, or you will experience something similar in another life time.

People ask me, how do you know? I have seen it happen over and over again. I am an observer and a student of the universe. Compassion can be learned by watching animals. Animals have been sacrificing themselves, through abusive food production practices, and neglect. When the animals are neglected, we learn to open our heart centers. There are many ways to develop compassion on the planet. The teachers are everywhere.

Patience: Patience is the spiritual quality of waiting for the universe to create, in its time, not yours. It is also the attribute of learning to stay in the moment. To learn this attribute, you may have been challenged to want something, and it may have shown up different than what you thought or in a different time frame than you wanted. Children are great teachers of patience, so are marriages. Having an illness or being unemployed helps to cultivate this attribute. You have to learn to work with the divine, and learn how to go within during these times to see what *Spirit* wants to teach you. Things will fall into place in divine time. This attribute is not easy for me as an Aries, but I drudgingly have managed.

Humility: Humility is a Soul attribute you acquire when working the energy of being humble, and responding to painful and difficult things in your life with dignity, respect, and self-pride. It is not enacting, being vengeful, vindictive, retaliatory, or aggressive in nature. It is a very willful attribute. It is will over might, strength over cowardice. It is taking the higher road, and turning the other cheek, if need be. Humility doesn't mean to walk away with your tail between your legs. You may need to fight, you may need to stand up for what is right. Losing your job when you are at the top of your game, and having to find another job with less money may show you humility. The essence of humility that it is a state of realization that though one may be accomplishing in life, one is also aware that they are still moving toward a goal. A truly humble person will be willing to serve and acknowledge the humanity in others, even though the service on some level may seem unfair to the humble person themselves.

Strength: This quality of the SOUL is when you have learned to be strong in difficult or dire circumstances. You learn who you are and you learn to be supported by your own will, and that of the universe. Strength is added to you if you have dealt with abuse, trauma or loss, successfully without acquiring malice or hatred, then your strength attribute has been upgraded. Even if you had a nervous breakdown or fell apart, most likely, you are stronger than you were previously.

You may have had to stand up for yourself; you may have had to testify, or be a whistle blower, or somehow, tried to right a wrong. Are you one of the people who tried to protect the down trodden, the vulnerable, the exploited? Working with clients, I have learned to reframe trauma to help look at how they have survived, recreated their life, or just help them heal. Strength is a powerful attribute. Remember how strong Jesus had to be in his various trials on the earth plane. Strength can be learning how to forgive with dignity, and without the thought of revenge. Martin Luther King Jr. did a wonderful thing with passive resistance and non-violence, a great quote to remember by him:

"Darkness cannot drive out darkness: only light can do that."

Remember, your soul is very strong.

Kindness: To give love, share, have understanding, and be gentle are attributes of kindness. To be kind to someone is to be thoughtful, caring, and true. Your soul appreciates kindness, and your heart does too. Your light expands when you are kind, and your *spirit* will shine. The vulnerable appreciate kindness; the young, the elderly, the frail, and many animals. They are here to help you practice this attribute. The bottom line is if you are kind to others, they will be kind to you. For sensitive people, sometimes you have to combine kindness with strength. When you begin to listen to your *spirit*, you become more sensitive. You have to be, the messages from *spirit* are subtle, gentle, and intuitive. If you are kind and sensitive, you have to activate your strength muscle, for it is easy to become a doormat. It is ok if you stand up for yourself, even if it does makes waves. Remember, these experiences are for your soul to expand, so sometimes the experience may not be pretty. It is your choice to make, and how you react to experiences that makes all the difference.

Forgiveness: means to make amends, to let go, to move on. Forgiveness never means to be okay with something that was wrongfully done. It means to not hold on to the energy of another's wrong doing so that it becomes toxic to your energy, body, soul, and life. Sometimes, not understanding why something was done is part of the plan of learning to let go. This isn't an easy one. I have a very analytical mind, and can analyze things ten different ways all at once. I have heard many horrendous stories, and have no idea how to explain how long it takes for someone to forgive. For each person, the journey to forgiveness is different. A word of wisdom, don't let anything affect you for too long. Use any method to rid yourself of this energy–sans revenge--to attract more positive energy into your life. As I mentioned before, your built-in legal system is divine retribution. What goes around comes around. It is universal law.

Self-Love: This is what most of us are here for. Self-love is when you make decisions from love, not fear. Self-love is taking care of yourself. It can be through making decisions for your family, your livelihood, your health, or your career. Self-love is working on your own self-esteem and valuing yourself and trusting your choices. Self-love can encompass a lot of things. Self -love may be balancing your finances, paying off debts, walking away from a bad relationship or job. It incorporates keeping your mental, physical, and nutritional health in a positive shape. It also means loving yourself and others, as best as you can. Self-love can take a lifetime to master, but it is part of your path to positive soul growth.

Now that you have a better understanding about some positive and negative qualities of your soul, you should be aware that you can create positive and negative energy in your life, with the law of attraction. Positive attracts more positive energy, and negative attracts more negative energy. That is why it is so important to move on from difficult situations. I have seen that if someone is in an abusive relationship, they may have work problems because of chronic fights in the home. It is possible that a neighbor could hear the fighting, and call the child abuse hotline. This then may lead to a person having chronic health problems, like colitis, IBS (Irritable Bowel Syndrome) or GI (Gastrointestinal) issues. The body creates emotional issues like anxiety and depression, which can lead to a person using drugs to escape from the abuse. Do you see how negativity creates more negativity? It is important to take negativity out of the situation, and actively create more positive energy.

On the other hand, a person who is unemployed may volunteer at a children's hospital, even though they may be down and out because of being out of work, they use their strength and compassion attributes, and may still push forward and be positive by helping kids. This person will begin to realize this is an interest that they have always had. The head of the clinic where they volunteer may then offer them a secretarial position to assist in the office and greet the families that are in need. The job may be below their experience, but it gets them working again. They may then move closer to their job, and get a cheaper, nicer apartment. They may then receive a promotion three months down the road, obtain a raise increase, and go back to school to study child development. So unemployment, a soul crisis, may be the road to a real passion. This has happened to me, as I outlined before, as it has for many of my clients. The person listened to their *Spirit*, honored their gift with kids, and then found themselves right on course. Always look for the seed of inspiration in the mix, it sometimes shows up at the bottom of the crisis. A seed of inspiration that is willing to grow, with just some watering. This is how I became a healer. I kept listening to *Spirit*, and through a crisis was led to look into healing myself and others.

WORKBOOK EXERCISE #5

- **What qualities** have you obtained?

- **What patterns** have you learned in your life?

- **How have you turned** tragedy into triumphs by listening to Spirit? What were they?

- **How has the universe** tried to put you on your path?

- **Meditate** on these things and **Journal.**

CHAPTER

6 Becoming an Intuitive Healer

I T WASN'T my plan to become a healer, but my *spirit* had a different agenda. If you asked me twenty years ago what a healer was, I probably wouldn't have been able to tell you. It wasn't until I worked as a therapist, and I would find that I became very drained by all the stories that I heard, which led to my understanding energy dynamics. I am one of those intuitive empaths that Dr. Judith Orloff talks about in her book, *Positive Energy*. The more compassionate I became, the more my clients would reveal. Many of the stories I heard from clients were very painful and soul traumatizing. Energy healing helped me to transform that negative energy into positive energy.

When I say I became a healer, a healer is anyone who holds the energy of seeing another individual as a *spirit* on a spiritual journey, and holds the highest vision of their potential. A healer, if their intention is right, can help a client transform their lower vibrational energy into a higher vibration. You can be a healer and be a writer, an occupational therapist, an esthetician, masseuse, counselor, Reiki master, minister, or a teacher, by inspiring and helping other people. I consider all of those people healers that look at that individual as a divine being of light. I myself worked as a hands-on energy healer, and was trained in Reiki, a Pranic Healer, Integrated Energy healing (IET) and Theta healing. Healing is a conscious effort to assist in that person's soul growth. Healing can mean holding the space for the person to come to their own self –realization, helping them see that they have the light within them. It can also mean sending light from the universe to the client, as I do as a Reiki practitioner. The client may not know it, at the moment you are working with their *Spirit*, but you are a witness to their evolution. As a healer, you help people to find their light within.

When people read or hear about someone talking about energy, they think it is a new age, wishy-washy, flaky concept. In day to day life though, we all talk about energy all of the time unknowingly. We say we are "burnt out," "exhausted," "drained," or "dead tired" on a regular basis. When we use these terms, we are discussing the negative aspects of element depletion. When we are *burnt out*--we are talking about *fire*. We are *drained*--we are talking about *water, exhausted*-- we need more *air* and *stone,* dead--we are referring to *earth elements*. Haven't you used these terms when discussing the management and assessment of your personal energy? As a counselor, I felt all four energetic leaks, and later learned that I needed to use the elements to heal myself, getting back to equilibrium through natural means.

A brief example of self-healing, with elements, is that when we are burnt out, we can use fire, through candles, or a hot sauna, or sage to relax and renew. Energy healing can also help with the burnt out feeling. When we are exhausted and need air, methods such as meditation and pranayama breathing, or even yawning, renew us. Aerobic exercise that gets you breathing hard, and accelerates our heart rate also heals. When we are drained, we need water. Take time by the ocean, and engage in baths with earth energy (like lavender or eucalyptus essential oils, and epsom salts) to regain your energy. Drink clean fresh water to become more hydrated and energized. When we are stone dead, we need rest, or crystal healing, or a masseuse to ground and earth our energy. Hiking in mountains or the woods also calms our *spirit*, and renews our health and reinvigorates us. Grounding can happen with healthy sexual relationships and food. I always sage my energy field after working in the hospital and coming to my private office. These offices are very different types of energy.

Sage is a plant, and when you burn it you clean the energy around your auric field or the space you are in. Sage incorporates all of the elements. Sage itself is the earth element (as a plant), and the shell you put the sage in is earth as well. The fire is present, when you light the herb on fire, air as you fan the flame, and water when you put out the sage. Sage quickly removes negative energy from your field. Be careful to watch the fire alarms, as sage is very smoky. It can give you a burst of energy. Even when we say someone sucked the life out of us, people are actually stealing our energy, sometimes unknowingly! Energy vampires are all over the place. By the way, people who are manipulative and selfish are usually energy stealers. Energy is a vital part of who we are as spiritual energy beings, so it behooves us to understand it, work with it, and enhance it when we are depleted.

We can also abuse our bodies and our environment with the elements. Positive and negative qualities of elements temp us on the earth plane. Such negative attributes of elements are as follows:

Air: When we smoke, we are putting negative toxins into our bodies. Smoke constricts our lungs and clouds them. We cloud our energy field which is connected to the air quality around us. Chemtrails also contribute to bad air quality. We do this on a global scale by polluting the atmosphere with smog.

Water: We can abuse water by putting liquids into our body that are not helpful. With toxic drinks, especially excessive beer or liquor, the element of water (or liquids) can be abused with these substances. We also pollute our water and ponds by dumping garbage into them.

Fire: Negative use of the fire element can be found in smoking, and using other drugs like crack and crystal meth. We are using fire in a negative way. You are not using this element in the positive way, as it should be utilized, as through candles or bonfires. Of course, forest fires and arson are the way the fire element is abused here on the earth. Also, nuclear bombs and other explosions that are made to harm others are a negative way of using fire.

Earth: We can use earth elements wrongly if we eat too much of the wrong foods that both makes us heavy and grounds us too far into the earth so that we are not able to create our earthly mission. Also, becoming involved in earth bound activities like sexual addictions,drug addictions, consumerism, violence and exploitation against animals and others, and anything that is only of the earth, keeps you off balance. We abuse the earth globally by pollution, land mines, and spraying plants with toxins.

If you are on a spiritual path, clearing your field regularly does three things: One, it helps you keep your energy field clear. Our *spirit* lies in our aura and energy field. It actually exudes out of the body. This is the sensing, perceptive part of ourselves that is highly intuitive. Two, when we are clear, we help clear our connection to Source and actually are more open to spiritual messages, synchronicities, and signs that come to us in life. Our antennas, so to speak, are prepped and open to spiritual signals. Three, it also gives us more energy as it removes the debris from others that are left in our field. Sage is a shower for our *spirit*.

More examples of understanding energy, in layman's terms, is how energy gets imprinted in our fields, our minds, and bodies is through music. Do you remember your prom or wedding song? What about the song playing in the background when you had your first kiss? If you pretend you are hearing it presently, don't you feel you are right back at that same time? If you can't do it now, go back and actually listen to that song on Youtube or iTunes. Can you hear the music and feel it in your body? Can you smell the room? Doesn't it feel like the memory is happening now? Music is *vibration*. So it is a vibratory rate-of-an-ion. It is an ion that moves at a certain rate; an energetic frequency. The cellular memory gets stored in your body, mind, and soul at the time of the occasion. It is part of your energy matrix, since your soul is energy.

It is no different when someone has a negative trauma happen to them, and they become restless, anxious, and nervous when they hear the trigger. For example, if a young child was in a house fire, and the family had to run out of the house as the fire trucks were approaching, the sound of a siren later in life may trigger a negative response. Anytime, even as an adult, when they hear fire trucks, they may have an anxiety attack because of that memory, hidden or otherwise, that was stored in their cellular body. Sometimes, clients don't even remember certain traumas. They may have been two or three years old, and have no conscious memory of the sirens, but the memory was stored in the unconscious part of the body, or in the energy field, and may be stimulated when they hear the trigger. It becomes part of who we are, and settles in our energy body.

A good energy intuitive, or healer, can pick up the blockages, tension, or energy cysts, and tell you spiritually, and emotionally, what is going on in your life. If the healer is skilled, they also can assist in removing it. A lot of energy gets stored in humans. Since my energy field is alive and aware of picking up these frequencies, I would become easily drained, as my energetic antennas are trained to be hypervigilant. I had to learn to, somehow, protect and shield my energy, and turn down the frequencies. Becoming an energy healer helped me to understand energy dynamics.

Within the African American culture, vibration and energy is a large part of our language and interactions. Music and dance are a huge center of activities and careers. With music, there is a multitude of genres including blues, soul, gospel, rhythm and blues, jazz, hip-hop, rock, and rap. Getting the right baseline and beat is an essential part of all music. The beat was supposed to be connected to mimicking the heart-beat. Unconsciously reminding us we are all connected as live beings. Also dancing is a great way to clear your energy field. Movement helps to shake of the negative things in your aura field. All cultures have rituatlistic and joyful dances as they are letting go of negative energy.

Even in African American language there is movement. Common expressions of relating to people are "I feel you," meaning that I know the vibration of what you are saying. "I hear you" is not that I hear what you are saying, it is that I hear the energy and the words behind the words, the essence of the story as to what you are saying. Even in slang, "what is up" or "what is going down," "what is shaking," "what is moving in your life." This is "how we roll," always with movement, because being stagnant is not acceptable. New music, and the better newer mix or rhythm, new hairstyles, and new dances are an important part of the culture. Even the street "hustler" job description is about constantly moving, to create opportunities and income. "What is happening" is all about movement, up or down. It is about movement and reading energy and environments, for self-enhancement or protection. I am sure that within your own culture there is an explanation of energy dynamics. There is within various cultures, and the culture at large.

Working as a counselor, I easily would have compassion fatigue from all the stories and sometimes within the social services and political settings of environments there was little I could do. I began to explore various healing modalities to keep me going. My thought process was: how could I be a good channel for my clients without being drained? Somehow, I found a Reiki circle and joined the group and could feel the powerful energy through the practitioner. I would go to a healing circle regularly in the Chelsea area of NYC, and loved the good feeling I received. It would help me sleep better, become clear, and feel more connected to the universe. I became initiated into Reiki, but didn't do it for several years. But, if I went to spiritual circles or meditation groups, people would often comment that my hands were hot.

One time, I was sitting in a dream group and my intuitive friend's rabbit kept hopping near me and under my chair. Out of all the people in the group, like musical chairs, he would hop around and then sit under my chair. If I moved, old Bugs Bunny moved with me. It was the strangest thing. Months later the rabbit was put to sleep, because he had cancer in his eyes. I wondered if the rabbit sensed that he needed help, and was soaking in my healing energy. These were little signs of my budding career. At the time though, I was focused on the mind, and therapy. It was "dangerous" to mix the two worlds of hands-on healing and therapy, which I never did.

Then one of my private therapy clients came to me suicidal and depressed. She was planning to hurt herself, and couldn't get the thoughts out of her head. My office was on 34th street, it was before the holiday in Manhattan, it was late and I had no backup psychiatrist to assist me. She had been struggling with depression for a long time and the SSRI (Selective Serotonin Uptake Inhibitor) she was taking was not working. I was concerned about what I could do with her. Without touching her, I decided to send her a Reiki symbol during our session. I sent her healing energy of the cho ku rei, and she stopped sobbing, lifted her head up and asked, "What did you do? I feel so much better, it was a wave of... good." I told her that I sent her a Reiki symbol and she was surprised, stating that it worked. She stopped the suicidal thoughts and we were able to continue the session with an assured confidence that she wouldn't hurt herself, and that she would be okay for the holiday.

What is funny is that I didn't tell her I was sending her a Reiki symbol, I didn't wave my hand or create the symbol in my hand. I just sent it with thought and intention. We continued with treatment for some time. She was a beautiful old soul with many challenges. She was black, gay, female, an ex-con (incarcerated for defending herself in a domestic violence situation), an alcoholic, a rape survivor, and a powerful soul. I knew she was an old soul because no one gave her the benefit of the doubt in life throughout all of her life challenges. I had to respect her old soul and talk to her *spirit*, which needed the energy, so her soul could remember who she really was. This client was a high achiever soul, a person who enrolled in AP classes on earth.

If I fed her *spirit*, I could help her gain her own insight and connect her back to herself. Our *spirit* needs healing and energy healing, acupuncture, Reiki, Pranic, chi gong, polarity therapy, and other methods of treatment to fix it. Just like your body needs a masseuse or a chiropractor, your *spirit* needs energy work and spiritual nourishment. Spiritual books can help heal the soul, as can an inspirational talk or music, as well as the love energy emitted by spiritual hands for healing. God, unfortunately, cannot physically touch us, so he uses his ordained disciples with good hearts, high intentions, and a loving touch to be his conduit to transmit the energy of the universe.

Shrinking pain

I will give you another example of healing a client energetically. This energy was stored in the body from trauma. One year I was volunteering as a healer at Rickie Byars Beckwith's Agape Women's retreat in Los Angeles. I was giving twenty minute energy sessions to the participants as a part of the well-being center's offerings. I did a healing on Rita, a young, bright woman who just said she had pain in her back and leg, especially when she was nervous and anxious. The minute I put my hand on those areas, I felt the energy of being slapped and hit and had a vision of child abuse. I also empathically felt incredibly surprised that this would occur, feeling what my client felt at the time. Later I asked her if she was hit by a male figure. She said that, as a girl, her dad hit her in those same places when she was stepping into her power, and she felt mortified to be hit. She said I was right on and looked shocked that I had picked that up. I described the anxiety, or tingling, that comes into that area whenever she is stepping into her power. The first time she stood up to her dad, or exerted her power, she was hit. Not a good reminder. After our healing session, I observed that she laid out on the canyon for a long time and let the energy seep into her for an extended period. It was a lot of powerful energy. She thanked me for the session.

She was on my email list and received my newsletters, but that was it, and I never heard from her. Several months later, at another friend's play in Venice, I ran into her. She stated, "I have been trying to find you for months, and you were on my mind to email you." This is how *Spirit* works; organizing synchronicities to connect people to restore the soul. She continued, "I was thinking of doing a holistic program of sorts, an informational alternative medicine day, and thought of you." She later said that the energy healing session was incredible. She stated, "It was like five years of therapy in one healing session." Her extensive pain was shrinked down in one session. She was also told by her dad to shrink her power down and to hold onto her pain. I was surprised by her revelation, but more importantly, she disclosed that she was a psychiatrist! As a shrink, she understood how long it takes to get to the core of issues. This was a real confirmation of and for my work, and conformation that my move from a traditional therapist to an intuitive healer was the right thing to do. She scheduled a couple more sessions.

I did another healing where I used the healing modality called IET (Integrated Energy Healing). There are different areas of the body where the energy trauma is stored. This modality was given to Steven Thayer, a holistic healer, by an angelic being. I like to combine it with Reiki and Pranic, for a powerful triple warmer healing session. IET has you practice on different areas of the body, or as I like to call it, hot spots. The "should" area is by the upper back. This is on the back, where your shoulders are, and you release the energy of should and imprint freedom. When I touched that area, she felt a horrid memory. She revealed that she had gotten into a horrible car wreck, wounding other people, and she had always felt it was her fault. Some of her thought patterns were "I shouldn't have done this, or that, to have prevented the accident." The healing brought up this issue to be looked at, rethought, and healed. The accident may have been her fault, but it wasn't her intention to hurt anyone, so she had to work on healing her own guilt. She later moved forward in her own work as a more holistic based psychiatrist. I was glad to be a part of her journey to her own purpose. Her body stored the answers to her healing. She seemed to acquire the Spiritual attributes of **Truth and Wisdom**.

I continue to explore healing including, Pranic healing, Theta healing, and IET (Integrated Energy Therapy). I would incorporate them in spiritual counseling sessions and spiritual coaching sessions. Since I had problems with getting my hours in California to be relicensed, it was a great way to still be of service privately, without doing therapy. No one was going to stop me from helping. I continued to do healing at Agape. I volunteered for the Sacred Energy Circles, and also at various sacred service events, and Agape's annual conference, Revelations. Agape is a great church that is based on the science of mind or universal law principles. The focus of the church is that each individual should take responsibility for their thoughts. The belief is that our thoughts create our reality, and you attract what your think about and also what you create. Everyone can have a different path to the light.

It was a perfect place to do healing, because the energy tone was so high. I basically practiced my Reiki Mastership there, with all the many events that I did. I would do volunteer healing for many, many years. At Agape, I began to see how volunteering and giving of *spirit* can turn into something more lucrative. Then, at one point when the universe pushed me out of my job, with the betrayal scenario or initiation that I described earlier, the universe set me up to not only get healing for myself but to continue to expand my work professionally.

At one of the Revelations conferences, I bumped into a woman named Cynthia, literally back to back as we both did healing on our individual massage tables which were parallel. She was a psychologist at UCLA and part of the Pediatric Pain Program (PPP). She said the program was looking for a healer to be part of their team. The team had various practitioners such as a craniosacral masseuse, an acupuncturist, biofeedback, physical therapist, hypnotherapist, yoga practitioner, and pediatrician Dr. Lonnie Zeltzer, who created and ran the program as well as the weekly rounds.

Work as a healer? I couldn't believe that could happen. This was right after the betrayal I had written about earlier, so I didn't have full-time employment, just weekend work, at a hospital that paid the rent, but was boring. When I interviewed at PPP, within fifteen minutes they hired me. I worked there as a voluntary faculty member. I didn't get paid until I received a case and would generally go to the kids' homes to do healing. It was interesting to work on a collaborative, holistic team effort. I worked with several amazing kids, many who were very intuitive, having much of their chakra centers and intuitive gifts open. I was again enhancing my skills as a healer and learning about the younger generation of gifted children. The universe just led me to this job by volunteering.

Diving into the pain

I will start with Courtney. Courtney was a high achieving, intellectual girl who was fifteen years old when I met her. She was athletic and smart, having done gymnastics and diving. She also wanted to be a doctor back than. Courtney had chronic pain in her lower liver and pancreas region. When I performed the energy healing on her, I would feel a blockage right around her pancreas. I would feel it on her body, and also in the energy above her. It was palpable. When I told her mother about it, they were surprised that I really picked something up. The family, from Orange County, and conservative Republicans, didn't seem that open to energy healing, but they were willing to try anything. The mother later corrected me that she had gone to a Naturopath in Arizona for years. With a sound head on her shoulders, I noticed that she had a firm balance of her male and female energy. She would tell me that she would scoff at the boys that thought she couldn't be as smart as them in math, because she was a girl. I liked the fact that she didn't cow tow to boys at that age, which is common for girls. She was distressed about her condition though. When I did the healing on her, she would go out to a trance and come back at the end of the session. I noticed that many of the children clients have the reaction of going out of awareness, especially the kids who appeared more open. Children generally feel the energy, and open up to the energy of the universe. You can see the results of this healing on my Youtube page, Carolyncole9.

The family told the doctors about the pain in the lower region, and they found a genetic medical condition there. The family didn't stick with the healing. They later continue with a much needed traditional treatment for this rare ailment. I was glad I got them on the right path. Many doctors dismissed her pain by saying the pain was in their head. Courtney went on to college. She keeps in touch with me on social media and her mom and seems to be doing a lot better. Through all that pain, she graduated with a 3.8 average and won several awards. She still used some of the healing techniques and breathing relaxation methods that I taught her. Hopefully, if she goes into the helping field like a doctor or counselor, she will incorporate energy healing as Dr. Oz does in his operating room. I think her SOUL seemed to gain the attribute of strength. To be a sick kid in high school that was able to graduate with a 3.8 average, with several awards, makes it obvious to see that she incorporated the Spiritual gift **of strength and perseverance.**

The Wilderness boy

Eric came to me through UCLA. He was about twenty-two-years-old with chronic heart pain. Medical tests proved there was nothing medically wrong with him, unlike with Courtney. Eric would drive an hour and a half from his home, twice a month, to come to the healing session at my office in Santa Monica. He looked like a throw-back from the movie *Lords of the Rings*. He garnished a beard, wild hair, and a dagger necklace around his neck (a small one). He had a wonderful soul and a kind heart. He loved the fantasy game *Dungeons and Dragons*. He was a big player in the game. When I asked Eric about the beginning of his pain, he couldn't place it. But he told me that he was exceptionally close to his grandmother, who died when he was twelve years old, when his pain started. His mother worked, so his grandmother was the primary caretaker for much of his early life. As a sensitive kid, he really appreciated the nurturing from his grandmother. He had a couple really good friends and was slightly overweight. Eric admitted to being overwhelmed by the energy in Camarillo, where he lived. He wouldn't even drive because he felt the intensity of all the energy on the LA highways.

I knew he was sensitive and clairsentient, because when he went up north, to the woods with his family, his symptoms would almost completely dissipate. He would sometimes come to the sessions holding his heart, like he was just stabbed and wounded in battle. Honestly, with his look, and the fascination with *Dungeons and Dragons,* I believe that part of his heart pain was due to a past life issue as well. At that time, and through the clinic, I didn't touch that past life issue. Sometimes with clients, it is the here and now. The emotional pain was physical, and real. He was an amazing artist, bringing in his pictures of his pain or other amazing creatures he created. He would often sleep all day and be up at night, just like a cat. He yearned to get one, but was allergic. I believe he was craving the connection to nature and his own spiritual self.

He was very in tune to the energy healing, and could completely feel the Reiki healing. He was very disappointed when the pediatric pain program was taped for Good Morning America, and the commentator ridiculed and scoffed at my energy healing. He stated that the healings helped him so much. The producers pretty much cut me out of the clip anyway. I often use crystals in my healing. I place them on the body over the chakras to assist in balancing the energy. I gave him a couple of crystals, and he would bring them in his pocket every session and have me place them on his energy centers. I treated him, along with the pediatric pain team, and eventually the pain was less, and then finally eradicated.

Before the energy session, his pain in his heart closed his heart to any relationship. During the last couple of sessions, he met a girl. The first girlfriend he let in. He said it helped him so much to have a girlfriend in his life, and it raised his self-esteem. There was no mention of a girlfriend, or anyone else, at the beginning of our sessions.

Another result of the healing was that he lost about thirty pounds. I believe the energy healing helped balance his metabolism. He stated that he was on the "get off your fat ass diet," but nevertheless, he lost the weight. Besides eating less, he would walk around in the woods. The trees and nature do heal our erupted energy field. He would hike for miles. Nature opens our chakra and calms our soul. The energy of the sessions, helped to realign his chakra, as his heart opened like a flower. He stated the relationship helped raise his self-esteem and allowed him to be in love.

As his heart was healed and opened, he was able to attract love in his life and replace the love he lost when his grandma died. The heart that was closed off for years and caused him the energetic heart pain was finally free. The *spirit* attribute that his soul seemed to acquire was **self-acceptance and compassion**, compassion for self.

HOW ENERGY HEALING HELPS CHILDREN IN CHRONIC PAIN
Healing Children with Reiki

7. Sx of feeling alone, not feeling connected to life and activities
headaches, head injuries, problems

6. Sx of not seeing their own parent's truth, negating intuition, head injuries, emotional or physical abuse

5. Problems with verbal expression, throat problems, thyroid, neck pains, parental oppression of communication

4. Depression or grief, and childhood isolation, physical and emotional abuse, heart problems, asthma, respiratory problems

3. Feelings of powerlessness, controlling parents, lack of confidence, kidney, stomach, and intestinal ailments

2. Lack of creative expression, identity issues w/parents, sexual abuse, urinary tract problems, appendicitis, eating disorders and body image problems

1. Problems with feeling secure in the world, unhealthy parental attachments, colon and back problems

Crown
Brow
Throat
Heart
Solar Plexus
Sacral
Base

Photo by Maxwell Aston

An Empath's pain

Ross was fifteen when I met him and his mother. He was from out of state, and he had an intense healing week, that we set up at the Pediatric Pain Program. He was scheduled with me and the other practitioners. I explained the healing method, Reiki, that I did, and used the aura and healing charts (that I often used) to explain to families what was going on. His mother said that she herself had many angelic experiences, and she resonated with what I was discussing. Remember, this was a pain program run by a traditionally trained, and highly intuitive, medical doctor, so for me to talk about the energy centers and the chakras was a rare gift. I was lucky that Dr. Zeltzer let me do what I wanted with the kids, and often the feedback from the kids was very good. Ross' father was involved in a major scandal. He was a high-up executive in a major organization, where there was a lot of fraud and deception and executives stealing money. If I mentioned the name, you would surely know it. Ross' pain was physical and emotional, with chronic headaches and stomach pain. The pain resonated in his third eye chakra and the solar plexus. Not surprising, because his *spirit* didn't resonate with some of his father's tactics of gaining money and other bad habits. Ross' sensitive heart couldn't "see or stomach" what his dad was doing.

I am not surprised that his energy centers went into overdrive with chronic pain. This very sensitive kid picked up the dark energy and absorbed it, trying to transmute it. Children often absorb toxic energy from their parents and work as energy buffers. Children are innocent and protectors of parents, so sometimes they can be energy sponges which may turn into toxic energy for them (SEE chart on page 167). You see this most often when the parents are having conflict, and the kids are put in the middle. Before parents start to feel guilty, know these powerful souls were aware of their soul contracts with these parents before they were born.

Working with the kids at UCLA, I always asked the kids what they wanted to do with their lives. I would speak *spirit*-to-*spirit*, soul-to-soul, and would hear soul answers. Everyone has and needs a purpose, and it is the easiest way to ignite their *spirit*, the healing part of them, by asking what gives them joy. Ross didn't miss a beat as he said, "I think war is stupid, and I want to do something for PEACE." I was surprised he had a "mission" of sorts at only fifteen. The most astounding thing about Ross were his eyes. They were huge, and lit up the room. His mother said that people always commented on her son's eyes, and she thought that was strange. His blue-green eyes looked like that of a two-year-olds, yet you could feel the spiritual wisdom and the light that resided in him. I readily remember what I read about a crystal child. When his mother read the book on crystal children by Doreen Virtue, she couldn't believe how much it resonated with him.

When I did the healing on him, not only did he feel peaceful and relaxed, but he also would see visions, colors, and light. He sometimes felt like he was upside-down, and would describe the profound visions. He had second sight. He hesitantly asked his mother, "Should I tell Carolyn what I see?" I encouraged him to share what he saw. I explained to him what spiritual sight was, and he and his mother thanked me for validating his intuitive gifts. His mother said, "Ross never knew what was wrong with him. He was so psychic that he thought he was going nuts." One time, they went to see a doctor, and he kept nudging his mother to leave the office. He said that the doctor had a dark, heavy mist around him, and he knew he was evil. His mother did listen to him and left the office. Ross didn't understand how he knew and saw that. My explaining to him about a sixth sense helped him to understand who he was.

While I was performing the healing, I kept getting the impression of Abraham Lincoln. I didn't know if the family was connected to this president, or what it was. The family didn't relate to this comment. Years later, I caught up with the mother on a social networking site. She said that Ross was in college, and he worked on President Obama's campaign. Many historical commentators had said that Obama's presidential inauguration, when he went to various cities on the east coast by train, where he made various speeches, was reminiscent of Abraham Lincoln's train tour to the White House. I thought it was more than a coincidence that I picked up that name. It is to be seen what he does into the future, but I believe he has an important mission in life with peace. His mother said he was doing better, came out as gay, and best of all that the healing did really help him. He does struggle with his sensitivity still and purpose, as I will get an occasional hello on Social Media from him.

I was surprised how many children were aware of their incredible missions. One little girl stated that she felt a need to clean up the oceans. When I showed her my crystals, she was so excited to bring out her supply of crystals, that she kept hidden. Another eleven-year-old said that he'd been speaking about global warming since he was five-years-old. Another girl, who looked like a mermaid, stated that she had always loved mermaids, and felt like one. One girl said that she wasn't able to work with me until she was able to see my aura. She had to see me first, and was excited to see all the colors dancing around. She actually felt overwhelmed with the energy healing, feeling that my energy was too much for her. She too had a father who was in a toxic job and practice. The energy healing brought up the truth in her life, and it was too much for her to resonate with the truth and then have to live in an environment full of lies.

There are more and more stories of how advanced healing helped these young souls. I even pulled a dark energy out of one kid, but that is for another time, as I have no permission to tell the story. The new spiritual guard is here. These children were suffering with the heaviness and darkness of the planet, partly, I felt, because all of us have not activated our own missions. We are like dominos, depending on one another to fulfill our missions so that we can help the others who have contracts to hear our songs, eat our organic food, practice with a new healing modality, or write their book. So get going! The universe, and others, are depending on you to be inspired by your light. We all have a 'peace' in this puzzle.

I remembered reading about the indigo and crystal children in Doreen Virtue's book, and was amazed that these children really existed. I didn't doubt her, but I have one foot in 3D reality, and one foot in the spiritual world. I was so proud to be assisting them. I felt like I had a mobile Hogwart's school. I would schlep my massage table and crystals to various locations and assist the young souls on their journey. I also realized that there is a change on the planet in consciousness. The planet is raising its vibration out of the dark ages, and into one of more mutual understanding with the interconnectivity of our souls. These children were representative of seeing auras, hearing messages, connecting to the mystical times (as with *Dungeons and Dragons* and mermaids). None of these children were delusional or psychotic, they were in chronic pain. Being in pain, or being sick, will also stimulate mystical experiences. When people are in pain, they often pop out of their bodies. The *spirit* separates from the physical form, and creates an awareness of the separation between *spirit* and body. Then the spirit's language as seeing hearing and feeling opens up, when they are out of their body. Many times their intuitive gifts become present. I have also seen this awareness of separation in people who have been abused or even after surgery or various accidents. The planet is changing right before our eyes.

As I began to heal myself by attending Reiki circles, I eventually healed others. I became a better therapist, often sending people healing energy if they were discussing exceptionally painful or difficult trauma. My aura was filled with Reiki energy, and clients would begin to heal. My intuition became stronger with the Reiki, Pranic, and Theta healing. My understanding of universal wisdom and vibration was enhanced. It nurtured my *spirit* and helped my therapy clients. The possibility of just being present for someone, with good intentions, can do wonders, talking to them soul to soul and *spirit* to *spirit*, knowing that they have the answer inside of them, seeing them as the divine being they are.

If you are a counselor, therapist, or healer, see your clients as actors in a play wearing a costume. If they are presenting a very sad or dark side, they may be thought of as a great actor, demonstrating an amazing performance to keep you at bay, know that their *spirit* lies under the makeup and costume. Relate to their *spirit,* and they will take the costume off, showing you who they really are. Although, if a client doesn't resonate with the belief system that they create their reality, this modality can be very uncomfortable to them, you can hold the intention in your mind and in your heart that the *spirit* will teach them in a way that they can now hear the message that it is safe for them.

Walk your own Path

You see, through tragedy, triumph will emerge. It is important to know that light is always stronger than the darkness. Some parts of the earth are very dark, but the universe is so full of light, it can be blinding. Always stay in the light. Stray towards what is right, fair, and good and the universe will repay you. Even if we cannot see the payment, know that your light is never wasted, if you lean towards what is good.

Even when I worked in the hospital, other healers were appalled I would work in a system that was corrupt, money hungry, abusive, and dark. I didn't really like it, but I learned first-hand how the medical system worked. I learned about over-medication, health care treatment, medical mistakes, and the devoid of *spirit*. What I did like was helping others and holding the light. I can speak more honestly to people who feel failed by the system, who are feeling scared, overwhelmed, and over-medicated. The universe always has a plan. I never wanted, or was interested in, working in a hospital. As a sensitive healer, the empathic nature of being around people who were in pain was physically difficult. I gained tons of weight, buffering myself from their stories of physical, emotional, financial, and institutional pain. Sitting near them on their hospital beds, and feeling every ailment, was draining.

But, as an energy healer, it helped me understand from the inside out the positive and negative aspects of hospitals. It was my training ground to be a professional healer. I could learn from experience what was helping and what wasn't helping, what patients went through, how the system is too big and detached, and how the different variables can help or harm a patient. I have seen how easily words can both help or hurt a person. I worked at various hospitals — over 13 — in multiple places, at one time. One job was very close to my home and provided me with a good income for part-time work, where I could pay my rent and bills, easily supplemented by private clients, and some speaking engagements. But as a *spirit* that likes to grow, I would get bored easily. This training at the hospital helped me understand how emotions get stored in the body. With my belief system training from Agape church*, and science of mind (what your mind thinks it can create), and working in the hospital, I would see easily what emotionally what was going on with the patients. How emotions fuel, but not always, create a lot of illnesses.

I highly recommend the CD, *The Body is Your Unconscious Mind* by Candace Pert, PhD, a neuroscientist and pharmacologist, who discovered at age twenty-four opiate receptors in the brain. She proved that the emotions and body are intertwined, proving scientifically what my spiritual practice of science of mind was saying. Our thoughts and beliefs create our reality in our world, and in the body. In the ER, I would often speak to clients about their emotional issues in connection to their physical ailments.

For example, if people had IBS, colitis, or GI gastrointestinal problems, I knew that was connected to the power center, or solar plexus chakra. After the medical test proved negative, I would talk to them about their emotional body, and where there was a leak or where they were giving away power. Immediately, the women would talk about an aggressive partner, parent, or someone in their life that was taking the power away. In the brief moments we had, I would attempt to help them feel more empowered, so that they could take charge of their lives again.

The classic CP, or chest pain, in the heart, was generally due to some emotional stressor. If the patient had no prior cardiac issues, and was under forty-five-years-old, I would talk about stress and heartbreak in their life. I wouldn't read them spiritually, but would ask, "Do you have any stress in your life in the areas of legal, financial, work, or health?" Generally, truth will pour out as to some kind of heartache that presented so seriously as to mimic a heart attack or anxiety attack.

The second chakra issues, I generally stayed away from in the ER. If people came in with problems in their sexual area, including fibroids, cysts, miscarriages, or prostate issues, this intervention would generally take a lot more engagement on the clients end, before I would open up to this kind of intrusive questioning. The crown chakra, and ailments in the head (headaches and migraines.) I find that normally the clients were in too much pain to talk. I do find that people with chronic headaches have issues with connecting to God and trusting him. Throat pain would also be something I would wait for a private client to address, because the ER is for crisis, and if you are in pain, the last thing you want to do is use your throat.

With every client, I would sense and feel if it was the right time to approach them. Mostly, *Spirit* would lead me. Usually, there have been deeper trauma that is stored there, that was not appropriate in an ER setting to dive into. The first chakra, with chronic back injuries, I knew the person probably did not feel supported, or had monetary issues. Understanding how the body speaks to us, to help us heal emotionally, is so important to healing. Your body is giving you a wake-up call to heal or deal with an emotional issue. Our body is a barometer of our emotional lives. Learning about the human body helped me understand the emotional issues of my clients.

So as a healer, I can speak from truth, and not speculation. I also see in many medical systems that they struggle to be more user friendly, or patient sensitive, in a cumbersome, massive system. As I look back, I see how God had a plan for me to work in various hospitals to pick up my skills. As a sensitive healer, it was never my desire, but my assignment, and I was always per diem, which in my mind I called

BECOMING AN INTUITIVE HEALER

"per freedom," so I could dedicate my life to my passion. I can hear God saying, "So, you wanted to be a healer: a true healer is a doctor, but this system of medicine is becoming just that--a system." So, God was training me in all aspects of this archaic healing system. He trained me in all types of healing, medical, holistic, and Spiritual. If you are one of those people in the system, know that you can shine your light in the darkness, for that is where your light is needed most.

Every time I wanted to walk away, I was pulled back to spread some light, or I was fighting to bring the light in. I often send energy to dying patients. Helping, ever so subtly, understanding the other side and where they are going. Making them feel heard and valuable, in a very clinical setting, where sometimes they are talked down to and belittled. I would help patients translate the gobbley-gook spewed from doctors, who talk too fast, and rudely, in hospital code words. For example, if a patient lapsed in consciousness and coded, a physician would check the chart and say to the family, "Your husband had a code blue and I know he is DNR (do not resuscitate), do you want me to forgoe CPR and let him go?" I have had patient's family members ask, "What are these code words?" I would help them understand what was going on, with compassion, often using metaphors, and telling them their patient rights. I would also help respect their spiritual belief systems.

I believe in the East West Connection. I believe that we need allopathic medicine, and other healing modalities together, a combination of both. So, I was a healer, working in a hospital, undercover, on a mission from the divine. You never know how the universe will use you. But remember, I made a contract with God after I felt betrayed by the same system. "Work for me," he said, "and I will never let you down." The work is steady, the pay is good, and the retirement benefits are out of this world.

Economically, and steadily, my purpose aligned with his. My wishes and desires aligned with what the Source's plans were for me.

Sometimes I would fight him, but like a good parent, he let me have my tantrums, and then would say, "You are ready now to listen." And, I did. If you feel you want to align with your purpose, ask Source for some insight. Gifts will be given as incentives by your employer to get you to work for them and to continue down that path. Usually, this is done by the universe giving you surprise gifts and consultancies. When I got kicked out of my job years ago, I had already gotten paid for my vacation time ($3,000), and I was down to a couple hundred in my bank account. I was starting my business as an intuitive reader and coach with no full-time employment. I thought, "how am I going to pay my rent, and my $600 loan repayment to Columbia, and $300 for my car note, and the many other expenses?" I was talking to my friend about it, and I looked at my bank statement, and $5,000 was "'gifted in my account!" I have no idea how it got there. I did know my company had underpaid me an hourly rate, and that they had to review my financial statements. Could they have overpaid my vacation time? When the financial department said that they had to review my hourly rate, I was sweating bullets. They said, "I am sorry Ms. Coleridge, it is not $36 per hour, you are getting $37.50." They gave me a raise, and never said anything about the overpayment!

I was not sure where the money came from, and then the financial department contacted me again, and said there was another mistake. They stated it was $38.50 that I was supposed to be making, but no mention of the $5,000. It was an advance from God, and I was always able to pay my rent and expenses with pretty good credit. Over the years the money kept steadily increasing. If you are in a dead end job, and you don't know your purpose, ASK. You will be surprised as your guides, angels, and energetic energy vectors, will start setting you up to align you with what you were meant to be doing. I will give you more examples of being a light and healer in a hospital setting.

CHAPTER

7   Emotional Sutures

WORKING *SPIRIT* to *spirit* is what I developed when doing multiple types of spiritual work: such as readings, healings, and coaching. I realized as a mental health practitioner, it is easy access to a person's soul, when you honor their *spirit*. It was very tricky doing this in hospital settings, but as clients gave me a flash of their soul mission, I knew that *their* souls needed some insight to healing emotionally. I would try to honor that part of their journey that I would partake in. Remember, I was hired by the universe. It wasn't easy balancing the light and the dark, the ego and *Spirit*, the traditional and the intuitive, but I somehow managed, and created a method that I called Emotional Spiritual Suturing. Basically, this method was to use spiritual principles to help a client heal.

In the ER, for many years, if someone came in with a major laceration from an assault or fall, I would often have to come in to help the person gain resources and services. In the crisis mode of ERs, doctors can be harsh and direct. As a social worker, I was often told to clean up their mess after insensitive or rude dialogue had taken place. I myself was a victim of bad medical treatment by medical staff, just another number. I also have been the one who has said the wrong thing at the wrong time, a symptom of always working in crisis mode and Ariesitis, a disorder that I and others who were born between March 23rd and April 19th suffer from.

Like a harsh brush fire, I can also be quick and direct. If I sat and meditated before the day began, things were different. I have had experiences really shifting a person's life in a quick assessment in the ER. If someone is in pain, the last thing they wanted to do was to speak to a social worker, or anyone. So, I somehow would have to help them be open to an intervention, before I got there. I would often send them healing energy, or a Reiki symbol. I would pump up their energy field with more light, and surround them with angelic beings. I would say a prayer, or give them insight about why this situation had occurred. I would speak to them *spirit* to *spirit*.

I was suturing up their spiritual body, which would then affect their emotional body. The *spirit* has the ability to self-heal, so to connect with it is half the work, as a counselor. I will tell you one experience of how I talked a budding lightworker, out of a 5150 psychiatric hold, and suicidal thoughts.

From Suicide to Wide-Eyed

Marciela was a sixteen-year-old Latina girl who came in to the ER suicidal. She was shy, withdrawn, and seemed frightened. Her father was very concerned about his daughter, and protective of any intervention. When I assessed her, she was guarded and had a very good family life. She was close to her father, mother, and sibling. Her mom was her best friend. She had friends, and even a little boyfriend. She felt purposeless and stuck.

An exceptionally sensitive soul, she felt overwhelmed and bombarded by people's situations and energy. Her parents, as immigrants, wanted her to do very well in school, which she did. They actually encouraged her to go into any career that she wanted. She wanted to go into a career in art. In my mind's eye, I saw her drawing. "Do you like to draw," I asked. She said, "Yes, but you can't make money doing that." I said, "Well maybe *you* can."

She felt unfulfilled, with no interest in anything, and overwhelmed by harshness in school. She felt that the best thing was to end her life, because she felt her passion could not be fufilling. She also felt ghosts all around her house. She said, "I can't sleep, I feel restless." I said, "Do you see shadows?" She said, "Yes, all the time. They keep me up." I asked, "Are they shadows or ghosts?" and she replied, "Ghosts, and they scare me." I gave her the awareness that many people see ghosts, and that doesn't make you crazy. "You see ghosts too," she said, and I said "Yes." She said, "My mom also saw ghosts, but she doesn't like to talk about it. How do I get them to go away?"

I told her to surround herself with the archangels, and to connect to the highest being she believed in, and she said that she believed in Christ. She said, "My aunt told me to do the same thing." I said, "Well, that is two people." She started to smile, and laugh. I explained to her that many artists are sensitive, and that standard school may be frustrating, because it is so structured. She began to understand. "I like to draw when I feel inspired and outside of the box." I encouraged her to stay in school and take art classes, or be part of an artist group. She started to relax more.

During our time, I sent her a Reiki symbol and started to pull out the negative energy in our field, but it really was my words that shifted her. Her eyes began to shine and light up. I love dropping a seed of light into the field and aura of someone in distress. I love igniting them with the energy of their own divinity. I love turning on their lightbulb of awareness to their journey. For someone who is suicidal, I don't like them making the mistake of opting out of life too early, when their soul contracted to come here for this soul journey in the first place. Many of us have forgotten that we come to earth camp.

I try to quickly read their book of life, and audit their *spirit*, and help them understand that maybe the skills that they are learning are in their roughest terrain. I knew she was a lightworker, and was here to inspire others through her art. I like to turn on a lightbulb that has become dull or is turned off. To see the brightness in their eyes light up is rewarding and inspirational. I never heard what happened to her, but the next day I saw that she had gone home and was not put on a hold.

Losing Their Mind or Hearing the Divine

Many clinics I worked at felt that spirituality and meditation together would not be appropriate. One coworker at a clinic said meditation was making his patients worse, because he was jealous he couldn't do it. For Gods sake UCLA has the MARC, mindfulness awareness research center. Haters will be around, step above them. Most of these places were concerned about liability, due to the fact that spirituality in mental health can be tricky because of patient's belief systems. I understand that, but what I see is that patients are screaming for a connection to their *spirits,* and an understanding of their condition. Every time I did a workshop on their *spirits*, clients, were lined up outside of my office.

I find it fascinating that when people are psychotic and have sounds of religiosity, they feel they are hearing God's voice. Are they sometimes messengers from God, but the messages are scrambled because of a trauma or abuse that they have not processed? Or were they screaming out for the divine, trying to ease their emotional suffering? Are they fighting darkness in their bodies and thoughts trying to connect to Source. Maybe their wires were crossed, and they could be trying to call out to God to help themselves.

Alberto Villoldo, PhD, and an anthropologist who has studied shamanism in many cultures has a different view of schizophrenics. In his book *Healing States*, he says that when people are schizophrenic in Peruvian cultures, they are considered untrained shamans. Maybe the dark side of the *spirit* is craving for their soul to be heard. Malidome Some, an African shaman, wrote an article entitled *The Shamanic View of Mental Illness.* He says the same thing about schizophrenics being untrained shamans. Why do most earth based cultures, from more indigenous cultures, describe hearing voices as something different? Are they more sophisticated in their understanding of the spiritual aspects of people and the maladaptive occurrences that can happen? I believe some of these people have gifts but are listening to the lower level frequencies and may have scrambled brain or too much trauma to hear clearly, like Some and Villoldo believe.

When I was on call, for over five years, as a psychotherapist in a step down mental health program, there was a lot of spiritual talk happening there. It was a great environment, and I was able to practice my clinical skills, run groups, and do a life purpose/discharge planning group. Two of the staff members, a psychiatrist and pharmacist, were also energy healers. The pharmacist, Nancy, performed energy healing on the patients. Getting patients connected to their *spirit* helps them so much to heal. Nancy taught them about chakras, energy fields, and performed hands on healing. The psychiatrist often discussed Louise Hay's book, *You Can Heal Your Life.* The *spirit* has naturally strong healing abilities.

I have seen schizophrenics that have gifts with music. I have seen bipolar people that are amazing artists. A vitally important practice for people with mental illness is to help to them balance their chaotic energy field by putting it into harmony. This can be done when they are stabilizing on medications. (*If you have a mental challenge, please don't get off or change your medications without consulting with a psychiatrist. This can be dangerous.*) It is important to help assist their spirits' by using grounding, protecting, and working with crystals. Find that seed within them of the divine, and it can help them to transform.

Connecting the mentally challenged to their *Spirit* is so healing, especially when many patients were traumatized by mental health practitioners telling them they were crazy to hear a voice, see an angel, or see shadows. With the other energy practitioners, I was able to discuss how our mental health patients had a lot of spiritual experiences of seeing ghosts, angels, auras, visions, etc. It was great to 'talk shop" in a traditional setting. I thoroughly enjoyed my time there, and it helped me to learn more methods of healing people energetically and emotionally. Doing readings and working as a medical social worker was concerning for me, because I missed being a traditional psychotherapist. I was really good at it, really good when I was in the flow. A part of me grieved that I didn't have that opportunity anymore. The other medical social worker job kept hiring younger cheaper people that never stayed, but I would often lose my hours. On a whim, I decided to ask God for another gig that would treat me well. I was led to connect with a temp company and was notified that I was referred to this Partial program at the same company, at another location.

After you apply to the universe, you may also receive invitations from it to work. I was invited by the universe to work in this step down program. The universe heard my call, and provided me this opportunity to go back to my craft. I always had a lot of clients that I would do intuitive consultations for. The universe set me up in many ways there. The one Middle Eastern woman, who helped me years ago, would sometimes work there as well. She remembered the trauma, and when others balked at my very high hourly wage, she stated the truth as she did, years ago, "You deserve it! The way they treated you there, it was atrocious. You deserve it, every dime."

I knew I was not in the wrong, because the monetary pay-out by the universe, and the consistent freelance work kept proving to me that I was in the right. I would clear over six figures on call, and couldn't understand how I did that, except to give credit to the universe. I never wanted to work with all of those betrayers again, and the one person who really supported me and spoke the truth I was able to work with again. The universe will keep you safe, if you have faith, and your intentions are pure. I have worked for various hospitals, and they would supplement my income, but if the environment wasn't right, within a year I was gone, by my own choosing. When things were slow, I would chant to Lakshimi, the ancient Goddess of abundance, and find another gig to pay my bills. With the ability to work freelance, I liked the practice of working with the universe by asking and receiving. I like chanting, because it centers me, and gets me focused on something that is spiritual which helps me to feel centered. Also, the synchronicities would abound, as the chant is giving homage to the Goddess of abundance. The chant is *"ohm shreem mAh-ha lakshimi Swah-ha."* Say it 108 times every day until things start to flow.

Some people think it is idolatry to chant in another language to a goddess, but my practice of spirituality is eclectic, and I personally practice universal spirituality. I draw from many different disciplines. The practice is also putting positive energy into the universe. I like the chant, as the energy of abundance stays in my energy field, and I cannot negate it by negative self-talk, since I don't know Sanskrit. My father's grandmother Edith, my great-grandmother, was half East Indian, and practiced Hindu, but also had a *spirit* circle, so I feel genetically connected to this language. In working on call for hospitals, I was truly practicing the law of attraction in abundance. Maybe, it was just a *coincidence,* but within moments or days of chanting, someone, or some situation would occur to abundantly help me.

Emotional Sutures

To assist a client to heal on a deeper emotional level is pivotal to a client healing on the physical level--at least that is my belief. The more traumatic the incident, the more the spiritual and emotional aspect needs to be addressed. One morning, I received an intake call from a plastic surgeon to assist a client, a twenty-four-year-old

African American female who had an exceptionally bad experience. She had been living with a mentally ill sister, with a long history of paranoid schizophrenia. The sister and the patient didn't get along. Her sister was often off of her meds, and at one point, was hallucinating very badly. She thought the patient was the devil, and that God wanted her to get rid of this evil spawn. In a delusional tirade, the sister ended up stabbing the patient about eighteen times. The patient was taken to UCLA, where she was sutured and stabilized, but she had to follow up in her home facility. She then had to follow up in the ER where I worked, to receive a consultation about surgery on her thumb. UCLA stated that the surgery was urgent, and advised her to go to the ER. Coming into the ER is hard for anyone, because the environment tends to be an intense, chaotic, fast, and is sometimes impersonal. Imagine coming into the hospital with multiple stabs wounds on your face, hands, and body, after just being released from another facility.

When the patient came to the ER, no one knew what was needed; her records were still at UCLA where she was treated. The plastic surgeon wanted me to assist in coordinating all of her care. Her primary doctor was in Bellflower, but the surgeon was in West LA. I spoke to the patient, who was surprisingly calm and collected, as she discussed her experience. One of the patient's biggest fears was returning home to where her sister lived, the perpetrator of this violent crime. Her mother wasn't supportive of the patient because she was both in denial and embarrassed by the assault within the family. This made the patient feel more alone and victimized. The patient was experiencing multiple system errors, her family and the medical center that was not initially responding to her needs in crisis. I knew she would need emotional sutures.

First, I engaged her and offered supportive listening. I assured her that I would help her get through the system. I knew any struggle to get treatment and services would feel to her like another assault. So, I assisted her in relocation, both for her safety and her emotional healing. She needed a safe place to sleep and heal. I connected her to Victims of Violent Crime; they would help with relocation expenses. Luckily, her sister was incarcerated, which bought some time.

I connected with her primary doctor in Bellflower, who was very responsive and helped authorize treatment. I called member services about her medical records not being referred in time from UCLA to our ER, and that is why the ER didn't know what was going on. Member services was right there to coordinate care. I helped her gain more support in her personal life. Her family life was in a shambles. The patient already had a wonderful minister who was supportive and had provided a spiritual understanding for her wounded, betrayed, and deeply hurt soul. I contacted psychiatry to assist her in attending therapy, to help to work on this emotional trauma of this family violence.

Every time I connected her to a resource and received a result, I felt like I was stitching up her emotional body. Every resource was a suture, helping her to feel heard and giving her energetic empathy her family could not provide. Lessening the enormity of trying to gain services in a massive health care organization, where it is easy to feel lost, was another stitch. Assisting the patient in feeling a personal connection to someone in the organization, who was a supporter and an advocate, was another suture. As a psychotherapist, I believe if the client can be emotionally taken care of and her *Spirit* supported, her body's healing would surely follow. The mind, body, and *Spirit* are intertwined.

When the patient described the incident to me, she said she had locked herself in the bathroom, for two hours, away from her sister. She should have died, with all those wounds, and being unconscious for that length of time. She then said, "You won't believe me, but my guardian angel came to me, and told me to get up". I smiled a knowing smile, and stated, "I believe you". She was in between life and death at that time. What are the chances that she connected with me, an undercover Spiritual counselor, as a social worker on the intake call. The angel told her to get up and assisted her in opening the door, even though her hands were extremely bloody and slashed, she was able to call 911. Her sister had fled the scene. It was very important that I validated her angel visitation and believed her. This was part of the healing process connecting to her *Spirit* and Spiritual experience.

The patient was very strong and confident about 'testifying' of her experience in church, and was positive she would heal. Someone attempted to stab her to death, but she was somehow stabbed to life, finding more of a purpose and reason in her tragedy. I admired her courage and felt satisfied that I provided her, if even for only a couple of phone calls, a healing experience.

Update: I called the patient to see how she was doing, and to ask her permission to tell her story without identifying names. She agreed to the story and ironically, the last time I spoke with her was August 28, 2007. It is August 29, 2008, almost exactly a year to date, since I last made contact. Synchronicities always mean something. She was thrilled to hear about her story being told, and is planning to go to law school to practice family law. She has moved out of state, and has restarted her life.

I wasn't sure how I impacted her, but she said that she remembered me, because she 'still had my voicemail message on her cell phone, and had it for a year, because she wanted to follow up with me.' I was stunned that she would save my message for so long, but I guess my voice was a healing balm, a positive memory during a nightmare. Maybe, I was another sort of supportive helper and her keeping my voicemail made her experience seem more real. My intention was to provide her with support and empathy in one of the worse traumas, probably of her life. She validated the services I provided, were, in fact an emotional suture, and she still had not removed that one last stitch.

A Dance With A Dead Man

I engaged in a dance with a 57-year-old drug abusing male client, well known to me at one of the hospitals I worked in. This patient frequented the hospital ER, rolling in his motorized cart, and through various demands asked us to partake in his various dances. This patient with cancer, and multiple medical problems, would come into the ER often dodging any serious questions, and try to receive food and housing for the night, if he couldn't get high on the street. He was mostly cheerful, though sometimes frustrated with his plight. He had a family, a wife even, and health insurance, even though most of his money went to his drug abuse. He had estranged his family, like a typical addict does, using drugs and alcohol, and causing havoc in their homes.

At one point, he was connected to a facility to live in, but he acted out so badly that he was kicked out. I had seen this patient numerous times, he knew me almost by name. "Ms. Social Worker," he would call me. When he was diagnosed with prostate cancer, I knew his time was running short, living on the street and using was not conducive to a major illness like that, and he would never follow up for chemo treatment.

Then one day the patient's very familiar motorized scooter, battered from being out on the streets, wouldn't start. Symbolically, I speculated that his life was close to ending. The scooter, usually, was able to be charged up, but this time, he tried to plug it in, and it would not work. I went with him to various outlets trying, to see if it would spark, but to no avail. The chair was not going to be activated again. Like the cancer that was eating away at his lungs, no amount of charging or chemotherapy would help him. I had spoken to everyone in his family about offering compassion, and taking him back into their home in his dying days, but they would have none of that. He had burned one too many bridges with them, and as a typical addict, had betrayed them many, many times, a complicated tango. Pt was not welcome back.

In the case conference, working with this patient, everyone was discussing trying to get him placed, medically stabilized referred and all of these systems in place. To me the intensity of this discussion was fruitless, at this point, because we were dancing with a dead man. We are doing this cha-cha for ourselves. I knew when his motorized cart died, and this homeless man had no movement, it would be soon after that his cancer would break him down too.

In his dying days, I took a moment to speak to him and find out what his thoughts were about the severity of his illness. As a social worker, I became a soul-worker, I have become very interested in the soul of my clients. As I had watched my dad, a minister, do numerous times, I was offering him his last rites, his Spiritual rites. The patient, in his typical homeless stance, was detached, defensive, denying, and dying. To die, knowing that you have hurt so many people, and no one there for the passing, was far worse for him, I believed, than having the cancer. To reveal and acknowledge it to someone else would make it real, and probably too painful. Whenever I saw him, he tried to smile, but I knew that covered a melancholy, that was irreversible. In essence, I was offering him his last rites, giving him the option to make amends with his family, and to heal some of his broken relationships.

The soul lessons he taught to staff and others is so much compassion, tolerance, self-respect, and dignity; rarely does the staff think about it, they just look at him as using and abusing the system. But who created this hustle? Weren't the system and the patient just playing a long game of musical chairs? My *Spirit* said to me, "I would engage him in a dance one last time." It didn't happen. He died alone in his room. His ex-wife was notified, and there was no worry of the protocol, his last dance was a solo, and the audience box was empty. I was glad that I had humanized his existence, provoking in him his deeper emotions about his illness and his feelings of his life, his soul. I had given him an option to make sense of his plight, and he had demanded that he have the option of living and dying the way he felt safest and most comfortable, a waltz alone.

> ## WORKBOOK EXERCISE #6
> - **What will your soul** think of you at the end of your life?
> - **What do you want** to do before you get there?

Heartache

Amy came to me after she found me on the UCLA Pediatric Pain Website. She worked at another fellow organization, and I thought she was going to refer a client to me. "No, I wanted to come myself." So Amy came in, tall, long-legged and blonde, a nurse. I explained my work, and sat down with the chakra chart. I started at the top and explained what each chakra meant. I then got to the heart and said this is where heartbreaks lie; before I finished my presentation, she was in tears. She was 38-years-old, successful in her career, but alone. She described some childhood difficulty, and we looked at it related to her relationships, currently. She said she felt bad for feeling sorry for herself, because of the way she looked, and has a lot going for her. She stated have a lot to be thankful for. "I think about how the black people were treated in Hurricane Katrina and think, what is my problem?" She then looked at me, and realized she was sitting with a black healer. I laughed, and realized I served as a reminder for her about how our differences can be a teaching tool.

We did a healing session on her whole body, and I placed three rose quartz on her heart, balancing out the other chakras with other crystals. I use crystals in healing the body energetically, because it helps to ground static energy. We are energy beings, and earth stones ground our energetic body in the physical plane. Just like lightning grounds when it hits the earth, our energetic body grounds when the crystals realign to heal our chakras. The various crystals correspond to different energy centers. For example, the *rose quartz*, which is the heart stone, resonates with the heart. *Amethyst* is perfect for the third eye. *Blue lace agate* is great to place on the throat for communication issues. *Citrine* works really well in the solar plexus, or gut center, to clear any debris there. *Carnelian* is great for women and men in the reproductive area. I like *hematite* as a grounding stone for the first chakra, *and clear quartz* for the crown. Many healers use different crystals in different areas, work with what intuitively works for you.

A great crystal therapist, Teddy Seraphine, taught me about the alignment of the crystals, and it has always stayed with me. There are some crystals to stay away from, in certain parts of the body, but I would consult a crystal book for that. Amy felt better, and came back later for another session. I gave her a rose quartz as a reminder of what we energetically created and the information that was given. She kept it by her bed.

I never heard from Amy, until several months later I saw her on Facebook, and saw that her relationship status had changed. I said, "Hi! Wow, there was a change there!" She typed, "Oh I met someone, not too long after I saw you. I met this wonderful guy, and things are moving along." I was happy, and surprised. She went on, "You helped me open my heart again, and it helped me so much. I saw things differently, and I keep the rose quartz by my bed as a reminder. I am happy." She later became engaged to him, as she opened her heart the other chakras realigned, and her life changed. She attracted exactly what she desired. She was later married. She came back to me one other time, for a different issue. It was just a 'touch-up,' but it helped her. I reminded her what her *Spirit* wanted, and her perceptions were right. She was able to move forward, again.

Healing our soul aches with our chakras teaches us what is going on in our emotional and physical body. The client's Spiritual heart, the heart chakra, is what told me about what she was going through emotionally. Her *Spirit* was aching for love, and it manifested with an energetic pain in her heart. Remember, it was when I spoke about the heart chakra that her truth hit, she teared up. She listened to her heart, and moved in the right direction. The chakra system is an excellent diagnostic tool for our Spiritual life. Energy gets store in us from emotional, physical, or Spiritual trauma. The energy is absorbed in our bodies, and it becomes part of our energy matrix. The maladjustment can be seen (or felt, as I do) in our aura field. She learned **self love and self esteem.**

Without Judgment

Anna is another example of how energy is stored in the heart center negatively, but can be more serious. Anna, a mature Mexican American female, met me at a Spiritual event, and received a healing. It was months later that she called me and told me she was in crisis. "I was in the hospital all weekend, and they think I had a heart attack." When she said that, it didn't ring true for me. She said she was in for a couple of days and all these tests were done. I listened intently. I scanned her heart energetically, but didn't feel like she had a heart attack. "They even put a heart monitor on me to walk around for several weeks!" My first thought was, "What insurance does she have that would cover that!?"

I deferred the final result, as I always do, to the medical workup, but intuitively I saw emotional heartache. She scheduled a healing session. The healing would help with the heart that needed nurturing energetically to be taken care of. Anna, in her mid-fifties, was approaching her Saturn return, this is an astrological term that means all of your planets are lined up at the same place when you are born, and issues regarding your soul purpose, health, life, traumas, wishes, dreams, generally the desires in your heart will come up to be looked at or created. Anna was a very successful lawyer and judge; she had broken many barriers rising to that position. When I read her heart, I saw visions of Anna singing and lots of colors and paints. I told her what I saw. She said "I used to sing! I loved singing before I went to law school. I had to prove to myself that I could do it, be a lawyer." She also was a painter, but hadn't picked up a brush in years. "I was given the impression by my parents that I had to get a real job." As the first born, in a Mexican American lower income family, it was important that she succeeded, and she did, but it was with sacrifice to her heart. She was the first in her family to get an education. She was also the secondary mother to many of her siblings. I saw her reading over things for her parents. I thought she was translating, but she quickly corrected me, stating she often helped her English speaking parents pay the rent and bills on time. She would often read contracts for them, as neither had graduated high school. She did this starting at age 7-years-old. Her childhood was for her parents, not hers. I am not surprised she became a lawyer, as she started reading contracts so young.

I felt she wasn't honoring her *Spirit*. The messages I received was that she could present speeches, and inspire the growing populations of Latinas and Latinos to help give them a sense of direction. Her eyes lit up. "I love talking to kids," she said. She didn't have to leave her job, but it would be good if she painted and sang and nurtured her creative side. When she emailed me back to tell me that her tests on her heart were negative, I was not surprised. I smiled, and my Spiritual prescriptions were to get a paint brush, a mic and enjoy that part of herself that is calling to her. That was her heart wake-up call. The Spiritual attributes she learned were: **Self-Awareness, Self-fulfillment, and Self-Love.**

A year or so later, Anna came back, she looked completely different, younger. She had a near death experience and energetic issues that affected her medical body, so severe she ended up in the ICU. The doctors were never able to find what was wrong, but her energetic body was very weak. Anna responds very well to energy healing and grounding. I discussed emotionally what I felt her brother and mother said to me from the other side. She stated, "that was so my brother!" I said, "Were you twins?" She stated, "No, but we felt like soulmates; he was my best friend." Since they both were gay, they bonded on a deep level. Her brother showed me fabrics and clothes. She said, "He so wanted to be a designer, but he died of AIDS." I said, "I think your energies are so intertwined that you almost have to experience creativity for him and you." She shook her head in agreement, "I feel his energy so strongly in the room."

I always tell her to ground and center regularly, especially going to the heavy energy of the courthouse and hearing such difficult cases. I gave her a hematite stone for grounding and anxiety. Her partner did buy her a hematite necklace, to help with the grounding. I have no idea how she is able to go to that job, without being drained, but she is well respected in her field, by her peers and superiors. The next time I saw her there was even more light around her. She said, "Guess what Carolyn, I sang at karaoke, and I am doing photography. I can't put my camera down." She was even featured in an art show, and her teacher voted her best in the class. Remember, Anna had suppressed her true desires for family obligation.

By this time, she had just turned sixty in the midst of her Saturn return, she was on the right path. You are never too old! Partake in your heart's desires and soul dreams. Until they pull the plug, or bury you in the earth, create! This is what we are here for, hopefully and Spiritually, to create something that serves some good. Anna began to live her life for herself, without judgement.

Our Soul is always calling to us. Similar to all this talk about 2012, our collective soul truth will come out. We are aligned with our galactic center on December 2012, our collective Saturn Return. Our collective souls aligned with the center of the galaxy, the galactic heart center. That is why more and more, you find people are searching for their truth, soul searching for the reason for being.

The backlash is the obsession with materialism, like the snake in the garden, to tempt us away from our purpose. It also makes sense, spiritually, why we are angry at our government, projecting our rage to our collective parents, but when we grow up, we realize we can no longer hold our parents responsible for what they did, or didn't do, for us as children. We have to take our own responsibility, we have to forgive and take action for our own lives.

I am not negating that there are things that need to be changed with the government, but we cannot keep externalizing our rage towards someone else or another thing or institution. We have to listen to those soul messages, to God—he broadcasts and we say, "Ok, how can I *empower myself?"* The galactic center will send out a signal to your soul about your soul's true calling, stronger than anything before. You know during a full moon, you are more emotional than usual, it is the same concept. It is the time of the Soul on this planet, a transformation of the material world. The end of times may be the end of times, as we know it.

Our time is evolving to be spent for good things, meaningful things, back to nature and green living, organic farming and raw food, cooperative markets and sustainable communities. Global tribalism may be the new trend, tribes of souls and *Spirit*, that we realize we need each other, and each soul has a 'peace' of the puzzle. Equality in healthcare and in health care treatment, an awareness that our inter-connectivity will sustain us, and not having it will create our demise. The awareness that our planet has a soul, and a lot of what you see out in the world with all the various environmental problems are our own soul aches being manifested in the earth plane. So, we must stop wasting time in purposeless jobs and lifestyles that don't speak to us. Spend more time listening to our *Spirit*, and learn the universal laws, so we can learn how to sustain ourselves in a more economically viable way, as opposed to the greedy self-absorbed way that has hurt our families, children, animals, and environment.

The concept of *the law of time* was written by Jose Arguelles, Phd the founder of Earth Day and the harmonic convergeance*, a brilliant man, and Princeton professor. Most people don't know he founded earth day. He was both Mexican-American and German-American, and went back and forth between Mexico and the US. His book *The Mayan Factor* was a popular book that many people based the 2012 phenonmenon on.

When I met him at the Bodhi tree a metaphysical bookstore in Los Angeles, he minced no words-- he was disappointed in how people misinterpreted 2012. He received this information at about age 14, at the pyramid Teotihuacan in Mexico, about the earth and 2012. He believed one of the greatest tragedies was that humans were the only beings who don't resonate with the natural rythmn of nature. I am paraphrasing here, but the gist of his idea was that, "We fight against time and nature to develop our own rules. Animals walk to the beat of nature, and the environment has its own rhythm, but we humans fight against time. We have very late hours, we sleep at chaotic times. We try to overpower the earth by taking down the trees, and end up contaminating our food sources. We torture animals for fun and sport, and pollute our environment and oceans. We try to fight against nature, which is our teacher, dumping crap on it and polluting mother earth's ability to breathe. Of course, she is pissed, she can't breathe. It is a global wake-up call, but one that we have heard before. We have individual wake-up calls, and planetary wake-up calls. This time it is louder, and bigger!"

One of the most powerful things he said is that we don't know we are powerful beings in the universe, more powerful than any beings on the planet. The whole room didn't speak for at least 2 minutes after he said that. It was a powerful moment. A severe alcoholic, he died just several months before December, 2012 occurred.

Family History

I had mentioned, before, that your family history may give an insight into what you should be doing in this lifetime. If you don't feel connected to your family, or don't like them, don't fear, that could be an incentive too. I know of people who grew up in horribly abusive family situations, with alcohol and physical abuse, who never drink that stuff and dedicated themselves to helping others become clean, or do something more constructive with their lives. Remember, older souls pick challenging lifetimes.

It wasn't until I was a lot older that my parents starting telling me about all the healers and intuitives in my family. It wasn't a part of everyday conversation, because the family and the culture honored their Spiritual part all the time. It wasn't trendy and exotic like the new age is now. It just was. My mother would always shake her head when she heard I was taking classes on healing or intuition: "You are going to let somebody teach you how to be intuitive?" In her mind, it was like someone teaching you how to take a shower, you know your body, you should know how to do it! Things have changed, and my mother didn't have all the technical distractions that we have now, all the seductive sales going on, the constant bombardment of consumer marketing that takes you away from hearing your *Spirit* and honoring your soul.

My mother had told my father that he would become the first African American Episcopal Bishop of Connecticut. She said she had a dream that he would be elected. My mother often had premonitions, so I was a pretty good kid, because she would often know what in the world I was doing. My father said he didn't have those gifts, but he believed his wife's gifts. Sure enough, someone from the Diocese of CT knocked on our door and invited my father to run for office as an Episcopal bishop. He became the suffragan, and then the head. In lily-white, old money WASPy Connecticut, my father was the first black Episcopal bishop. Many people attributed his popularity to his love of spirit and God and putting it into practice. He came from South America, almost penniless an immigrant and rose to a high position in his field. If my mother hadn't said she had a dream, I think my shyer father would have forgone the invitation to run.

My father also got a 'message' from *spirit* to become a minister. He was studying at Howard University, planning to become a veterinarian. At the time, he heard that Martin Luther King, Jr. was doing a speech. Dr. King's house was at risk of being bombed. My father and other students went to his house to support him. My father was excited to meet this rising star of the Civil Rights Movement. He was able to shake his hand. Dr. King said, "What are you studying, young man?" and my father said to be a minister, even though he was in veterinarian school. Dr. King supported him, and said that is great, but you should be at this university. My father agreed, and changed schools. My dad had no idea why he said minister, but a message came through Dr. King, a man who greatly influenced him. It was a good decision, at the end of his career my father had three honorary doctorates, including one from Yale, and numerous awards including Habitat for Humanity, building five houses in his name, the Coleridge Commons.

Premonitions and messages can be powerful, pay attention to them. Your family history can teach you, from a genetic and soul level, what you should be doing. Don't worry if you don't know your family, or didn't respect their choices--that doesn't mean that you don't have a soul purpose. Many people incarnate into families to change the negative genetic attributes or family addiction issues they were born into.

Mommy Dearest

I had a client that I read when I worked at a metaphysical bookstore. She wanted to do something with her career, but couldn't figure out what it was. She was a teacher and a dedicated mom, but found that she had a hard time achieving her purpose. As I was reading and scanning her, to find out what her gift was, I saw a woman who looked earthbound show up. I asked the client if her mother had passed on, and Tameka said that she had. I felt this pain and shock in my head quickly, and asked if she had an aneurysm, or had been shot. She said, "My mother committed suicide, by shooting herself in her head." Her mother showed up and showed me a lot of personal pain and addiction to drugs. There was also a history of abuse and sadness plagued her soul.

As I tuned in, I said to Tameka, "I feel hungry. Did your mother not feed you?" In tears, she affirmed this. I also felt a lot of havoc in her household, and she affirmed this too. Tameka had never been to a reader before, and was taken aback by all of this information. Tameka grew up in South Central, LA and had a street keenness and intuitive awareness of bullshit, but was buying my words. She said, "I feel chills as you are saying these things." I also said a son of hers was communicating with his grandmother. Tameka was surprised because she said, "my son says that, but I didn't believe him." I also said he was helping another relative with her leg. I discussed severe abuse of her mother, and that is part of the reason she was using drugs so much.

Tameka wasn't sure what to make of this information, but I told her she needs to pray for her mother, because her mother felt earth-bound to me. Tameka confirmed she often feels her mother is in the shower, and around the house. She thanked me for my time, and left it at that. A couple of months later, I heard from Tameka. "You were right," she said, "I spoke to my sisters, and they said mother was severely abused as a child. She had never told that to me. They also said the information you mentioned about her was right." Tameka continued, "My sister and I had some relief in understanding my mother on a soul level."

Because Tameka didn't have a good role model, it was hard for her to move up to higher levels in her work. She began to forgive her mother, and then the next time I saw her, her mother's energy was lighter, like she had transcended. Tameka recently reminded me, that I had sent her mother towards the light by telepathically talking to her. Tameka was already a school teacher and she had created very healing environments for her young adolescent African American classroom. She was an amazing teacher, and had helped many girls help themselves to heal. Her life experience helped these other girls, many of them in foster care, and without revealing her story she helped them on a deep soul level. I encouraged her to create after school seminars and different topics.

She is still working on this. Her family is doing well. She has a loving husband, and 3 great boys. She was able to become a good mom, often missing my classes to be with them. She has broken her mother's pattern, and is a great parent and mentor to others. I didn't plan to talk to her mother who passed over; I planned to help her find her purpose. I had other visions about her life, but she never pursued it seriously, the glitz and glamour in Hollywood. She dabbled in it. She had to realize that sometimes we are looking for our purpose, but we are already sometimes doing it. She continues to inspire high risk girls, and is strengthening her intuitions. Tameka then referred a friend who was also struggling with depression and medical problems.

Cellular Grief

Aisha was a kind hearted woman who called me to clarity her life goals. She was in Detroit when she called, but before she called, I saw this man out of the corner of my eye in my office. I kept looking around, and thought I was imagining something. She asked me about her life, and immediately I clearly saw this young man, an African American man, in his thirties, on a basketball court with work boots. Then he kneeled on one leg and presented me with a ring. He was in my office between the frame of the door. I knew this was symbolic for him, being in-between dimensions. He had not transcended, and was earth bound, that is why he was so low and close to me. Aisha busted out crying, "That was my ex, Reggie, he worked in construction, and he died 3 days ago on a basketball court. He had asked me to marry him, and then cheated on me, after I accepted." He played basketball also, this is why he showed up in work boots on a basketball court, so I could recognize the symbols and translate them to her. I said, "Well, he is apologizing, and presenting you with a ring." He said to me telepathically, "I was foolish and had made a mistake, and I always wanted her." She sobbed some more. "He didn't act like it," she responded. I said, "I think that is why he showed up, because on the other side, he realized what he had done wrong."

Then a white women with red hair showed up over my head. She had white light all around her, and a shimmery white dress on. Her energy seemed high and clear. Aisha was African American. I said, "Was your mother white?" She said, "No, but very very fair, and she could pass for white." I felt a sadness as I saw a severe history of abuse and rape imploding on her mother. "No one took care of her, they were ashamed of her, and much of my family abused her." She was not around for Aisha, as she died when she was young. Her mother too apologized, saying, " I didn't know who I was. And I was working through my own heartache. I wish I was there for you." Many other people showed up and gave her various messages. Aisha said she began to feel lighter. She had felt stuck, and said she felt very relieved. Funny, I didn't pick up at the time that Aisha had fibromyalgia, probably because it wasn't what she wanted to work on, and it may have been a weak medical diagnosis. She thanked me, and said she would write a testimonial.

Three days later, she left a voicemail and stated, "Carolyn, I have to tell you something: I waited to write the testimonial, because I had to make sure, in a couple of days, that the miracle was real. I have had fibromyalgia for 10 years, and you healed it! I feel the information from my relatives from the other side healed my cells, and all the grief that was stored in them. It felt really amazing, like years of sadness lifted. I truly thank you." My intention was to help her with her life purpose, and what happened is that her *Spirit* had a different agenda. Every loss, and thought of these losses, was too much for her cells to carry. The cells closed down, but her body was screaming out in the physical. Many clients I see with fibromyaglia have unexpressed pain and grief. I never had a healing occur though, just through my words and messages. She immediately took a yoga class, with a cohort I happened to know in Detroit, and the last I heard she was starting her own business and traveling around the country. Amazing, sometimes *Spirit* had its own agenda, and you as a healer can just be present for the highest miracle to occur. I am still shocked myself. I sutured her emotions with *Spirit* messages. I wrote down her testimonial on my website, to remind myself what miracles can occur when you trust *Spirit*.

Like I mentioned, sometimes souls come in to heal their ancestor lineage pain. Tameka with being a great mom and mentor, and Aisha living the life her mother could only dream of while healing herself. It is important to learn that the most painful situation sometimes helps you, and others. There is always a seed of inspiration in a tragedy. Look for it.

Many times ancestors pass on gifts, or genetic gifts, that our elders may not have been able to finish. I believe, as I study healing, my grandmother Francis may have passed on her gift to me.

Healing Hands from Heaven

When my maternal grandmother, Francis LaMaizon Jervis, passed on, she promised me that she would come back to visit. My grandmother grew up with my family and me in my household, in New England. She was like my second mother. She was a very Spiritual woman, with a pure devotion to God, and a determined will. She had many Spiritual experiences, and even with limited education, could memorize Bible verses. We shared a lot of similarities, especially our love for angels and cats. She was an amazing healer, in her own right. One story she told me was that she was a great runner in her homeland of South America. One tragic day, she fell while running in a race. She hit the back of another athlete's shoe, and her eye was spiked by the cleat, which blinded her. Determined not to be blind the rest of her life, she prayed to God to help heal her eyes and felt a presence, miraculously she was given partial sight back. She believed, and it happened. Obviously, she was a Spiritual inspiration to me and one of my earliest teachers.

My grandmother was diagnosed with pancreatic cancer when she was 87-years-old. The most aggressive and deadliest of cancers, my family knew it wouldn't be long before she passed. Grandma, though, always promised me one thing--that she will come back to visit me after she died. When I saw my grandmother in the hospital, she didn't look like herself. Frail and thin, the smell of cancer, as it was eating away at her, had enveloped the room. It was painful for me to see, and I am sure, more painful to her.

In her final stages of the illness, unable to respond to me, I told her I loved her and I would miss her. All I could hear was her struggling with her breath. My *Spirit* told me to tell her what she had meant to me. Intuitively, I knew her *Spirit* would hear me. This was one of my last chances to express myself to her. I told her that "she taught me about unconditional love," something I was not aware of until that moment. Even though she was semi-comatose, my grandmother coughed coarsely, and tried to speak!! I interpreted this as her acknowledging what I said. I KNEW she heard me.

A couple of nights later, I had a dream about her dancing with me. She was at some kind of outside gathering ,with many elderly people and some younger people I didn't know. She was dancing, barefoot in the center of the grassing clearing (the grassy earth, and everyone being barefoot represented to me that these souls were close to returning to the earth). I remember I had shoes on. She saw me on the sidelines and ran up to me, grabbed both of my hands and pulled me onto the grassy dance floor with her, tightly holding my hands. She couldn't walk in her last days, so I knew the dream was a premonition of her soon passing, and her ability to dance when she passed to the other side. It was that morning that I got a call from my mother that she had transitioned. Her passing left a big void in my life. She was the first close family member to die. My mother was always the disciplinarian, but my grandmother was always the playful 'Ma,' with unconditional love. I wondered what she was doing, and how she was transitioning.

I was saddened, because she was gone, but it was bittersweet. My grandmother had always wanted to return 'home' as soon as she could. She had 2 near deaths experiences prior to her death. She had told me about the other side. One night, when she was in the hospital, her symptoms grew worse, and the staff called 'code blue.' The hospital staff revived her. When she came to, she said that she went to the other side and there were tons of angels around her. She stated that the angels showed her a scroll with her name at the top. She had 3 more things to do before the golden seal was put on the end of the scroll, and she would 'graduate' and pass on to the other side. The nurses thought she was hallucinating, and that she was imagining the white uniforms of nurses as angels. Funny, I don't remember nurses wearing white anymore! Mostly scrubs. My family knew that she had seen her angels.

The funeral was, of course, painful. It was the most difficult when I saw her hardened body lying in the casket. She TRULY didn't look like herself. I held onto her hands, as a reminder of our dance together, and wished her love on her journey. I admittedly felt distraught with the stone cold feelings of her hands and the lack of warmth. I wondered about her promise to me, before she died, to contact me.

My grandmother died on November 16th, and soon after my co-worker told me that she had a black kitten that needed a home. My grandmother loved cats, often feeding them outside our kitchen door, as I did as well. I thought this was a sign! My coworkers said that in another couple of weeks, the kitten would be ready to leave her litter. When I asked my coworker what day the kitten was born, I was shocked to find out it was November 16th, the same day my grandmother passed! Surely this was the sign, her sending me a black kitten, born on the day that she passed. This must be her message that "life does continue after death." I didn't realize this was only the beginning. I named my cat Lavender, as representative of that flower being an emotional healer.

A month later, I returned to my parents' home in Connecticut for Christmas. I thought about her during the holidays. That night I went to sleep and it was colder than usual that night. My bedroom was always freezing, so I tend to layer up in bed and use this old electrical heater, along with the house's heating system that always turned off during the night. That night I had a dream, and visitation. My grandmother walked out of the closet in my dream, and came up to my bed. She was heavy set, and looked healthy and she gave me a warm hug--I really felt her hug! I could feel the strength of her arms and the intensity from someone who you truly missed.

She said she came through dimensions, and was very happy where she was. She spoke telepathically, and told me things about heaven, which I barely remember, but what she said was impressed into my soul. In the background, I felt she wasn't alone and she stated she had to go, because she was still being 'adjusted.' One thing I did remember my grandmother say, "God was like a King, but like one of us." Now that is not something I would say living in the human body, or even think about. God, a king? She hugged me again, and grabbed my hands and I felt this warmth of energy penetrate into my hands. It felt so real, warm, healing, and heavenly.

When she left and I woke up, it took a long time for me to open my eyes. I wanted to keep that heavenly feeling and her warmth close in my memory. When I finally opened my eyes, I was surprised to find my covers had fallen off of me, and the heater had turned off, and my body was fairly cold, but my hands were still hot!! I held onto them, and realized it was the only warm part of my body. I ran out to my mother, and told her to feel my hands because grandmother had come to visit. My mother, who had numerous medium experiences, didn't even blink and stated, "What did you expect, she said she would!"

Grandma's healing hands from heaven helped me believe in the afterlife, with an intense physical experience. Truly, she kept her promise, and I still continue on my Spiritual journey, helping others believe in the continuity of life. As a medical social worker, I relay this story to other grieving families in the hospital, it helps to soothe their souls. Hopefully, it will do the same for you too.

She is still healing from the other side. Through all the synchronicities of her hands, in the dream with her grabbing my hands when she was dancing, at the funeral when there was no life in them, and then the visitation in my room and the heat that came from them. All these messages were synchronistic. I believe she transmitted healing energy to me, or perhaps her healing gifts. So healing was a passion I had and also inherited. It also helped me when I was drained, finding out later that I had a genetic disposition to become a healer.

Disappointment In the Universe

Sometimes the universe doesn't always feel friendly, if the earth or the universe was on a site on Facebook, at times I wouldn't be a fan. What am I talking about? How can I say that after I am teaching about how the universe can give you all you want, and you create from love and all that good stuff? I have noticed studying the human soul that not everyone gets everything they want. Sometimes, they run into something that I call nexus points. These are difficulties and painful experiences on their path that they have to hit and move through. Sad things, horrific experiences, stories that make you doubt the goodness in humanity.

Un-Model Behavior

One story involves a mother who came to see me to check up on things. I met her in Santa Barbara, where I had worked at a new age bookstore — Paradise Found, on call. The mother gave me permission to tell this story. She came in to discuss her life and situation. I gave her some various insights. She then asked me about her grown son. I don't always like to read on people's children, but she was checking in on her son who had previously had a substance abuse problem and her other son.

When I picked up information, I kept getting information on her older son. Everything I said she commented, "That is Ken, my older son" or "no, that is Ken's personality and issues." Her younger son's soul was blank to me, it was like a wall I couldn't get through. I wasn't sure what to make of it. A week later she called me to tell me that son was hit by a car and died. I was so sad, and thought she was mad I couldn't see it. But since I work with God when I do my readings, I knew God prevented me from seeing this tragedy. I am glad, because I wouldn't have told a client about a death of a child.

When I made an agreement to do this work, I said I don't want to see death, or births, meaning the time someone will give birth, or die. These two information sources always seem fuzzy to me. One client, I knew her mother was dying, but I literally could not get it out of my mouth! So, I was horrified I was so wrong and spoke to God to block my ability if he felt I was causing harm. I thought the mother would have been mad, but she agreed that she wouldn't have wanted to hear her son would be killed. Her son, Eric, was a Versace model, but was off his path. A sensitive soul, with some demons, he turned to drugs and alcohol.

His mother asked me if I could reach him. I felt uncomfortable with the whole idea, and at the time wasn't doing that much mediumship. I told her I would do it pro bono, because of the tragedy. I also thought it was too close to his death, but I was talking to her on the phone, I felt a strong presence. I heard, "I am here," and his energy was around me and through me. I kept feeling chills. I did the read, and she said, "That is him!" Within the week, she wanted his whole family, including his girlfriend, Tanya, to be in the reading. They called from Sacramento and the whole family, including his born-again Christian brother (who thought I was doing devil's work), his mother and step-father, another cousin, and Tanya. I had no idea in the room, but I told them exactly, where people were sitting, and the messages Eric wanted to give to them.

I remember Tanya was also skeptical. Tanya, strikingly beautiful Korean and white gal, had met her Soulmate in Eric. They both were drugging together and were working on getting each other clean. They had an instant and deep attraction, and through trauma bonding were able to begin to heal each other. Eric mentioned in the read, "all our losses together were tragic." I didn't know what he meant. Through their partying together and deep love, Tanya became pregnant. A week before Eric died, she had terminated the pregnancy, because of the drug use and timing. She lost a baby and the love of her life. His mother gasped, and the room fell silent, as everyone felt the sadness of losing a grandchild and a son, such loss.

Tanya also just lost a best male friend to a drug overdose the same week! She was really enraged, and not easy to read in this family parlor setting. Many insights came in during the reading from Eric. He felt unsettled, but knew he was meant to go. He felt such a pull to Tanya, it was almost unbearable, as his energy was all around me. He spoke about these beautiful balloons from friends, and was floored at the planning of the funeral. His mother didn't know about any balloons. He spoke about the work he wanted to do with kids and charities. None of this corresponded to his life as a Versace model. Tanya though confirmed his unhappiness in the modeling world, and his love and passion for helping kids. He also was really connected to music on the other side, and he brought in Jeff, Tanya's friend, who overdosed the same week that he died in the car wreck. The insights were deep. The next day, Eric's mother emailed me. His friend bought many balloons to send to the funeral, which made the final touches perfect. His mother was convinced. Eric's mother said, "I know you don't do mediumship readings a lot, but that was my son." As the reading closed, he thanked me and I felt the 'swoosh' of energy leave. I felt relieved, as I had felt I failed the mother, and God gave me the gift to say one final goodbye. Mediumship has always been challenging for me, because in grad school, I was haunted. Also working in the hospital settings, I don't want the *Spirits* to try to talk to me, so I close this energy down. I never know when someone will come through, or not.

Three strikes and you're out

Tanya though, wasn't finished. Several months later, she called to speak to Eric in private. She was skeptical, but when she sat down, Eric and Jeff swooshed into the room. She was so sad, drained, and almost suicidal. I did a reading and healing to help her through this tragedy. When I did the healing, I thought I felt energy on her second chakra that felt off. I didn't know what it was, and didn't mention it. She lost a soulmate and a baby and a best friend, so I figured her second chakras was in overdrive. To many strikes against one person at one time was overwhelming.

Tanya ended up moving in with Eric's mom for several months, as they all needed healing. She was really depressed, and I felt despondent also. Three deaths for one woman would have knocked anybody out. A month later, Eric's mother said she was thankful for my healing. I said, "Of who?" She said, "Tanya." She had a positive pap smear for maladaptive cells. Tanya didn't mention it to me, and now I knew what I felt. Eric's mother told me that after she went back to the OB/GYN after my healing, the cells were fine, and had miraculously gone back to normal. I felt the creator, through me, was giving her a gift. Tanya later found another nice guy, and became a good producer for major projects. She keeps in touch, and is one of my favorite clients.

She has a funny sense of humor, and a good heart. She flies back and forth from New York to California, so I like working with her New York direct humor. I am glad with healing and insight, she has gotten through that God awful tragedy. She still misses her soulmate, but has dated some other guys since the tragedy. She didn't give up though and still perserveres.

I have heard them all. Like the story above, a beautiful 30-years-old male who just met his soulmate, and after years of substance abuse, finally pulled his life together and was killed by a hit and run driver. A woman who surrounded herself with animals, after she found out her father was a pedophile, so she decided to save other vulnerable souls, abused animals. I have heard of the woman who spent years creating a wonderful movie project, only to have it stolen right from under her to become a major blockbuster. The stories are devastating to hear and experience, but I have trained myself to hear and listen to the soul lesson in the midst of the sadness. Why, you ask? Why these ironic and senseless tragedies? For the growth of the human soul, which is here on earth to grow. That is why we are here, to gain Spiritual attributes to our soul belt that can grow and expand and hold more light. This earth is really an illusion and not our true home. If you do work with your own gifts there will be a lot more good times than bad times, but that cannot be guaranteed. The big honcho upstairs has the divine script, the whole movie, and the ending. Sometimes intuitives, like me, hear a message from your higher self or other guides, that we can help you understand. On the Spiritual path, sometimes, you must learn to ACCEPT WHAT IS, that is that you have done the work, and have been kind and listened to your soul and something happens that helps other people. I will give you an example:

Since I have been working for the universe for several years, I never know who might come to me, where my next assignment will be, or what will come next. I have had many great opportunities. People can say a lot of things about me, but almost everyone knows with all the various sites I work, I am hardworking. I always have multiple jobs, doing multiple things. I worked in hospitals, and psychiatric facilities, usually two, never full time. I work in a private practice doing healings and readings, and also teach classes. Usually the universe arranges my schedule so everything fits in place, but I tend to be very busy, yes, I am a SOULaholic*. Soulaholics feel like the work to evolve their soul, or the soul of others, is more important than anything else. They often think about karma and choices, looking at everything through the lens of Spirituality. It can lead them to working incredible hours, mostly giving of their heart and time, and sometimes never seeming tired. I felt happy doing my work, my part in helping down here, listening to universal wisdom, and transmitting messages to those who need it. I was at peace with my work, or so I thought.

CHAPTER

8 Dharma or Karma

DHARMA IS an individual's duty, fulfilled by observance of custom or law, and conformity to one's duty and nature. Karma is the energy that what you sow, you will reap. Since I was working with the universe, being ethical and hardworking, I didn't expect anything so tragic to happen to me. Then the universe throws me a curveball. This experience taught me there are triumphs, and tragedies, on your path.

After that crazy job, being kicked out of the darkness, and promoted by the Universe, I had to deal with the fact that I did need surgery on my uterus. My fibroids were very large, and I had done various holistic things to help them to shrink. Women in my family, going back three generations, had massive fibroids though. I decided to get a myomectomy, by a surgeon that was recommended to me. I had avoided it for a year and a half, as I didn't want to lose my job, my health insurance, my ability to have children, or my dignity--that was too much for women of color, like me, who have struggled to feel accepted and valuable in life. I also didn't want the system to win in devaluing who I was.

I had saved a good amount of money, and wanting to have a child, I went to a private MD, with high regards. I was labeled as self-pay, even though the surgery was done in the hospital, but in a different area. Everything went wrong. I was labeled 'self-pay,' by mistake, to the nursing and hospital staff, who interpreted that as me having no rights, it somehow meant that I didn't deserve any respect.

I woke up, post- surgery, in the recovery room, after a 5 hour uterine surgery, this hospital made multiple mistakes. The nasty and lazy nurse let me 'bleed out' of my Jackson Pratt bag, so the chux sheet was covered in blood when I woke up. I felt like I was a gunshot wound victim. I was horrified. The nurse laughed at me while she was cleaning me up. She thought it was a joke, and for some reason let me sit in the blood. This was when I was on heavy anesthesia, and could barely open my eyes. I called out to the woman who looked like she was in charge asking, "Are you the charge nurse?" She looked horrified when she saw the blood around me on the chux sheets on the bed. I was saturated in blood.

My heart rate sky rocketed, so they had to put me in the cardiac care unit, because the doctor whispered to me that "he didn't trust the nurses on the other unit." What does that mean? Should I trust them? Not really supportive of my feelings of safety. I was shocked that I was admitted, because the MD said it was an easy outpatient procedure, but he never really did a full exam on me, and I had brought x-rays from my previous ultrasounds. I have no idea why this MD never did a full exam, but I was ok, because I don't really like male OB/GYNS. How a cardiac oncology surgeon didn't do a thorough exam, I don't know. Yes, I should have known better, but he is the expert right? They gave me Percocet, even though my red arm band said I was allergic to Percocet so I kept throwing up! They took forever to get my 3 bags of transfusion blood, so at one point I woke up FREEZING, deathly cold , when all the blood ran out of my body, so close to death, that I know what it is like to die, bleeding out. When I asked for covers, or something else, I seemed like a nuisance, a pain in the ass. When they changed the Jackson Pratt bag, from me bleeding out, the nurse didn't use gloves, so I became septic. They didn't put the sequential compression devices on my legs, post-surgery. I had to ask them after I had enough consciousness post surgical. They attempted to give me a vq scan twice in an hour, until I told them I already had that procedure. I felt like an extra person filling up a bed, which I didn't deserve.

After my first surgery, the doctor was concerned about the amount of blood leakage into the Jackson Pratt bag. He offered me two decisions: a hysterectomy or an embolisation by an urologist. The embolisation was to be awake, but under light sedation. I didn't want to be in so much pain already, and have surgery, and then I didn't want to go back under anesthesia. Besides not wanting a hysterectomy at 38, I also knew I wouldn't survive another dose of anesthesia. I knew I wouldn't survive another surgery. Don't ask me why, but a voice in my head told me not to do it.

I agreed to the embolization, with this disgusting sexist and degrading urologist. He kept trying to talk me out of the surgery with his tall dominating stance. He kept talking all of the medical goobley-gook. Thank God, I worked with doctors so they don't intimidate me. He even talked about how this surgery would ruin my sexual lifestyle, that I wouldn't have an orgasm. He actually said that several times, in front of my family. Everyone was shocked and didn't understand what that has to do with me having children, shocking how many misogynist doctors are in the hospital. I felt very vulnerable because if I said no, I would get a hysterectomy, but if I said yes, I had this misogynist doctor operating on my uterus; and I would be awake. I was stuck between a rock and a nightmare.

That whole conversation was completely disrespectful to a woman, but a lot of health care professionals have little respect for patients, women, people of color, people without insurance, high risk issues, I could go on. I think, even drugged out, I can spot a liar a mile away.

My Aries temper was rising, I was like *what the hell*, now you think I really wanted surgery with a local anesthesia with doctor misogynist. I really wanted to take the scalpel, shave off his balls, and have a woman surgeon say to him what he said to me, but I needed the surgery. I was enraged.

There were multiple times he and the nurse were making fun of me, because they were too lazy to do the surgery. Remember I was self-pay and my HUEmaness didn't help either. Thank God, they gave me a strong anesthesia, because I couldn't feel anything, but I really didn't want to have his energy around me, especially not in that area, but I did want the potential to have children. When you are in the hospital, sick and medicated, you are very vulnerable. It is easy for abuse to happen, and unfortunately, because the hospital has become a business, and businesses tend not to be sensitive, abuse happens all too often. As a medical social worker, I see and hear it all the time. The complaints about doctors, nurses, and treatment come to social services. I wasn't prepared for this rude behavior, because one of the primary hospitals I work for was so liability oriented that I rarely see that kind of blatant rudeness, sloppiness from nurses or medical personnel, and especially not to patients. Though I have heard stories. I just wasn't prepared.

When I finally had the embolization, there was a large angel over the operating table protecting me. The surgery was successful, as the doctor and nurse snickered at me. But the abuse didn't stop, the urologist reminded me they needed to ambulate me the next morning. He said it to me three times. The next morning after two uterine surgeries, I was incredibly weak and in SEVERE pain. The morphine was worthless. The worse experience was when a nurse yelled at me that she was too tired to 'get me out of bed,' because she was busy. This East Coast hospital had an insane rule that nurses in ICU get 5 patients, per shift. In ICU (the intensive care unit) on the West Coast, it is two... so this inexperienced nurse figured she can leave me without ambulating, post-surgery, after the MD told her twice to do it, and the urologist once, to get me out of bed. She told me she didn't have the time, at 6 a.m., and being on morphine, I didn't have the energy to fight and the time lapses feel different when you are medicated on morphine.

'I Can't Breathe'

Around 3 p.m., I wasn't sure what was occuring, but I couldn't breathe. I knew something bad was happening, the bad nurse checked my saturation level on the oxygen, and it was 50%, that is when I was rushed down to get a VQ scan, and found out that I had 3 blood clots. These blood clots could have killed me, or left me with a stroke. Blood clots! Only the elderly this happens to, or because of neglect.

I then realized I was a victim of **hospitalcide**--this is when hospitals commit homicide, or shotty bad treatment on patients, because they are too expensive, no insurance, or their health issues are not considered serious. Even the night after the embolization, a resident came into the hospital and said, "Haha, you are the train wreck, we were talking about you in rounds." My near death was funny. I called her, because I had this extreme pain that radiated from the center of my uterus out to my ovaries after the embolization. It was an intense painful feeling; I was already on pain meds. So the nasty resident told the nurse to give me another pain medication dose, and you won't believe this one, *the nurse actually left me in pain, and said that I didn't need the pain meds and went against Dr. orders.* Her actions were sociopathic, so I had to hold my tongue and use a method I learned from a holistic healer-- that eased the pain in the uterus and for cramps so it worked...but the fact that the nurse left me in pain,

I will never forget that--it was cruel and inhumane. I didn't want to confront her, because I was vulnerable and working in hospitals, I see how the staff works when you confront them, they get more passive aggressive. Plus, I was in a lot of pain, so my defenses were down. I started documenting everything, because I had to. When I woke up the 2nd time from the surgery, the MD said, "You probably won't ever have children." The meanness and callousness of doctors never fails to surprise me. I could barely open my eyes. After the blood clot, the staff got me on heparin, but just barely. Their sloppiness almost killed me.

To be a layperson in the hospital, and seeing everything they were doing wrong was like being on an episode of *American Horror Story*. I knew exactly what they were doing wrong. The name of the hospital was Holy Cross, and boy, did I feel I was being crucified. In some ways it may have been an initiation to my true path or a higher path. I say that after I read an article by Lissa Rankin MD, "*10 Signs You Are a Shaman and You Don't Know it*." I identified strongly with, "1. You sense that you're meant to participate in the global shift in consciousness that is currently underway. 2. You've been through a difficult initiation, which has prepared you for this leadership role." There are ten other signs, like feeling sensitive, or being in home in nature, I highly recommend this article. Well this was surely an initiation of some sorts! What bothered me the most is that I worked so hard in the hospital, I wasn't like other people I see really lazy, barely doing their work. Sometimes, I would cover the whole hospital on the weekend; I would be the only social worker there and would still be very thorough.

Since no one can honestly call me lazy, why did I almost get killed in the hospital after I had given so much to others? A nexus point, a lesson from God, or the universe, or something I attracted in. I know at that point, I wasn't a fan of the universe. What you give out comes back. What you reap, you sow, right? My soul had a different plan... the night before in the hospital, when the blood clot was probably festering...I had a profound out of body experience. I was lying there exhausted, and in a lot of pain. I realized, all of the sudden, I saw stars, like I was in the cosmos. I felt free and light and was floating around the galaxy, it felt normal. I saw this being, a man, standing in the middle of the universe, he appeared to be some sort of gatekeeper. I moved towards him at lightning speed. He looked like a court jester to me, with a funny hat, but more serious and neutral. I pressed, it looked like a big glowing button, and this screen transmitted information to me about my life. The man told me I could not go any further, and when I asked, he showed me what I needed to do on earth.

I felt shock in my mind and heart, that I had not accomplished anything. I clearly felt like I was in kindergarten. *Oh, I have to go back*, I thought, but before I did I asked to see God. The court jester wouldn't let me go to the light, but it seemed like Source seemed to hear my request. I felt God's presence all around me, above me, and in me. It appeared to be God. I realized that he was the universe. I was living in God's energy field, his aura, and I was a part of it. God was the stars, the air, the galaxy, everything. I feel like we are all living in God's auric field. This energy force seemed to know everything about me. I couldn't make this being mad, or disappoint him, it made absolutely no sense, and was non-negotiable. *I had* to go back, my soul wanted to complete my mission.

When I came back into my body, there was a lot of beings around me in the hospital bed, they were talking to me, and trying to get my attention. I couldn't understand why there was a crowd in my hospital room. This one woman, named Diane, came up to me, it was a while before I realized that she, and the others were ghosts and deceased, because they looked real to me. She said that she was killed erroneously from hospital errors. Many of the other people agreed to that, and said it happened to them too. That had pleaded with me to do something, to help them. I was a bit frustrated and angry, there I was ill and sick and post-surgery, in the hospital, and I was still doing spiritual social work! I didn't promise them anything, I just told them to go away, because I had to heal.

When I came back into my body though, I remember there was no line between dimensions. There was no darkness, meaning that when I closed my eyes I didn't see black, I saw the past when I blinked my eyes, I saw the present, and when I blinked my eyes again, I saw the future. It was amazing, and spooky. I kept blinking my eyes to see past, present, and future, but no darkness. I would tell the nurse what she was going to say, and tell her when she left the room that she would come back and say it. It freaked the nurse out, she dismissed it as medication, and I think they upped my medication to shut me up, but I know what I saw, felt, and experienced. My ability to see past, present, and future increased incredibly, but it was never the same as it was at that moment, when there was no darkness, when I was closer to the other side, where there was no time.

I was still angry at the universe, and God, for what had happened to me. I had been working so hard, and getting abused and neglected at the hospital, I almost met my death in the hospital, a place where I have given so much.

This was a soul question for me: why did this happen? I did go to the other side briefly, and was able to gain some Spiritual energy. I remembered when I got my aura picture taken shortly after this incident, it was all white light around me, probably energy that I pulled from the other side. My healing sessions do appear to have gotten deeper, a lot of clients tune out and go into a trance, and wake up at the end of the session. God had a plan. In that hospital, the death rate of people with pulmonary embolisms, at that particular hospital was probably about 80%! I found it on some internet site--Health Grades. The people that had come to me were the dead people that were killed for no reason. I also filed every report possible to the Department of Public Health, and also JCAHO. I sent JCAHO and Public Health in the southern state a summary of what happened, to let them know step-by-step the 18 huge mistakes the hospital had made. The nurse from Public health called me back and talked to me for 2 hours!!! Without asking, a nurse on the CCU unit actually gave me the names of all the nurses and MD's involved and encouraged me to report them. She stated, "that was neglect. " Than I knew that she knew that blood clot could have been prevented. Trying to sue this facility for abuse and neglect was to no avail, as the primary doctor mocked me. He mocked me on the phone to "sue me, sue me," when I called the MD back about the sloppy and abusive behavior he wouldn't take my calls. He knew. His surgery was $3,000, he charged me $1,200--he knew. Many lawyers I spoke to in this southern state, stated, "You are you black, and because of that, your case would never win, especially not down here--hospitals, surgeons, and doctors are local and the law would defend their own," they all told me. So I didn't call risk management, I was too traumatized. They made way too many obvious, and careless mistakes. So as a social worker, I have to report bad treatment at skilled nursing facilities. I began to realize why God may have put me there.

My insurance didn't cover it, and my bill was $30k. I did go out of my network, but at the same facility, in another state. I spoke to the administrator at the hospital, and she sounded very annoyed, "Ms. Coleridge, do you know how many meetings we had about you? We had at least 12 meetings about you, and all your complaints." I said, "Miss Administrator, you almost killed me! You are acting like my life doesn't matter!" She barked back, "We have better things to do, than to have meetings about you!" I retorted, "Well maybe my life doesn't matter to you, but it does to me! My black life matters." She gasped, "What Ms. Coleridge?" I snorted back, "Have a nice day, Miss Administrator, and a nice life time."

I got a $30 K bill and realized I basically paid for a murder attempt, hospital style. It took me a good 6 months to heal from the surgery, and calling those lawyers was physically exhausting. Funny, I couldn't even breathe while talking to them. I also had to wear a cast because my arm had been so badly infiltrated that it swelled to two times its size and had to take louvenox shots and was on coumadin. I also had to go to OT for several months to get my arm working well again.When I was first out of the hospital, I couldn't watch TV, either, especially the ads with pharmaceutical drugs, anything that wasn't pure, or for the highest good, exhausted me. My dip in eternal light made me see things differently. I had to get candles and healing music, and would repeat Sanskrit chants, things that were light, positive healing ,and holistic energized me, anything else drained me. It took me a while to figure out what this lesson was about. What was very strange is that when I came back to my sister's house to heal, I felt like I was still in the hospital. I would have dreams of being in the cardiac care unit, with the ineffective hospital staff in my room with me. It was deeper than trauma, since a part of my soul was stuck in the hospital, the part that had been traumatized. I now understand on a personal level, what it feels like and means to lose a part of your soul. I learned how a part of you gets stuck, and you are frozen at that time. Most people think I am that age, when that trauma happened. Soul retrieval, or losing a part of your soul, is deep because you miss a part of your soul essence.

When I read a client, I can always tell the age of someone when some tragedy happened. I can somehow see into that dimension, where the soul essence resides. I asked a client from Istanbul once, what happened to you at 4 and 7, and she looked stunned. She had come in to deal with her difficulty with finding a good relationship. She said that is when my dad left, came back, and then left again. The trauma was still in her body. I picked it right up. She had come in to discuss her difficulty with connecting in relationships with men. We were able to change some beliefs attached to that time period. She found somebody briefly, and then I lost track of her. The healing was profound, as she has pictures or memories of her dad leaving appear before her, that she didn't remember. She also remembered Dad saying, "It was not you honey." It was these words that she had never remembered before. Every time she had relationships that didn't work, the men would say to her, "it is not you honey." This traumatic event was stored in her cellular memory field, and kept playing itself out, because it was a hidden belief, meaning her father leaving the house was not her fault. During any trauma, or difficulty, we have a choice of what reaction we can have, whether it is hate, anger, rage, or acceptance, or guilt, forgiveness. Our reaction and choice as to these very difficult situations helps our SOUL to grow, expand, and move closer to the light. Light is knowledge, and the more knowledge we obtain from difficult situations the higher our SOUL expands.

What Spiritual qualities did I obtain? **Strength and Forgiveness.** Having survived a murder attempt, hospitalcide style, created out of sloppiness and neglect, I took that anger and rage and turned it into real compassion to my clients in the hospital I worked for. I have had patients complain about the multiple mistakes that were made, and I can truly say, "Yes, I have been there," and I was able to somehow help them in the situation. When a woman who had a tragic surgery, and the doctor minimized and ridiculed her pain after a double masectomy, I didn't defend the insensitive doctor's flippant rudeness, I agreed with her and told my story: "I understand, this is what happened to me..." I never defend a company or physician that was wrong, I tell the clients their rights, and offer true compassionate empathy. Not superficial bullshit, company policy standard rules, that I told them: it was on the East Coast, and part of the story that was relevant, like a mean nurse who refused to give me my pain meds, and took it herself. I am really assured of divine retribution. It is not God making a list of what we do, and then when the time is right, slam dunking us with some ugly karma. *It is energy, and what you put out comes back to you.* You may never see when, where, or how, but energy returns to its source. Being positive is not about a silly Pollyanna type reality, it is about understanding physics and energy.

The true reason of the hospital death, I probably won't know until I get to the other side, but I did hear God's voice when I asked him a question about why this experience happened in the hospital. God gave me an answer. His thoughts were in my thoughts. The voice was in my head, and sounded like a voice I knew so well, and had heard before, the same energy that expanded around the universe, as the universe and star, when I almost died, the same voice that spoke through that messenger when I was 27-years-old, that no matter where I go, or what I do, I am never alone! It was an opening into my own consciousness. I won't repeat it, because I only see a small part of his prediction has come to pass, but he did gave me a SOUL assignment. Of course, it made me even more sensitive to peoples' treatment in the hospital.

It was a long time later that I realized that I learned the lesson was one of **forgiveness**, this was a soul lesson on a very deep level. Forgiveness can be minimal, or very large. Forgiveness is a huge energy on the planet to help your soul move forward in life. It is not easy when you have a $30,000 hospital bill, and I did pay it off on a freelance salary, and it only took about three years. Paying for neglect and abuse doesn't sit right. Strength and forgiveness are two of the big energies I had to work on, in this incident and in this life. Many people work on these lessons. Jesus, a great master of transforming the earth plane through his life, taught a huge lesson in forgiveness.

If you don't resonate with Jesus, pick a master teacher, or any person whose story you resonate with. It could be Buddha, Krishna, or Mother Teresa. I was speaking to this lady on the airplane; we were both speaking about Spiritual lessons and belief systems. She was Jewish, and helping to build summer programs for children to keep her culture alive. We were both talking about forgiveness, from different perspectives, regarding something tragic that happened in the media. She said to me, "Why Jesus? He was just a Jew." I said, "Yes, he was, but with a really good publicist and agents, 12 of them, no less." We both laughed heartily, and connected on the humor, in just knowing we both knew of this being, but had very different viewpoints about him. Pick your own guru, but model after a person who has transcended the earthly existence, and has inspired you on a deep level.

These are what I call nexus points, a point on the stage of life, a mark you must hit (things that I probably needed to hit to help the others). The CNN video, which showed healing in hospitals, has inspired people to receive energy healing. Many healers have put it on their websites. In some ways, it puts positive energy into hospitals, and possibilities. Or maybe I created this. I won't know until I climb back home. My sister did say, "You seemed sooo nervous, before the surgery, more nervous than I ever saw you." Maybe, my soul knew before the surgery that something tragic would happen. I remember when working around the hospital, prior to this incident, and I saw the word 'pulmonary embolism' in some elderly persons chart, the word looked so familiar to me. When I asked a nurse she said, "Oh, don't worry, you are too young for that." But it was like déjà vu, the word looked familiar to me. It was clearly something I had seen before. Your soul knows, it remembers.

CHAPTER

9 An Application to the Universe

WE ALL have a path, and if you are on the path of your own soul's evolution, than you will be motivated to do something that helps the planet, helps others, and does as much not to harm others. As I mentioned, when I worked for an environment that was very toxic, leaving the environment, I heard a voice in my head that said *why don't you work for me.* When I questioned the voice, it repeated the statement. *Why don't you work for me?* I knew the voice, as you would know your own parents voice. It was that of the Divine.

My first impression was, how is this voice in my head, and all around, me at the same time? It was like his thoughts were in my thoughts, but separate. We all hear God's message, the question is whether it is something that you recognize and acknowledge, or will you be able move forward doing what you hear. God's voice can also be our gut instinct. I asked the voice how, and there was no answer, the voice actually moved away, and I was left with my own thoughts. I then thought about it, in severe honesty, and almost humored the voice, and said, "Ok, I accept." Then the voice said, "The pay is good, the work is steady, and the retirement benefits are out of this world." The voice humored me back in this satirical stream of consciousness. I felt a sense of peace. My friend April helped me pack up my stuff, in my car, and I couldn't understand what I was going to do or how I was going to do it. Before I could ask God how I was going to support myself without a full time job, he impressed upon me, as a demand, command, and request: "Honor *your Spirit*." I knew in my SOUL, I didn't belong there at that clinic. I don't do well with putting up with abuse, I knew they weren't respecting me, or honoring me.

Another important thing to know if you are pushed out of a situation where you feel you were contributing to the good of the organization, is that you may not belong there. Lightworkers can sometimes be challenging because their light shines the truth on the darkness. Also, whistleblowers, or people who stand for what is right, are always a problem when people are shady. God can see the whole plan, and there may be a bigger assignment for you elsewhere that you are not aware of yet. God sees your whole life plan, we see just a segment. If people don't respect you, and you're doing good, they don't know you. I teach this spiritual redirection in the work stress class in a major HMO, where I teach meditation, and also an after care group called Plan P. Plan P is "What is your Purpose."

I went to Agape church on Sunday, and Rev. Michael hammered in a message about working for God, and signing the song, "Use Me," and the realization hit: we are simply here for God. Suddenly, everything made sense to me. I thought to myself, *is this what Rev. Michael means about "we are here for God,"* I didn't quite put it together, because my logical earth mind felt: "I need to pay my rent, and get something stable," but my *Spirit* said, "TRUST." The music at Agape was inspirational, and so moving that it feels like you can do anything. Now, I could put this inspiration to a test. Something in my heart felt it was right. Was this more of the same message by Jesus, walk by faith, and not by sight. Be careful where you get your Spiritual knowledge, you will be influenced subliminally, and directly.

So I left my job, with expensive health insurance, a 10 cm tumor, a bit demoralized, but I wasn't going to let these losers, or lost souls, win. My friend, Jaina, checked in on me. She is an intuitive herself. She and I became friends in New York when we were in a mini-intuitive support group. Since we had become close, we decided to never read for each other, because it gets too confusing. She is a much more accomplished reader than I. She said, "You will be alright, I see you working in a lot of different jobs, freelancing." We both had lost all of our incomes from the material world, and had to depend on the Spiritual world. This was a lesson in **Trust**.

Her lesson with a crazy shaman who I warned her about, he stole her money; and my life in the corporate world. Jaina had grown up an orthodox Jew, and she left that religion when her psychic abilities had picked up. Her whole family was incredibly intuitive. When I was working at the predominantly Jewish owned firm, on Wall Street, with a corner office, she was working in Brownsville, a rough area of Brooklyn, teaching Haitian first graders. We laughed that we had each other's jobs. She would help me understand sensitivity, about her culture, and I would educate her on West Indian culture. She had called me out of the blue, though, and told me to get out of the job. Since we didn't really read for each other, I knew it was a warning. Jaina chimed in, "Your boss is really racist, and he resents you. He is also trying to figure out a way to fire you." Jaina also stated, "He has been sued for racial harassment before, and he is threatened by your intelligence. His whole family is really racist, for generations. He gets a thrill out of humiliating black people."

Don't you know, later, I went out with a group of black professionals and another woman, upon hearing my story, said, "I think I know this guy, and he was allegedly sued for racial harassment." This was the second message for me. *But God knew that would push my buttons enough, that I would have to leave and I believe source wanted to use me elsewhere.* That supervisor and job were toxic but the dark side is addicted to power and uses the dirty tactics I had mentioned before: lies, manipulation, deception, cruelty, abuse--that is their bag of tricks. The hardest thing is that my health problems were acting up. The stress of the work situation surely made my health problems accelerate. My experience though has helped many other take spirit oriented changes that were for a higher good.

Then things started to fall into place. Work freelance, and not for a company, work your heart's desire, and not what looks good. Honor your *Spirit*. I decided to work on my own, not easy when you have $600 a month in student loans that you have to repay, from grad school, alone! $300 car note, and tons of other debts, including rent, but remember I was gifted $5000. Many clients began to call me that month for Spiritual advice, information, and readings. I worked on the weekends in the hospital, and then did readings and Spiritual coaching during the week. I made $1,500 that month, and with my weekend work, was able to pay my bills. Every month, the money increased just slightly, and I was feeling this work could really take off. During that time, I did very little advertising. The universe was sending me clients. So many clients would say, "I am glad I found you. Just in the nick of time, you really helped me." Or "Your messages were God sent." To me, that information was a message, from God, that this work really was God's work, and I really was working for him. I also had conflict doing readings, and all the negative press about intuitive readings, healings etc., but as a trained therapist, I saw the change in people after they were inspired. God said to me, with intuition, "Go with your heart." My heart loved to sit, and read, and do research about other dimensions, metaphysics, and other Spiritual topics. These events came to me as the ghosts showed themselves to me. It was like I fulfilled a position that was somehow waiting for me. I liked doing it, was not drained, and it felt fulfilling. I thought, *I should have been doing this all along.* I realized then, I wasn't getting kicked out of my job, but promoted by the universe, and fulfilling my mission. That is why sometimes a divorce from an abusive spouse is a gift. Or a car accident that puts you on disability, so you can write that music you always wanted, these things may be a wake-up call.

Applying to work for the universe is an easy process. No resumes are needed, and you don't need references. You don't have to go through someone's secretary to set up an appointment. Working for the universe doesn't mean you need to give up your job with benefits, as long as it is fulfilling to you. What it means is that you are doing your heart's work, and also fulfilling your mission. Usually your purpose is something that fulfills your heart. What does that mean?

So many people negate their heart, for their head. The planet is shifting though, and when so many systems are breaking down, it is forcing individuals to move with their heart. Health care costs are out of control, and can easily cause bankruptcy, if you don't have insurance, and even if you do have it. Some drugs, for major diagnoses, are very expensive. We are a consumer society, and we buy so much that we don't need, then we become unfulfilled inside, but externally look successful. Heart focus work is about something that 1) makes us feel good, 2) we love doing it all day long. 3) We felt called to do it, or are passionate about the work, 4) something that piques your interest, and 5) we feel inspired, and fulfilled, when we do it.

The illness that helps you become more holistic for your health is a blessing. It may be a Spiritual redirection*. I thought to myself that maybe I should be a healer, and realized that working in a hospital setting with patients was draining for me. I realized that they were taking my energy. I also realized as a sensitive healer, my energy conflicted with the harsh energy of the hospital. I also remember what my boss said to me years ago, when I worked on Wall Street, "Your energy changed the energy in the room." On the Spiritual path, you will get words of wisdom that stir your soul, and leave *an impression.* Pay attention to these subtle messages, the messages that stir your mind and makes you reflect. Most likely, you are connecting to your destiny. I was always wondering, *how did I change a room's energy?* What is energy? As a social worker, or therapist, you learn about energy very quickly, as we need to tune into our clients and what they may need.

When I learned more deeply about it, and after I had sent that client a Reiki energy symbol, I realized that there is always an energy exchange. One experience builds on another. I was doing readings and Spiritual coaching during the week, and some healings. I remember saying out loud, "Maybe I should be a healer, God." I didn't realize he has his ears primed to my requests. While I was doing healing at Agape, I bumped into this woman named Cindi and she got me to work for the UCLA Pediatric Pain Program like I mentioned before..Working for the program was on a volunteer basis, and we had rounds at UCLA every Wednesday, at noon. What about a full time job? After being screwed over by, and not supported by staff, I felt it was safer for me to work for myself and the Universe.

As a hard core Aries, and an overgrown *Indigo** adult, I don't work well in environments that are out of integrity, and abusive. I couldn't give this *Spirit* driven opportunity up. I couldn't get a full time job when my schedule was chopped up on Wednesdays at noon. It was such a gift to be part of this program and the universe provided my needs with clients. When I worked in Manhattan, years ago, I fantasized and visualized myself working in a team approach, and doing speeches on visualization and meditation. It was years later when it happened, but it did. Seeing clients for readings privately, out of my home, doing healings at UCLA, and I also felt I should be speaking more, and was soon set up with various speeches. I was writing, and had other opportunities to perform for events, or on television. These dramas made me really learn how to trust. *I also had to develop my Spiritual muscles of asking and receiving, trusting and having faith, praying and meditating.* The universe was my employer, and it always kept me busy. It honestly was a privilege.

This is when I started my per diem (per freedom) work. I use the word 'per freedom' because the medical social work job gave me the freedom to pursue my passion for three reasons: 1) It was close to my house. I was about 7 minutes away, and I hate commuting in Los Angeles traffic. 2) It paid well, for years, I could pay my rent and some bills on only 2 to 3 days work, and occasionally, I would work weekends intermittently. Sometimes, I would work more and sometimes, less, but it always seemed to work out financially. 3) Work was light, it wasn't that challenging in the hospital. Since much hospital work is based on the medical model, social workers roles are greatly limited. Also there is a limitation on what kind of counseling you can do in the hospital, when there is family and multiple disciplines vying for the patients' attention. Since I was on call, I could not work if I didn't want to, or work if I wanted to. 4) It taught me about my craft. Many healers would never go to a hospital, never mind working in one, but I can speak honestly on the pros and cons of medical and alternative treatment. I have seen the numerous problems of hospital care, and also the positive aspects of Western medicine.

Working in the hospital taught me about the human body, medications, side effects, limitations of health care--the healing and non-healing aspects, liabilities in treatment, and so many other things, so there were many lessons and limitations, but since I wasn't that invested in the system it gave me the energy to go and fulfill my purpose. I was invested in the patients, though. Over 10 years I worked on call, with no full time job, just various gigs, at various hospitals, and my private work. I was working for the Universe and, as God promised, the pay was good, the work was steady, and the retirement benefits are out of this world.

If you are not sure about your path, apply to the universe. It can't hurt. The Universe will not take away your full time work, unless it is off your path and YOU don't want it. Sometimes the universe will have to be VERY dramatic to get you back on your path. Your *Spirit* and God made a contract, before you came here. The universe's plan is to help you fulfill your destiny. The universe always wants to get your attention, and sometimes it can be in a very overwhelming way. If anything, it will clarify what you really need. Your *Spirit* knows why you are here. As I fulfill my purpose, I feel I am paying into my karma bank by helping others grow, learn, and trust. I haven't seen my retirement package, but I feel it is good, and in the universe is a feeling energy that is the only measure that you have. I did take a part time job with full benefits after the 10 years stint. Insurance was expensive and as I needed the coverage without a high premium. I am doing therapy again with a spiritual twist and the response of patients has been overwhelmingly positive. The Universe will give you essentials on your path, without a lot of stress, lies or manipulations to get it.

My Office

As I began this work for the universe, and freelancing for God, I developed a class called *Dialoguing with the Universe.* There, I would teach people how to connect to the universe and start communication. I would also help them become aware that the universe is constantly broadcasting information to them to help them create their purpose. It is like a sun beaming information. First, I started with Spiritual Life coaching classes in my home, which was a lot of work to clean, and move things around. I would fit from 8 to 12 people in my apartment. I always check in with God, to see if I am following my path. It was a lot of people in my personal space. I felt there must be a better way. Shortly thereafter, I got a knock on the door and the landlord in my apartment building said that there was a pipe problem, and they had to break through my apartment wall to fix the plumbing. This called for the extensive work of opening up the walls and tearing down the pipes. First, it was the whole bathroom wall they would tear down, and then my whole kitchen wall. This was very inconvenient, as I had been running my classes in my place. The offices around where I lived in Mid-Wilshire were extremely expensive. I told the manager that I saw clients for coaching in my place. She was aware, "I always smell incense coming from your space," she said, "Well, you can use the apartment next door, as I know that this inconvenience will affect your work."

The apartment next to mine had been vacant for some time in the slow economy, where many weren't renting. I accepted the offer, and I just happened to have an extra kitchen table that I had used for an extended desk in my home, and was able to put it in the apartment next door, for my coaching and reading table. I also moved my massage table into the bedroom, which created a healing room. The living room in the new vacant apartment was my meditation room. I purchased some large pillows to put in there as meditation mats. With nothing in the apartment, but a few items, the energy in this new place was very clear and clean. It was great!

Ironically, a year before there was a hole between my wall and the apartment next door, as the pipe problem had started on that side. I was able to see into my neighbor's apartment, who was a musician for a major film director. I would look through the hole in that wall, and think, "Boy, this would make a nice healing center." I dreamt about what it would be like to have an extended apartment, and then let the daydream go. I didn't believe it would happen, but loved daydreaming about it. Then with no attachment to this idea, it happened, no attachment in the Spiritual manifestation process really helps something to occur.

About 4 weeks later, the repair job was done, but I was loving my new 'office' space. On a whim, I asked the landlord if I could use this apartment as an office. She said, "Well no one has ever asked that before, and we have never done that." I, again, let it go thinking it would never happen, but at the same time keeping the energy neutral. Within two days, the manager spoke to the landlord and said, "The landlord says 'yes,' but how much do you want to pay?" I almost fell over in my tracks--here I was in Miracle mile across from LACMA, in a high rent district, and she asked *me* what the going rate for office rent is?!

This renovated apartment rented for $1,500. My unrenovated large one bedroom rented for $1,250 so I said, "I don't know $250 a month," and she said, "OK!!" So, I rented the apartment next door for only $250 per month, a large renovated one bedroom. My wifi worked with my computer, because it was right next door. I had an extra phone, which I put in the room next door, so when people buzzed up I didn't have to leave my apartment to let them in. I was renting 2 apartments worth about $2,700 for only $1,500--the universe answered my question of where should I be teaching classes. Yes, you are to do classes, and here is your space. Since the room was bare, the meditations went really deep. I saw a lot of clients, and built up my clientele, because now I had a space. I was able to stay in that space for 8 months!

One of my friends, who was fear oriented, felt I was doing something illegal, and thought I was colluding with a shady landlord. I was nervous as she put this pill of fear in my head. I asked for assurance from the universe, as I always want to stay in integrity (working with the Universe, you must keep your integrity, or else things will backfire). The next day I went to the gym and my saw my neighbor, who used to live in that exact apartment I was leasing. I hadn't seen her in months. We exchanged formalities, and right away she asked, "Did they rent the apartment next to you." I was told not to talk about this arrangement, by my landlord, with anyone, so I kept a poker face. She then said, "Well, I am having a dispute with the management, I moved out because of the smoke. As an actress, it affects my voice. They want me to pay the rent for the broken lease, but if they rented it, then I have no obligation. Did they rent it... is someone living there?" she inquired.

Well, I wasn't lying and told her, "No one is *living* there." But I was *working* there, there was my answer from the universe, why they let me rent this apartment on the down low. The management couldn't rent it, or they would lose the money, and the legal battle with the tenant who broke her lease. What are the chances I would see her at the gym and hear the story?! I never saw her again, and my heart was assured that the universe set this up.

At the end of the 8 months, they wanted the apartment back, and I was thankful for the time. I moved people back in my space, but it was not the same. I had created a professional clientele. I started to look around for space, but everything was really expensive, then a client came to me and said she was renting space in a nice area on Beverly. I didn't think I could afford paying two rents, on a freelance salary. Was I being reckless? I saw the space, it was small, but I felt I could do it. Last minute, the landlord told me that he was switching the office I decided on, and wanted me to rent the room by the garage! As a healer, I didn't want myself, or my clients, to smell the fumes from the cars. I felt swindled, and decided it wasn't the place for me. I let it go.

Almost 9 months later, after using my home, apartment office, I was sitting in Starbucks, and had a vision (read daydream) of that former Beverly office, but I kept seeing myself upstairs in a larger space. I went back to the same office, on Beverly, because I liked the area, and really needed a professional space. The landlord stated, "Well, there is something upstairs, but it is bigger," and it was a lot more money--over a $1,000 more than I had paid in my building. I couldn't do it, I thought, but there was a healing room in the back, a midsize meditation common room, and a desk area. As I looked across the courtyard of the building, there was a hummingbird caught in the room, pecking in the office across the way, I felt it was a sign.

Within a couple of weeks, I had an impression, a vision to call the landlord. An impression is when a thought is put into your head that seems to interject all of your other thoughts. People call these impressions, insight, "Ah-ha" moments, or hunches. I called the landlord immediately, and struck up a deal. I would pay him 6 months in advance for a substantially reduced rate (on a new credit card that I just got). The deal just came out of my mouth, before I could think.

He agreed, and I rented an office on Beverly Blvd, with two rooms--a healing room and room for clients to meditate, and an area for administrative work. Within a couple of months, he sold the space, as I later learned--he was in debt. I understood why he had settled for such a deal. The new owners renovated, and upgraded the office to a very high end building, and barely increased the rent. When you are on your path *Spirit* will provide the way, the place, the job, the clients. Trust, ask, believe, and move forward. I have rented there for 5 years, and have no problems paying my rents. Thank you, God.

If something is just a goal, activity, or a place that is not right for you--it will close down really quickly. The contracts won't work. There will be mistakes, missed appointments, etc. You have to trust that there will be signs to move you forward, or stop you in your tracks. Pay attention to the signs that help you to create what you want, and move from the situations, people, or environments that do not support you. Your life path is precious--don't waste earth time in situations that do not serve your highest good. I, myself, am trying to close up this earth deal to never come back again.

When you dialogue with the universe, you will receive messages, signs, and synchronicities. When this happens, you begin to align your hidden desires with your purpose. You begin to open up a conversation. I look at God, and the universe, like a sun, constantly shining information down onto us. If you are open to the universal broadcast, you can align you life with the life you have dreamed up. Sometimes, though, there is static on the airways. When I say airways, I mean your own awareness to consciousness or your brain awareness. The more you meditate, you clear the signals, and can hear the messages. Meditation and quiet time in nature helps to clear the cluttered airwaves. Being quiet helps you to hear. The clearer the signal, the more you hear those signals from *Spirit,* and align to the synchronicities and signs. Negativity, anger, confusion, drugs, alcohol, and other addictions will also cloud your airways. You have to take time to tune in.

After I had been on the path for some time, I realized there are steps to walk the Spiritual path. 1) *Seeker*--As a seeker I was looking for what I was here to do, what my path and mission was. 2) *Learner* – Once I figured out what I wanted to do, I began to learn everything about Spirituality, and metaphysics, including, energy, intuition and healing. Any experience that helped me with my path as a counselor, intuitive, healer, and my experiences with *Spirit*, became my priority. 3) *Creator*--I became a creator of the work. I started doing healings at UCLA and privately, readings privately, Spiritual life coaching, and Spiritual counseling and writing. I created my path as a teacher, counselor, healer. 4) *Teacher*– I would have 3 or five clients with the same issue, so I would create classes to help them synchronize, and help people learn how to create their own paths. I was shocked when people use to write down things I said. Now I expect it. 5) *Master*–I feel writing this book puts me into the master level in my field, or just for myself. I have been on panels, on TV, on radio, and in print.

The title master comes when you perfect your path, your calling, and you have accolades, and testimonials to prove it. I won an award from Master Pensuk in Thailand for Spiritual coaching; I have 94 testimonials on Linkedin, and receive high scores at the clinic I work in, as a psychotherapist. I can say I master the work I sought, learned, and created. 6) Avatar –This is the last part of someone on their path. An avatar would be Jesus, Gandhi, Mohammed, Krishna, maybe even Oprah, or Mother Teresa--they make history, and inspire men and women. I haven't gotten to that level, and probably won't in this lifetime. This 6 step system comes from how I created my path, it resonates with the path I walked.

Energetic Payback and Good Karma

Working for the universe is a lucrative commitment. Lucrative does not, necessarily, mean money, but it is lucrative for your soul. Remember, your SOUL came here for a reason, and your SOUL can be abundant, if you choose that, or don't have some karmic issue you are working through. So, you might as well listen to your *Spirit* and fulfill that contract. Sometimes your 'agreement' has to do with creating and doing things you do want to do. I worked with a company that had grievances; if you had problems with management, work hours, or job responsibilities, you could 'grieve' your issue. These grievances rarely worked for me because in my experience sometimes the union was in bed with the management, sometimes not. I also don't like people who speak with split tongues by speaking out of both sides of their mouths. This, unfortunately, happens a lot with corporations for profit.

I would grieve to God about situations I didn't like. Sometimes, I would go up and whisper in God's ear, like, "NOW, I need help, or I need an answer." God would listen to the 'grievance,' and give me more of an assignment for my *real* company. Sometimes, he would connect me to a healer, or a new teacher, or guide me to a Spiritual community. Sometimes, it was a detox, like Optimum Health Institute, or a raw delivery program. The grievances I sent to God would have me look at the current situation from a higher perspective. The people that lie for a living, and the call it corporate policies, or supporting toxic environments, are killing their souls. They create more negative energy that is stored in their energy field. If you speak up for truth, YOU become a problem. God forbid, you tell the truth. Any grievance I had with God usually directed me up, in some way, to listen more deeply to the universe.

Grievances in the Spiritual world are not punitive, or negative. They are like prayers, but it is more specific, and it creates a win-win situation. It also helps you to get back on your path. I grieved to God to show me the truth in the situation, and he did. He would say, "Who do you really work for? Or what is your purpose?" Going **to Human Resources (HR)** is also something you do when you are disgruntled with your job. HR, as it is known, is different when you are working for the universe. **HR is working with the Higher Realms**.

You can file a grievance, but also go to HR--the angels, goddesses, Spiritual teachers, and other energies that are here for divine good. God is always there, but if you have certain things you want done, you can gain assistance from other evolved beings. Let's say you want to write a great novel and get stuck. You can go to HR and ask a higher teacher, who was a great writer on the earth plane, or Spiritual muses to come help you, and assist you.

Whenever I write, I always call in the creative muses or my *Spirit* guide to help. God doesn't send us here alone. We all have an entourage and teams that help us on our Spiritual journey. You have to have pure intentions to connect to the right kind of positive guides. The writing comes more smoothly. Some other benefits are also available, when you are employed by the Universe. You get **a** 401K package. The **401 means** *for one karma*. What it translates into is, that we are all one. So, what you do to someone else, you do to yourself. You do something good, you pay into the karmic bank of the universe. Every month, you will have energetic money put into your retirement package. This helps the global evolution of the planet.

We are all here to help one another grow and learn. Hopefully the growth is from a positive perspective, but sometimes it will be from a negative perspective. So, if I spent days and hours in Spiritual work its called good Karma. So, as you're helping other people through healing, counseling, music, art, medicine, crafts, etc. a donation goes into your universe fund--for one Karma (401) savings account. For example, I have worked with many women who have been severely abused, who turn around and create a program for girls that are abused, and help them to have a positive perspective, helping these girls build good self-esteem, self-awareness, and to have the ability to heal in a safe environment. That kind of work, when you work for the universe, fulfilling your mission, the surplus is put into your 401K. As you are setting good (God) intentions with your deeds, good karma will come to you in your next life, if you choose to come back, it might be a bit smoother.

Even in this life, as you deposit high energy, you may get space to do your classes, gain a discount at a spa, get a very low interest loan. These 'gifts' have happened to me, many times. I stayed at the Hilton in Sedona for 4 days, for $250 total. I had some reward points I had forgotten about and somehow *Spirit* reminded me, and I received a great deal on a beautiful room facing Bell Rock. You don't know where it is coming, but you will be withdrawing good karma from your 401k, but remember, this account doesn't have any penalties, even if you withdraw early. All you have to do is to look up to God and say, "I need a loan," and it will come. Even before you muster up the courage to ask, it is already in the process of being given because your employer is the universe, and they take care of all of their employees well.

That is the biggest difference when working for the universe, this helps you and others and the universe. You withdraw from your 401K by just asking the universe to show you a sign, synchronicity, or message and then if you align your wish and desire, it will happen quicker, just like how I got my office in my building in Mid-Wilshire. The 401k deposits can only be qualities deposited that are uplifting--kind, supportive, and loving. Deposits such as tolerance, patience, kindness or strength are readily accepted. Anything you try to deposit that is mean, manipulative, vindictive, or hurtful goes into your penalty plan. You will have to pay back those deeds, as they are not of the highest good, and they go against the awareness that 'what you do to another, you really do to yourself.' Simply, they get stuff into your auric field that are recreated. In many ways, we are the same person, a '*Spirit*' having multiple experiences.

There are NO traditional penalties for withdrawing early from your 401K. You don't have to pay the government or IRS for a traditional IRS withdrawal. There is a specific penalty payment to the IRS. This IRS is different than what you think. It is not the government agency. **An IRS, is an Individual Receiving Support account.** This means that if you do something against the universe, you receive an energetic penalty, and then have to pay back to an IRS account. These are people who are part of the IRS (Individual Receiving Support) who need your continual support--the homeless, poor, emotionally disabled, or cognitively impaired person. It also could be a friend with a substance abuse problem, a victim of a recent trauma, or those that are bullied. You may not know how the IRS will show up, but know they will come, and they will find you! The difference in the penalties for the IRS is that once you pay them back, it reduces the penalty. There is generally no interest on the penalties. The *only* *interest* is your *interest* in how you can help someone else or create something that helps another.

Fringe Benefits: The dictionary says: "A fringe is an ornamental border of threads left loose, or formed into tassels or twists, used to edge clothing or material, or it is not part of the mainstream; unconventional, peripheral, or extreme." When you think of fringe, it is something that adorns your clothes, but is not the whole garment. Your *spirit* adorns your body, but is not your own personhood; it is like your fringe. Thus, when you work for the Universe, your fringe will be enhanced. If you think of fringe, it moves, shimmers, and shines, and hangs off the clothes. Like your aura and *spirit* moves, shimmers, and shines when you are on your path. It starts to grow and glow, and people are attracted to it, like they are attracted to the movement of fringe. Remember, when it is ignited, your *spirit* vibrates and moves within you much like the fringe on clothes. Fringe is something on the edge and peripheral, also like your *spirit* will be as it listened to its messages. The fringe benefits with working with the Universe are enhancing your *spirit*.

Let's talk about other fringe benefits when working for the universe--you may get free parking spaces, when you need them, meet random people at the right time that will help you on your path. Sometimes in the regular world, corporations give out cell phones at discount or reduce your plan when you work for them. Don't be surprised if your cell phone is that your body cells will respond when you have a direct communication with the divine *Spirit* beings, or angels--chills, flips in stomachs, hair on the back of your neck that remind you your *Spirit* is being activated. These feel like text messages. When you accept this position, your plan may be upgraded so you are feeling chills, goosebumps, and butterflies regularly as communication from your universal employer. The quick cellular communication we are now accustomed to is just us getting used to the stream of younger people who will be born telepathic, and souls who have been around who will be remembering, and uncovering their telepathic gift.

Working for the universe there is a language requirement that you will begin to develop, the language of intuition. This is the language of the *Spirit*, and can guide you to your Spiritual path, and not just another job or career. Listening to your *Spirit* directs you to your passion and your purpose. You know the language of intuition--it is an ancient language of your SOUL.

Vacation time and sick days are also built into the package. Usually, when I am sick, clients seem to not call. My *Spirit* guides and angels seem to orchestrate that. Somehow, when I am going out of town, I get a lot of calls from clients. When I am packing for a trip, I must send out a frequency of not caring if someone calls for an appointment or not.

One time, I had to fit 13 clients into my schedule in two days to accommodate the demand, but they paid for my trip. Mind you, I don't put in my newsletter or on voicemail that I am leaving. The clients, somehow, telepathically pick it up--that my energy is leaving. I feel it has to do with the element of detachment. When you are detached from an outcome, it usually happens quicker. **Detachment** fits into the universal wisdom that you TRUST the universe will give you what you need. *Worry and fear* are telling the universe that you do not trust the universe will provide, and also you are vibrating on a more earth energy frequency. *Faith and trust* are telling the Universe that you trust your highest good is at hand. I also know when a client will be contacting me. I often feel their energy or get a thought in my head, of that person's name. Sometimes, it feels like pressure in my thoughts. Within a couple of days, that client will call. It is the same as a mother's intuition. We are telepathically more interconnected than you think. We just need to connect to that frequency.

Job evaluations are often done whenever you want when you work for the universe. I struggled for years, wondering if I should be doing this work, because it was the exact opposite of what I was supposed to be doing as a psychoanalytically trained psychotherapist. I would state out loud, "God show me a sign, if I should do this work." The phone would usually ring, or I would be asked to speak on a clairvoyant panel at the Conscious Life Expo, or some TV show would call me looking for a healer, or Hay house would contact me to do mailings for their top authors. This was all BEFORE I wrote my book!! I would promote mailings for *New York Times* authors, and had not written a book myself! That would be a sign! If I asked for a more detailed review of my work, I sometimes would meet random editors or virtual assistants, or an in-person personal assistant who also was a web master that charged me nada!

One time, I got validation that therapists would be interested in this work. I was in Ojai for a holiday, and watching the *Long Island Medium*. It was a marathon, and I was intrigued by how much Teresa Caputo touched people's souls. I went to my favorite book store, Soul Centered. I was chatting with my friend about crystals at the shop. Some people overheard me, and said that they loved my store. I laughed and said it wasn't my store. They then asked me how I knew so much about crystals and energy healing. I told them about the work I do. As I left the store, three of the women followed me outside and asked me more about the work I do, and they asked to get a reading from me when I am in Los Angeles. They happened to be from Los Angeles too. We agreed. Then later, I was near my hotel walking down the street, these same women bumped into me, and

I found out they were all therapists! They were mesmerized about my work, and didn't think it was weird at all. They all asked to get readings from me at my hotel.

I was reluctant, because I was on vacation, but I remembered I had asked the universe for a sign. Later one of the women, Ojai Jen, I will call her later, referred a lot of people to me who were all therapists. They also came to get training with me on Intuitive development. It was an uncanny coincidence that I was watching the *Long Island Medium* and asked if this was my path, because of my profession, and walked outside with no expectations, and met three therapists who appeared moved by my reading, and then continued to refer others and stay in touch. The universe is always listening. I have had reviews for years, and have been both stunned, and humbled, how my employer keeps me on track.

Being humble on the *Spirit* path is important. If you become ego oriented, you contract with the lower earth energies. I try to stay positive and minimize criticism of others on the path. It isn't easy. I grew up in a very intellectual family that likes to analyze and pull things apart. Also, my Ivy League education plays into this critical analysis. My health problems have kept me humble. I am not a fan of these, but to do higher Spiritual work you have to be gracious, ethical, and humble--not a doormat, but resonate with humility. It is not me doing these things, but source. I am just open to assist with the divine plan.

I have had people in my field supporting my path. I have taught other therapists about intuitive development. I have had many small groups, from 4 to 8 people, with whom I train. I teach a six week course about how to trust the intuition and hear, see, feel and know intuitively, and how to work more intuitively with the clients. When I sent out an email about offering this class, six women, all of the of Latina descent came to my office. Only five ended up taking the six week class. It was right after 2012, so I was intrigued they were all

Latina. My *Spirit* guide, a Peruvian healer, who I call Eagle Feather, was on high alert. He kept me up half the night giving me messages for the group and individual women. I think he felt connected to the culture. For example, the first two classes were progressing a little slow since they are all therapists, they felt the conflict that I did of trying to heal, feel, and see *Spirit*. They also were all very Catholic, and some of this work seemed against their religious background. Besides teaching them to become more intuitive, I was teaching them how to work with the Universe. My guide, Eagle Feather, broke down the Lord's prayer for them as a metaphysical way to look at how to work with the Universe. The interpretation goes like this:

Our father who art in heaven – We are all one and have the same father.

Hallowed be Thy name-- God's name and vibration is sacred no matter what you call him--God, Allah, Jehovah, Wantanka, etc.

Thy kingdom come- we will inherit the kingdom of heaven when we make it there. It will come.

Thy will be done on earth, -- may God's will be done on earth

as it is in heaven.- AS it is written in the book of life in heaven that we wrote with God before coming here.

Give us this day our daily bread. – asking God for our abundance, by learning the laws of abundance from the universe.

And forgive us our trespasses – We will do wrong, we are not perfect. God, please forgive us.

As we forgive those who trespass against us. – Others will betray us and we should learn forgiveness.

And lead us not into temptation, --Stay in the light, and do not go into what is wrong.

but deliver us from evil:-- Protect us from the dark forces we may run into so we are not tempted.

For thine is the kingdom, - God will give us the kingdom if we go along his path. Freedom peace and all our dreams.

and the power, and the glory, - the power is in good not in the dark. *forever and ever.* – we are eternal souls and will retun to the kingdom. Amen

The women felt more open that the new age concept of the Lord's Prayer was similar, as a reinterpretation of traditional prayers. They were resistant, because many of the men in their families looked down upon this work. The infamous Bruja interpretation of seeking dark spiritual knowledge was present. There was disdain and ridicule of women who wanted to enhance their intuition, as the women were unconsciously told to be secondary in many of their relationships. These were women with Master's degrees in therapy, so the contrast was strong. The women talked about brothers making fun of them as children when they 'knew' something. I recommended books that were more culturally sensitive to their path, *Women Who Glow in the Dark*, by Eliza Alavarez and *Women Who Run with the Wolves*, by Dr. Clarissa Pinkola Estes. The books were about Latina women, who were intuitives and healers. Ms. Estes is a PhD in psychology, Ms Alaverez was a psychiatric nurse.

Three of the therapists, the week before had dreams about wolves, this corresponded to the book and their own power animals, the synchroncities were clear. My spirit guide also explained how spirituality was deep in their culture and not from just being Catholic. He interpreted the word *hola* to containing the *oh* in *ho* like the sound 'ohm' and La' like the sound *ah*. Ohm meaning peace and the sound of creation and ah meaning the sound of God. For example, Allah, Jehovah and God all have the *ah* sound in it. So Hola with regards to saying hello means *I salute the peace that represents the God in you.* This is very similar to a Spanish Namaste. Namaste in Sanskrit an ancient Hindu language means, 'I salute the divinity in you'. So when you are greeting people you are greeting the divinity in them. The Latina women resonated with that interpretation of a spiritual greeting right in their language.

It was nice to have a group of therapists who learned and grew in this class and validated that therapist-as-healer was important and viable work. They all felt less drained, and more empowered when I showed them various techniques for enhancing their energy. This is how I validated the work I was doing, when I asked God should I continue. I believe lots of the knowledge of healing will be coming to heal through the earth, its plants and herbs. With many of these women coming from indigenous cultures, much of the knowledge will come from these earth connected cultures. I feel that is why there is such a spotlight on this group. Now, whatever is spotlighted needs to be focused on. Just like with the African Americans in the sixties, and all the emphasis on the Civil Rights Movements, there is going to be more knowledge that comes out of Central, Latin America and South America.

I just met a powerful healer in Sedona who grew up on a farm in Pennsylvania who had powerful healing experiences. He grew up a Mennonite. There are many people who grew up in the mid west on farms who also talk about knowledge connected to the earth. God has planeted healers in every culture in every part of the world. It is the people who are closest to the earth that the earth speaks with. I believe every culture and person has knowledge, there are just different times under the sun. Earth is a teacher, and it is speaking to those who have their hands in the earth. My friend Ramirez, a fellow therapist, says he often hears a sound that comes from the earth. He sends it to patients and to his sons, and it calms them down. He can't explain how he heard or got it, but he never has a complaint from patients, whenever I see him, he has this large purple glow around him. He also had an experience in Mexico, healing people on another plane of existence when he was ill and out of his body. He was excited as a therapist to tell me about these experience without feeling it was strange or weird. There are different ways to heal, and different methods out there. Go with what resonates with you.

At the clinic I worked in, I also created a group for African American women on my caseload. Many had spiritual experiences and needed assistance and a spiritual lens how to interpret signs or messages or God's voice. It was fun to work with them, some therapists and some teachers and other professionals and help them to dialogue with the Universe. The group was popular and it was nice to have Christian trained women look differently at spirit. They also were healing their depression and anxiety through spiritual self awareness.

Does this sound like something you want to do? As your life purpose recruiter and path pusher, I also have gone through this process of application, and I can guarantee you--it is the best job I have had. As a recruiter, I too get a commission, when I recruit you. This commission does not come out of your salary, like the old recruiters. It is a direct payout from my employer, God. He said, "Carolyn, bring them back to me. So many of my children I sent to Earth and they never talk to me, they don't write, and I don't even get a phone call. Can you get them to pay attention to all the messages, and help them remember what they went to earth camp for?" I said sure, send me a check, and he did. Remember the $5,000 that showed up in my account? God then sent me an application package, through some tragic work, health crisis, or financial drama which got my attention to work for him. I am now passing it onto you. The only thing I ask you to do, is to do the same--be a light of inspiration on the planet, and it will ignite others' light. I accepted the job as Spiritual recruiter for the soul, and hope you will too. Your SOUL is waiting.

WORKBOOK EXERCISE #7

- Do you want to work for the universe?

- What are your pros and cons?

CHAPTER

10 Mending Your Spirit

MOST PEOPLE come to the earth to mend part of the *Spirit,* or their soul. They can do this many ways. Trauma is an important way that you move towards the light--abuse, tragedy, mental illness, job loss, divorce, there are multiple ways to move deeper into the light. Another way to look at this is, do you want to be in the light, or in the dark. Talking to a good therapist, Spiritual counselor, or advisor can help. Regular healthy food or exercise, of course, Yoga, and tai chi, or a great energy healing can help. Of course, energy healing, which heals your SOUL and *Spirit,* is so helpful. Here are some ways to strengthen and to activate your *Spirit*:

Ways to Heal Your Spirit

1. **Stand in Your Power:** When you lie to others, and yourself, you age and affect every cell in your body, physically. When you hold back the truth of who you are, your spirit will cry out. I have taught people in my class about kinesiology and how if they say negative things to themselves, that their body becomes weak. We are programmed for good. You can read the book by Candace Pert, PhD, *Feeling Good or Feeling God.* If you say positive things

to your cells, your cells will respond, and vice versa. You are valuable important and are supposed to be here. It is imperative to stand in your power, knowing you have a spark of the divine. Self Love is key.

2. **Watch your relationships:** There are relationships that help or heal. There are ones that help you to rise, or others that hold you back. People can really support your light, or take from it. Sometimes there are good natured people that may not be good for you. You have heard this saying: if you cannot change the people around you, then change the people around you. Sometimes, family members are part of this plan that you have to remove from close proximity to you. Toxic relationships can affect your health, your income, and your life. Watch who you keep company with. **Also your relationship with earth and heaven.** When the commandment says to honor your father and mother, it not only means your birth parents, but if they weren't good people, forgive them, and honor father God and Mother Earth, or the father of humanity, Adam and mother Eve, if you resonate with that story, who are also the mother and father of the human species.

3. **Don't give into hatred or abuse:** When something really bad happens to you, especially some kind of negative or abusive situation, it is easy to want to get the person back. Becoming vengeful and vindictive is a common trait that you see on the earth plane. Revenge is common in movies and literature of the old way of dealing with conflict. That is why the planet and Spiritual evolution keeps going in circles. We don't forgive, we seek revenge, and make new energetic contracts. That is why I have practiced forgiveness. If you understand universal laws, you know it will come back to them. Walk away if you have to and don't give into hatred or abuse, and practice forgiveness. You know when it is time to fight, and time to withdraw, and remember, the truth always comes out later. Years later, I went to another job, and was happy to hear that person that was so difficult was pushed out of their job.

4. **Forgive self and others:** Forgiving another person frees you up on a deep level. When you hold onto anger and resentment, you create negative energy in your aura field, which creates a fine place for more of the same experience to occur again. We live in a magnetic universe. So the energy you vibrate will attract more of the same experiences. This is an important concept. What you focus on expands in your life. Forgiveness does not mean that you support what the person has done to you. Forgiveness means that you do not want to hold onto this energy anymore. It does NOT mean you condone what has happened to you. It means you no longer will allow that energy to rule your life and to affect you and your decisions. A friend of mine that I met at a writing class gave me this prayer. You say it to help release yourself of a bad situation. The understanding is that on a SOUL level we created various circumstances. She was a student in a Course on miracles, and really helped me to understand.

The energy of creation according to the Course:

I forgive myself for dreaming the dream of
_____ (cause)

I forgive the dream of _____(effect)

I ask Holy *Spirit* for peace with this above, all in space and time, all the higher self, united equal, the Christ, we are that could not be separated.

In essence, the course says that we created this experience of pain or drama, and we take responsibility for it. It was in essence, a dream. Remember the earth plane is a school, so all of these experiences are not really real, they are just experiences.

Then, you take responsibility for it, and nicely with the last part, ask it to go away as you have learned the lesson, if the experience no longer resonates with you, and it no longer serves you. I have said this prayer numerous times and bad situations have seemed to disappear.

To take responsibility for what you created is very hard, but I don't say that to blame you. It means that your SOUL may have created powerful experiences to grow on the soul level. It stings and hurts on the personality level though. If this information doesn't serve you, there are many different philosophies out there.

5. **Watch judgement of self and others:** This is a tenet of mindfulness meditation also. We are here to learn and grow. This path should be more joyful, than nerve wracking. I also have noticed this pattern: what you ridicule, becomes your rule. This is how others will treat you. Ridicule another, and it is coming back to you. When you judge, you nudge the outcome into existence. I remember, I was judging a friend who got into a relationship with a guy who was bipolar and selfish. I was lecturing her in a nice way that she deserved better, within six months, the same thing happened to me. I was duped by this clown, ok, he was hot, and I immediately thought of my friend. Within a day, she called me, out of the blue, as we parted ways, because of my criticism and she said, "Ha! It is coming back to you... see!" She was right. When you judge, you nudge. When you make fun, you have begun the path of experiencing the same thing, just like one of the other tenets above. Make fun of someone mercilessly, and you WILL experience the same thing. By paying attention to the outcome, you are calling it into existence. When you hate, you make a date. The universe is just waiting for the right date and time to write something into your karmic calendar, to have you experience a similar hatred. If you belittle, you go straight in the middle of a future mess of the same type of situation. These are laws to follow when working with the universe, and trying to remain an active and important employee. To recap, here is *the Poem of karma* expanded. *When you judge, you nudge; what you ridicule becomes your rule. When you make fun, you have begun. When you hate, you make a date; when you*

belittle, you sit right in the middle. What you do comes back to you. When you open your heart, you will start, when you understand, you lend a hand, when you love, inspiration comes from above, when you give, you truly live, when you spread joy, you will be employed. When you inspire, you will be hired. This is an easy way to understand the rules of working for the universe. The choice is yours.

6. **Use Essential oils, homeopathic remedies. or flower essences:** If you are going through a hard time, and feel you are in a Spiritual crisis, try alternative methods to help yourself heal. If you are on antidepressants or prescribed anti-anxiety medications, please don't STOP them, or do anything before you consult with an MD. Many clients, who are on psychotropic drugs, will also use homeopathic remedies, essential oils like lavender, rosemary, and frankincense to enhance stress reducing relaxation. These types of products also speak to your *Spirit* and help it to heal on a soul level. Rescue remedy is wonderful, and others in the Bach flower essences. There are many other flower essences, check them out at a holistic pharmacy. Remember, you are feeding and healing your *Spirit*. Your *Spirit* needs enhancement and support during crisis, because it is in overdrive. Don't forget to support it. Your *Spirit* likes natural ways.

7. **Ask for the higher understanding of this situation:** When people have a hard time forgiving or letting things go, it is sometimes important to understand the reason something happens. Most things that happen to us are lessons for our SOUL's growth. They help us to be more compassionate, more tolerant, or take us out of our comfort zone. I have had clients that have been abused several times, who then learn to become incredibly compassionate healers, therapists, or advocates for animals. It is not easy to go within the darkness of your lives, and come up with the light, but it can be done. I had a client who was always left home alone. He ended up drawing to comfort himself. He would create super heroes with incredible powers, as he found comfort in thinking his characters would come out of the blue to save him.

He ended up becoming an electrical engineer when he was laid off, because of a recurring anxiety disorder that prevented him from hitting deadlines. I asked him what he did when he was scared. He said, "I used to draw when my mother left me alone." I said, "Why not draw." He said, "I always wanted to be a cartoonist, but it's not stable work." I asked him to ask the universe to see if he could find work in this field, and if he was going the right direction. Later, the client said, within a week, he met someone at Starbucks that was interviewing people to do cartoon-like graphic design. He thought it was a sign, and asked the guy if he needed more help. The man said yes, but only people with experience. The fact that Jim had an electrical engineering degree got him in the door, as an apprentice of sorts. Within 3 weeks, he was a trainee. The job still didn't make a lot of money, so Jim opted for contract work as extra money, working also as an electrical engineer. Eventually, he made good money and was able to live well. The client's higher understanding was that his SOUL wanted him on a different path, and the job loss was a way to get there. He did forgive the employer that let him go. The employer he had worked for 15 years had laid him off to hire his lover, a less competent younger woman. If he didn't like item 5 he said, he may have been really angry when the guy at Starbucks said, "I only want someone with experience." If he scoffed, and felt slighted by the suggestion, Jim would never have had this opportunity. Also, when he was offered an apprentice type job drawing cartoon graphics, if Jim was very negative, it could have prevented God from getting him a better opportunity. The freelance life worked better for Jim, because he was so anxious--he liked the outdoors which healed his energy field, and working on his own time schedule allowed him to spend time with his animals and garden. I almost fell off my seat when I attended a movie, and saw he had done some of the graphics. The universe always has a plan and it usually is for our higher good.

8. **Thank Source and Universe for your journey:** Gratitude, gratitude, gratitude is a high vibrational attitude to have. Remember, we are in a magnetic universe so

gratitude begets more gratitude. It also helps you see the truth in the situation clearer. If your eyes are filled with anger, your vision will be clouded. If you accept the little things graciously, the little things will grow into bigger things. If you want to heal your *Spirit*, make a gratitude list every day—list five items you are thankful for, then the next day, five more, and the next, and the next. If you appreciate the little things, others will appreciate you. Whenever I am down on myself, like I had mentioned in the beginning of the book, I always saw a blind person that reminded me of what I do have. I am not saying blind people have it worse than me, but I think of it as a very high SOUL challenge on the earth plane. Working in the ER for many years, I would run into many homeless people. I was always thankful I had a home. The *Spirit* needs different things than the personality. Some of you older souls know that you will be not be judged on the other side for eternity, and we are here on earth just for a short lifetime. Have gratitude for the little things.

Listen to your heart

If your heart dies in the physical body, you die. *If your heart chakra dies in the your energetic body, you will emotionally and Spiritually die too.* You may feel unfulfilled, sad, and empty. The chakra doesn't really die, it closes down. You may have the physical things in life, or not, but inside, you feel off and dissatisfied. You may fill this emptiness with addictions, food, serial dating, objects, or drugs and alcohol to stuff down those feelings. Sometimes the feelings of nervousness have to do with fear of moving on your path or being on it. How do you feel the difference? If you feel nervous, but something is right there, like a job opportunity, do it. If you feel nervous, and then you miss appointments, or have the wrong directions to get to an interview, and turn up 20 minutes late, that may be a warning. You may make many mistakes that were, in the past, easy assignments. This may mean you are not on the right path. Pay attention to these signs and messages. The universe leads you through *feelings,* and it is important to pay attention to them. The universe is a feeling energetic force field so if you work with the Universe, you have to go with your feelings. Remember these two statements:

If you feel nervous about a decision, *Ask God or the universe to block it, if it is not right*-- "God block it if it is not right." And if you are not sure about someone, say, *"God, show me who they really are."* If you are past 28-years-old, you will be shown. Sometimes, before the Saturn return, you have to walk this path of challenges and karma before things will be revealed, even if you ask. The universe needs wants and encourages dialogue, so go along and do it. But, it is, first and foremost, created to have you grow.

Universal laws

I received these laws from Verna Aridon Yater, PhD. I took a workshop with her, and resonated with the laws that she presented. Many other people have various interpretations of the laws of the Universe, so go with what feels right to you.

The Law of Attraction: Where your attention goes, your energy flows. Negativity draws in and experiences negativity. You can only attract to you those qualities you possess. If you want peace and harmony, you must become peace and harmony.

The Law of Personal Return: This is another way to view karma. If you think negatively or send hateful thoughts, they may harm a person, but in due course, return to the sender. Also, this works in reverse and the positive is returned to you.

The Law of Duality: The universe is a ying-yang balance of positive and negative. Everything contains these dual aspects, and this tension is necessary for structure to exist.

The Law of Self-Worth: You can only attract to you what you feel worthy of. The more you like yourself, the better others like you, and the more worth you feel.

When I learned about the universal laws, it helped me understand, far beyond the law of attraction. It helped me understand how to work with the universe correctly.

The Law of Compensation: You alone are responsible for what happens to you. All results come from your attitude towards life and life experiences. This comes in rewards or problems such as confusion, trouble, and heartbreaking experience.

The Law of Growth: There is no growth without discontent. You know what is best for you. Strive for more awareness.

The Law of Restriction: Man cannot create anything higher than his own level of understanding. Work from the inside out, and incorporate the power of harmonious thinking. The only solution to poverty, limitation, and desire to heal the world is first heal yourself.

The Law of Release: Let go of anything that is no longer useful, or purposeful, without resentment, such things as beliefs, lifestyle, books, etc. Pleasure is in the moment of experience, and by letting go, you free yourself to get another learning experience without being bound by the old.

The Law of Vibrational Attainment: The entire universe changed when Einstein discovered that matter is energy. He opened the door to metaphysics. You don't die, you only transform. Energy can move only forward to backward, it can't stay still. You are energy. Your skin which appears solid is trillions of molecules moving to the rate of what you earned in the past and current life, to this point in time.

The Law of SOUL Evolution: Everyone on earth shares the goal of soul evolution, whether they realize it or not. We have reincarnated to Spiritually evolve. By rising above our fear based emotions, and learning unconditional love, we raise our vibrational rate. Even though it may appear that you are not evolving, you are! Remember how you fell off of a bicycle before learning to ride easily; every failure was a small success bringing you closer to accomplishing your goal.

The Law of Free Will: You have free will on this earth plane to do, thank, and feel the way you want. *Spirit* and God will not intervene, until you ASK. There are Spiritual laws to follow and if you don't follow them, you will reap those consequences.

The Law of Manifestation: Everything manifest begins as a thought or idea. Ideas and experiences create belief, which in turn creates reality. We must change belief if we feel unhappy. When things are not working for you, program what will create success and harmony in your life. Through dedication, awareness, and training within the physical laws, you can manifest any reality. Decide which disharmonious behaviors you want to eliminate. You don't have to change how you feel about something to affect it, if you are willing to change what you believe.

The Law of Reflection: The traits you respond to in others are in yourself. That which you admire in others, you recognize as being in yourself. That which your resist in others and react to is something which you are afraid exists in you. That which you resist in yourself, you dislike in others. Let go of fear for more unconditional love.

The Law of Dharmic Direction: You have a guiding principle, which is a duty to you and society. It is your dharma and karma to have a character to fulfill your destiny. The secret is to listen to your inner direction. Fulfill your dharma and resolve your karma.

Conclusion

W **E SOULS** come here to experience the duality of the earth plane. We are valiant beings of light, that incarnate down on 3rd dimensional reality to experience the contrast of the light and dark on the physical plane. It is our *Spirits* that brings us here. So, I find it fascinating that we don't listen to it. We are energy beings. The energy we love is what we will take when we leave earth. It is the only part of us that transcends. Our bodies don't continue, but our Spiritual minds and *Spirits* do. We listen to the media, our parental programming, our teachers, and society as they tell us what we should have or be. Living in Los Angeles, I see how many worship actors and honor them. Actors are play acting and that is why I believe it is why we honor them. Actors are exemplifying what we all do. We are spirits and have different costumes of being black, asian, indian, male or female, smart, disabled etc. We are playing during our time on earth and after we leave those suits are left behind. We are spirits. Are spirits are pure and whole. What about our *Spirits*? Our *Spirits* want to grow on earth, and they orchestrate a contract with God to have an experience down here. Our passion in action is what we should be doing. There are *Spirits* who seem to have simple lives. They appear to just go through the easy issues with experiences. They may experience little life challenges, career, marriage, work, some minor ailments, and death. They may not be drawn to a book like this. Don't judge them. This may be their vacation lifetime as they may be here to assist others, or they had some tragically horrible experiences in previous lifetimes (if you believe in past lives). There are Spiritual teachers that believe that we only really have one lifetime, but that debate is for another book. Check into multidimensional lives if you feel drawn to explore. We don't always know the totality of the soul. Think of a crystal prism. We only see through one part of the glass, the others part we don't see may be distorted. Stay centered in the now. What is it that you want to create? When I worked in hospitals, we would have code blue when the physical body crashed. When you are in a Spiritual crisis, you may have a code purple. Purple is connected to the crown chakra, which is connected to God consciousness and global consciousness. So, if you have a code purple or are in your Saturn return, and you are wondering why you are here, reach for this book, or another one like this. Learn about the universe and the laws that govern it. Check into your heart as to what lesson you learned, and what you really want to do while you are here. Work with the universal laws, and the laws of nature. Listen to your heart, and your intuition, and pay attention to your soul. Honor your *Spirit*.

Resources

Book List

You Can Heal Your Life by Louise Hay

Embraced by the Light by Betty Eadie

The Lightworkers Way by Doreen Virtue, Phd

One day My Soul just Opened up by Iyanla Vanzant

Spiritual Liberation by Rev. Michael Bernard Beckwith

Life Visioning- Rev Michael Bernard Beckwith

Positive Energy by Dr. Judith Orloff, MD

Women who run with the Wolves by Dr. Clarissa Pinkola Estes

Chakra for Beginners by David Pond

Women who Glow in the Dark by Elena Avila

The Dream Book by Betty Bethards

Dreams and Visions by Edgar Cayce

Think and Grow Rich by Napoleon Hill

Open your Mind to Prosperity by Catherine Ponder

The Dynamic Laws of Prosperity by Catherine Ponder

In the Spirit by Susan L. Taylor

Healing States by Alberto Villoldo

A Course in Miracles by Helen Schucman

Power Versus force by David Hawkins, MD

Love Medicine and Miracles by Bernie Siegel

Your body is your Unconscious Mind – Dr. Candance Pert- CD

The Shamanic view of Mental illness – article - Malidome Some

Ten signs you are a shaman, and don't know it - article. - Lissa Rankin, MD

Websites
Chakra --www.westwindflags.com

www.Agapelive.com

www.intuitivesoulhealing.com

http://www.lawoftime.org/jose-arguelles-valum-votan.html

Movies
The Secret by Rhonda Byrne (also a book)

Glossary

Chakras: (in Hindu thought), each of the energetic centers or wheels of spiritual power in the human body, usually considered to be seven in number that contain emotional energy.

Lightworkers: are people who are here for the purpose of raising the consciousness of mankind. They serve in a variety of different ways to help expand light and spread goodness to humanity. Lightworkers are in human form.

Mayan calendar: The Mayans, an ancient indigenous group of scientists and artists had an elaborate calendrical system, no longer in use, which obviously evolved in complete isolation from those of the old world. This system ended with the fall of the Mayan civilization. Most of the remaining knowledge of it was destroyed by the Spanish, during their conquest. It was not until very recently, during the 1990's, that archeologists have finally been able to fill in many of the gaps in our knowledge of Mayan civilization, including the calendrical system. Mayans are located in Belize, Guatemala, and Mexico, among other places.

Spiritual redirections: When a tragedy, trauma, or initiation happens on your path, and you are redirected to doing something from your heart, either a new job, purpose, or passion. Your *spirit* may be leading you to change direction.

Intentions: Are spiritual vectors who create reality by putting out specific energy vectors and wishes to the universe.

Indigo kids: Sensitive and intuitive children who are programmed by *spirit*, the interpretations of these beliefs range from their being the next stage in human evolution, in some cases possessing paranormal abilities such as telepathy, to the belief that they are more empathetic and creative than their peers. The tend to stand up to what is wrong and have a hard time dealing with unethical behavior in adults.

Agape Church International: A spiritual center created by Rev. Michael Bernard Beckwith, that is based on science of mind principles. It is a metaphysical church in Los Angeles.

Soulaholic: A lightworker who feels the evolution of their SOULs, and the soul of others, is important to the evolution of the planet. They work, think, and act in accordance to what would be right for the growth of the soul and the spirit. Sometimes becoming obsessed with the soul's journey.

Soul Nutrients: Information, insights and messages from others that make your soul growth could be lessons, dreams or insightful experiences.

Manifestation: Putting focused intention out to the universe to be able to create with spirit.

Life Review: When you pass over you get a life review of all your experiences on the life plane. Thoughts feelings, occurences and how you made other people feel will be played back to you for review.

Harmonic convergence: The name given to one of the world's first globally synchronized meditation event, which occurred on August 16–17, 1987, which also closely coincided with an exceptional alignment of planets. The timing of the Harmonic Convergence was allegedly significant in the Maya calendar, and organized by Jose Arguelles, Phd. Jose was all the creator of Earth day. The chosen dates have the distinction of allegedly marking a planetary alignment with the Sun and Moon.

Reiki: A healing technique based on the principle that the therapist can channel energy into the patient by means of touch, to activate the natural healing processes of the patient's body and restore physical and emotional well-being

Theta healing: A meditation healing technique By Vianna Stibal utilizing a spiritual philosophy for improvement and evolvement of mind, body and spirit

About the Author

Photo by Maria Rangel

Carolyn B. Coleridge, LCSW is a licensed psychotherapist, who is a Spiritual life coach, an intuitive and healer with 20 years of experience. A graduate of Columbia University, with a Masters in Clinical Social Work, she has been licensed in NY, NJ, and CA. Carolyn has appeared on CNN International demonstrating energy healing and the USA Network. Carolyn was a former Voluntary faculty member of the Pediatric Pain Program @ UCLA, a Complementary Alternative Medicine program, where she performed hands on healing with children in chronic pain.

Carolyn has incorporated spiritual healing practices into her work as a psychotherapist, including teaching Mindfulness Meditation, and Energy Awareness at major HMOS and psychiatric hospitals. She has a private psychotherapy, healing, coaching, and intuitive counseling practice in Los Angeles. She is a Reiki Master, Pranic healer, Integrative Energy Therapist and Theta healing Practitioner. She is part of the healing ministry at Agape International.

Publications

Carolyn is published in 4 books, *Visits from Heaven, Divine Visits*, and *The Spirit of Woman Entrepreneurs*, by Josie Varga and *The Caring Book* by Kaiser Permanente. Her first book, *Honor Your Spirit*, will be out in May, 2016.

Awards

Photo by Maria Rangel

She was voted the 11th best healer in the book *2105 Best Psychics, Mediums, and Lightworkers in the United States* by Maximillen de Lafeyette, in 2014 was votedat the 24th best healer by the same publication. She was also **Winner of the** *Master Award* for her distinctive Dedication as a leader of Spiritual Healing for all Mankind by Master Pensuk from the foundation of **Save the World.**

Acknowledgements

To God the Creator, thanks for the journey. To the Christ light and the Holy Spirit, thank you for the inspiration.

To my ancestors, who didn't have a voice and created song, who didn't have rights but stood up for equality, who didn't have justice but created freedom. A long journey of honoring their spirit.

To my biological ancestors, Ina and Charles paternal grandparents. Ina who did spirit readings and Charles who had premonitions. Francis Jervis, materanl grandmother. Your wisdom, insight and healing naaure stays with me forever. To Edith my great grandmother from Hindu and African ancestors who created spirit circles. Shelyva my great paternal grandmother of South American aboriginal ancestory from the woods of the Amazonian rainforest, your connection to the earth I feel it.

To my parents Euna and Clarence who taught me to think for myself, stand up for what is right and help others along the way. Thank you for setting the path of honoring your spirits and reminding me spirit matters. To so many who have helped with my work over the years, my heart goes out to you. I appreciate you.

Rev. Michael Bernard Beckwith and Ricky Byars Beckwith and Agape. Also the Agape Well Being Center.

To Lightworkers, shine shine shine! To my global brothers and sisters, the journey is yours, take the first step. Thanks Laura Febres and Rosario Luis my right and left hands who helped me at numerous events. Thanks for listening to me endlesly lecture about spirit. Thank you Amy Rice ,my editor, and Doug Williams, my designer.

My many assistants at events and expos. I appreciate you. Thank you my clients' who inspired me to keep going by your stories. Thank you Graphic designers, Erika Wilmore, Lucinda Rae, Maxwell Aston. Erika thanks for the amazing cover, and Lucinda Rae for digital art of my golden heart and dove.! Eagle Feather my gate keeper and guide, Namaste.

Made in the USA
Charleston, SC
20 July 2016